RIO

N

D0407174

DISCARD

JON SPENCE

Becoming Jane Austen

The True Love Story
That Inspired the Classic Novels

MJF BOOKS
NEW YORK

Published by MJF Books
Fine Communications
322 Eighth Avenue
New York, NY 10001

Becoming Jane Austen
LC Control Number 2007931188
ISBN-13: 978-1-56731-894-4
ISBN-10: 1-56731-894-0

Contents

Illustrations

Illustration Acknowledgements

The author and the publishers are most grateful to the following for permission to reproduce illustrations: the great-grandsons of Admiral Sir Francis Austen, no. 4; the Jane Austen Memorial Trust, nos 2–3, 5, 7–10, 18, 20–22; Bath City Library, no. 13; the British Library, no. 19; Hampshire Record Office, no. 12; Helen Lefroy, no. 14; Major Jeffrey Lefroy, no. 15; the National Portrait Gallery, no. 1.

Introduction

When I wrote this book (first published in 2003), I assumed that no one would read a biography of Jane Austen unless they had already 'met' her before in her novels or perhaps in dramatizations of her work. With Miramax Films' *Becoming Jane* that no longer holds true. The movie might well cause people to seek out a biography of Austen in order to find out what happened to her outside the time frame of the film or to discover how much of the film is 'true'.

Becoming Jane Austen was the first biography of Austen to challenge the long-held view that Jane Austen and Tom Lefroy never met again after his visit to Hampshire during the Christmas holiday of 1795, and to marshal the evidence that their relationship was serious and more enduring than the brief flirtation that previous biographers had assumed. Only one of Austen's letters (a letter of condolence) from the period of the autumn of 1796 until the autumn of 1798 has survived. (Jane's sister Cassandra destroyed many of her letters.)

The scriptwriters of *Becoming Jane* have imagined what might have happened during this time. Although the plot and incidents of film are fictional, the writers have striven to give us a true picture of Jane Austen's character, personal circumstances and social context. The 'story' of Jane and Tom's romance may not have played out in the way the writers have imagined, but the film is, I believe, true to the spirit of Jane Austen's character and to the forces that came into play at that time in her life.

As a biographer, I welcome the film *Becoming Jane* for another reason: It allows us to see the young Jane Austen. Some will argue – have already argued – that Anne Hathaway doesn't look like Jane Austen. But then, do we know what Jane Austen looked like? The only visual likeness we have agreed to call Jane Austen is the sketch Cassandra drew of her in about 1810 when Jane was in her mid-thirties. The picture is problematical.

In the sketch Jane is thin-lipped and careworn around the eyes, which are averted and gaze into the distance. Her arms are crossed in an unwelcoming gesture – annoyed, irritated, perhaps self-protective. This Jane is tetchy, not at all agreeable. Perhaps Jane didn't want to have her picture drawn. If she meant to sabotage the portrait, she succeeded. The picture was apparently considered unsatisfactory at the time it was done. Cassandra applied a little watercolouring to parts of the sketch and then left it unfinished. But she didn't destroy it.

It was the only likeness she had of her sister, and perhaps she knew Jane was not likely to be induced to sit for her picture again. However precious the sketch was to Cassandra, made more precious by Jane's death, it has fixed an image of Jane Austen in our minds that is an impediment to our freely imagining both what she looked like and even who she was.

Cassandra's sketch, it seems to me, has been almost single-handedly responsible for creating a general idea of Jane Austen as a dry, homely spinster that no words of description from people who knew her when she was young ('handsome but with cheeks a little too full', says one) have managed to dispel. Could this woman really have written the novels and letters? Rather than satisfying us, the sketch makes us yearn for a more 'recognizable' Jane Austen.

The film *Becoming Jane* has given us an image of Jane Austen that liberates our imagination. I envy readers of my book who come to it with Anne Hathaway's image of Jane in their mind's eye. You will not have to struggle against the image Cassandra created to see the Jane Austen who was young and pretty, lively and in love. Anne Hathaway's skilful portrayal of Jane Austen in *Becoming Jane* shows that art can have as much power to bring us closer to the truth as facts themselves can.

Double Bay   4 December 2006

Acknowledgements

I am grateful to the following institutions and archives, their staffs and archivists, for their support in the course of my research: All Souls, Oxford, Balliol College, Oxford, the British Library, Clemson University Library, the Family Records Office, London, Fisher Library of the University of Sydney, the Hampshire Record Office, the Huntington Library, Jane Austen Memorial Trust, the National Maritime Museum, New College, Oxford, the State Library of New South Wales, the Shakespeare Memorial Trust, the Society of Genealogists, London, Tulane University Library, and the University of Georgia Library.

Of descendants of the various ramifications of the Austen family, I would like particularly to thank Helen Lefroy, who has given me information about the Lefroy family that would have been nearly unobtainable from any other source. The late Joan Austen-Leigh, Major Jeffrey Lefroy, Richard Knight, and Margaret Usborne generously answered inquiries.

The following people have given support and advice in the course of my work: Guenda Abbott, Diana Allan, Professor Charles Beaumont, Jewel Spears Brooker, the late E. C. Bufkin, Lila Duckworth, Joyce Flager, Anna M. Fleming, Susannah Fullerton, Penny Gay, Winter Giddings, Kate Hardy, Meg Hayward, Professor Richard Hosking, Patricia Huff, Professor Clair Hughes, Professor George Hughes, Professor Tajiro Iwayama, Professor Hubert McAlexander, Helen Malcher, Miranda Miller, Leonée Ormond, Richard Ormond, Christina Silk, Patricia Spencer-Silver, Professor Peter Spencer-Silver, Elizabeth Terrill, Samantha Weir, Professor Joseph Wiesenfarth, Susan Williams, and Professor Nobuyuki Yuasa.

Sappho Charney has been the most diligent and indefatigable of research assistants, tracking down and sending information I required over continents and seas: I salute you.

Professor Richard Gilman and Professor Yasuko Shiojiri have given me time and patience beyond reckoning, and no words could properly express my gratitude. Professor Gilman has been my great teacher and without him this book would not exist.

To

Phyllis Yohe, Franklin Dyal
and
Mary Stevenson

friends of my youth

I entirely agree that a historian ought to be precise in detail; but unless you take all the characters and circumstances into account, you are reckoning without the facts. The proportions and relations of things are just as much facts as the things themselves.

Dorothy L. Sayers, *Gaudy Night*

1

Legacies

In 1704, the presumed heir to the Austen family fortune, John Austen, lay dying of consumption at the age of thirty-four. He was leaving behind seven children and was troubled by what might happen to his daughter and five younger sons. He was his father's only son, but he feared that his father, also named John Austen, would now leave everything to the eldest grandson and do little to provide for the other children.

Old John Austen was in the wool trade, as the family had been for several generations, providing wool to weavers, overseeing the processing of the cloth, and selling the finished product to cloth merchants. The business was run from workrooms in their large house in the village of Horsmonden in Kent. But the old man had decided that with his son the time had come to leave the trade behind and had brought up young John as the heir to a large fortune. When, after his son's death, old John made his last will he referred to himself as John Austen, Clothier, but to his late son as John Austen, Gentleman.

Young John's widow, Elizabeth Weller, later wrote an account of the family circumstances so that her children would know exactly what had happened. She believed her father-in-law had made the eldest son rich and left the other children 'but as if servants'.[1] She sketched the scene following her father-in-law's death: 'His housekeeper informed where his will was, which was opened in the presence of his daughter and son [-in-law] Stringer, his daughter and son [-in-law] Holman, and also myself. We heard it read though I think myself the only stranger to any former knowledge of it.'[2] The bulk of the estate was left to her eldest son, Jack. His sister received £400, and his younger brothers £40 apiece for an apprenticeship and £200 each as their stake in life when they reached the age of twenty-one.[3]

Even in a society in which primogeniture was an established tradition, old John Austen's will was unusual. Common as it was for the eldest son to inherit the bulk of the estate, younger sons (or grandsons) of a rich man would be left the means to establish themselves in professions – the church, the army, the navy, or the law. Daughters would be provided with sufficient dowries to give them a certain independence (unmarried women generally lived with a married sibling) or to attract husbands who were gentlemen.[4] Old John Austen, though, was determined to make his eldest grandson rich and to leave the other children to make their own way in the world.

Jack was only nine years old when his grandfather died and would not have personal control of his inheritance until he was twenty-one. Elizabeth hoped that he would undo what she considered the injustice of her father-in-law's will when he came into the property. This hope must have been her principal motive in writing the document she endorsed as 'Memorandums for mine and my Children's reading, being my own thoughts on our affairs 1706, 1707, a rough draft in a retired hour'.[5] She related that her husband 'on his death-bed desired his father to consider one child was dear to him as another and though he desired his eldest son might have a double portion [twice as much as the others], yet hoped the others [his father] would well provide for'.[6] And she makes explicit her reason for recording this: she hoped that her husband's last wish would 'open the heart of the eldest son to his brothers and sister, that in some measure he may perform his poor dear father's desire'.[7] When Jack reached the age of twenty-one, he would have a choice. He could keep everything for himself as his grandfather had wanted, or he might accept an obligation to provide for his sister and brothers as his father had wanted him to do.

Elizabeth's father-in-law had foreseen the possibility that she might try to persuade Jack to diminish his wealth by helping his siblings, and he designed his will to prevent this. The will demanded that the boy be removed from his mother's care and placed under the guardianship of his uncles Stringer and Holman. If Elizabeth refused to give Jack up, which she had a legal right to do, the boy would receive no income from his inheritance until he was twenty-two. In her already straitened circumstances, with six other children to bring up and very little money for the purpose, Elizabeth could not afford to undertake the support of her eldest son, so she had to agree to his being separated from her and the other children.

The will is a cold, clever document. It is carefully, subtly, even cunningly, constructed. Elizabeth rightly observed that in the will she herself was 'never mentioned unless as it seemed necessitated to make me appear as no friend, nay rather an enemy to the family'.[8] In her father-in-law's eyes she *was* the enemy because she wanted Jack to provide for his sister and brothers. As Jack's mother she would have the power to influence him to consider this his duty. Having Jack removed from her care was meant to put an end to her influence. But it also cut Jack off from his siblings, leaving little opportunity for forming bonds of affection that would make him *want* to help them. The deepest evil of the old man's will was not its material injustice but its studied intention of destroying the affection that unites a family into a single entity. The scheme was successful.

Jack seems to have been indifferent to the plight of his brothers and sister. He alone was his grandfather's heir; he alone was to be rich; he alone was to be a gentleman. He was educated by tutors and was sent to Cambridge, as befitted a gentleman of means. At the age of twenty he married his first cousin, a daughter of his guardian uncle Stringer. He died even younger than his father had, and left only one son, who inherited the fortune. Jack's only son was long-lived, not dying until 1807 at the age of ninety-one. He had failed to produce a son, and his only child, a daughter, had died unmarried. He left the fortune to a grandson of his father's second brother.

When Jane Austen heard about the will of Jack's son (also, as usual, called John) in 1807, she wrote to her sister, Cassandra:

> We have at last heard something of Mr [John] Austen's will. It is beleived at Tunbridge that he has left everything after the death of his widow to Mr Motley Austen's third son John; & as the said John was the only one of the family who attended the funeral, it seems likely to be true. Such ill-gotten Wealth can never prosper![9]

Jane seems to have known the whole sorry story, begun when the family fortune had been in one stroke transformed into the 'ill-gotten' wealth of a single individual.

Elizabeth Weller's widowhood was hard, but she triumphed and emerges as a figure who accomplished much without sacrificing her integrity.

She had great strength and ingenuity. She put off the brocade and pearls she had worn for a portrait painted in her earlier days, and providing for her children became her life. She perceived that her husband's plan to see that the children were well-educated was not just desirable but now essential. She made their education her duty:

> It seemed to me, as if I could not do a better thing for my children's good, their education being my great care, and indeed all I think I were capable of doing for them for I always thought if they had learning, they might the better shift in the world, and that small fortune was allotted them.[10]

Educating the children was not easy. There was no school in the neighbourhood so they would have to move to a town with a school. To pay for the move and meet the school fees, she had to find a way to supplement her income. With few possibilities of earning money open to a woman, she decided the only feasible way would be to take in boarders.

An elegant solution to her problem presented itself. Sevenoaks School offered its 'schoolhouse', as she calls it, for rent to anyone who would agree to board the master and a few pupils. She undertook to keep the school boarding house at Sevenoaks and negotiated an agreement with the school for her sons to receive free tuition. The boys got a solid education, and Elizabeth later scraped together the money to pay the difference between the £40 their grandfather had left each boy and the real cost of a good apprenticeship. Of the four apprenticeships recorded for the boys, three cost more than £100 and the fourth £60.

Elizabeth's daughter, Betty, the eldest child, probably received little if any formal education. The school was only for boys. Already about fifteen when they moved to Sevenoaks, Betty's main role was probably to help her mother with the housekeeping. There is no indication in Elizabeth's account books that the girl received any instruction. Limited as the prospects of her brothers might be, Betty was in the most difficult position. With hard work the boys might eventually achieve economic security, even affluence, but as a woman in the early eighteenth century Betty could not expect to earn anything beyond her keep. Her only real prospect was to marry.

Elizabeth believed that with just £400 as a dowry Betty lacked one of the most important assets in the marriage market. When she heard how little her father-in-law had left to Betty, she had exclaimed: 'Sure my father takes her for a bastard.'[11] She feared 'he had cut [Betty] off from any prospect [of] future hopes'.[12] This was no exaggeration, and in fact Betty's situation was even worse than her mother suggests. If a woman had no money and didn't marry, she was dependent on her brothers to support her and give her a home. By leaving so little to five of Betty's brothers, their grandfather made it impossible for them to take responsibility for her. Jack was the only one in a position to help her, and he no longer figured in the family as a brother in anything but name. Betty was going to have to make her own way.

Elizabeth's account books tell at least part of the story of what she did for her daughter. When Betty reached the age of eighteen she began to receive a special allowance for clothes, and the amount doubled from one year to the next. Decked in her finery, Betty had to go out and find a husband. She married a man from Tonbridge, the town where Elizabeth had grown up and where she still had family and friends. Elizabeth seems to have turned to her friends there to help find a suitable husband for her daughter. We know nothing about the man Betty married except his surname, Hooper, but the fact that she did marry relieved her mother and brothers of one of their most pressing cares.[13]

Tonbridge was the last of Elizabeth Weller's many gifts to her children. Not only did Betty marry a Tonbridge man, two of her brothers went to the town to pursue their careers after they had finished their apprenticeships. When Elizabeth died in 1721, she was buried in Tonbridge and left behind the abiding influence of her extraordinary character. In the lives of her children and even her grandchildren we find over and over again signs of Elizabeth's legacy: her determination, her belief in the benefits of education, and above all her belief in the importance of family affection and her abhorrence of the destruction of family ties.

Jane Austen's grandfather William Austen was Elizabeth Weller's fourth son. He was apprenticed to a surgeon and then set himself up in his profession at Tonbridge, where his brother Tom, an apothecary, soon joined him in his medical practice. At twenty-six William married

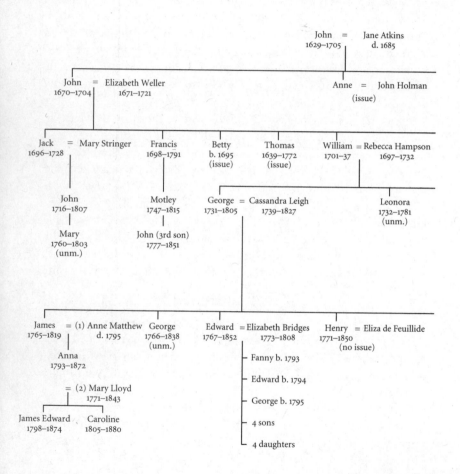

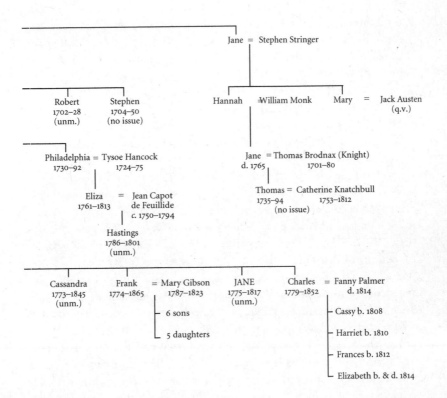

Jane = Stephen Stringer

Robert
1702–28
(unm.)

Stephen
1704–50
(no issue)

Hannah ~~William Monk~~ Mary = Jack Austen
(q.v.)

Philadelphia = Tysoe Hancock
1730–92   1724–75

Jane = Thomas Brodnax (Knight)
d. 1765   1701–80

Eliza = Jean Capot
1761–1813   de Feuillide
              c. 1750–1794

Thomas = Catherine Knatchbull
1735–94   1753–1812
(no issue)

Hastings
1786–1801
(unm.)

Cassandra
1773–1845
(unm.)

Frank = Mary Gibson
1774–1865   1787–1823

JANE
1775–1817
(unm.)

Charles = Fanny Palmer
1779–1852   d. 1814

6 sons

5 daughters

Cassy b. 1808

Harriet b. 1810

Frances b. 1812

Elizabeth b. & d. 1814

Rebecca Hampson, the daughter of Sir George Hampson, a Gloucester physician, and the widow of William Walter, who had also been a physician. It was a good match for William, better than might have been expected. He was a thriving young surgeon and had married a baronet's daughter. His prospects looked good.

Over the next five years he and Rebecca had four children, three of whom survived. After the birth of the fourth child, Rebecca died, leaving thirty-one-year-old William a widower with three children under the age of three, and a stepson (the child of Rebecca's first marriage) of eleven. He married again four years later. William's second wife was thirteen years older than him, an advantage because at forty-nine she was very likely already past childbearing. But it was a needless precaution. A year after he remarried, William died, probably believing his children had a mother to care for them.

His will shows how conscious he was of his grandfather's injustice and reflects his mother's belief in the importance of education. [14] He named as trustees the two of his brothers who were still childless and requested they use his money to 'Educate and bring up in such sort as shall seem most convenient to them my said Trustees my three children'.[15] When the children reached the age of twenty, the trustees 'shall in as equal manner as possible having no respect to sex or eldership divide all the residue and remainder of my said estate after the charge of educating my said children and all other necessary expenses are deducted and paid for between my said three children'.[16] The girls got the same as their brother; the younger children the same as the eldest. To make the division absolutely fair, he asked that his property first be sold and the money apportioned equally.[17]

The will was made before William remarried and was still valid, but his second wife had the legal right to live in the house and to receive the income from his property during her lifetime. The children would not come into their inheritance until she died. In the meantime, she was in control and apparently declined to keep her stepchildren with her. Someone else had to provide the children with a home.

William's stepson, William Walter, now went to live with the Walter family until he came of age and received the substantial fortune his father had left him. His half brother and half sisters, aged five, six and seven, were for the time being destitute, and someone among their own relatives had to assume responsibility for them. The care of orphaned children was often split along lines of gender. The father's family took in the boys; the mother's the girls. William, however, had made no mention of his wife's family in his will, and there were plausible reasons for the Hampsons not offering Rebecca's daughters a home. When William died, Rebecca's only brother, now Sir George, had just married and was about to leave for Jamaica where he would spend the rest of his life. Only one of the Hampson sisters was still living, and she had two children of her own as well as the care of the three orphaned daughters of another sister, Margaret. Margaret Hampson had married Cope Freeman, a plantation owner at Guanoboa in Jamaica, and on a return voyage to England in 1734, accompanied by their five children, Cope and Margaret had both died from a disease that swept through the ship. Their younger son probably also died during the journey.[18] The surviving Freeman children were luckier than their Austen cousins in that they were left rich. Their father's will appointed his wife's brother-in-law George Cure guardian of the boys, and his wife's only surviving sister, Jane Payne, guardian of the girls. [19]

Jane and Capel Payne were themselves rich and moved in high social circles. She was a Woman of the Bedchamber to the Princess of Wales.[20] Perhaps the Paynes made some financial contribution to the support of their Austen nieces, but with two children of their own and the three Freeman girls in their care, it doesn't seem unreasonable that they left it to William's family to give the Austen children a home.

In his will William had named his brothers Francis and Stephen as guardians of the children. Francis was a solicitor in Sevenoaks and well on his way to becoming the most successful of Elizabeth Weller's younger sons, but he was not yet married and the children needed a woman to take their mother's place. Stephen, a bookseller with a shop in St Paul's Churchyard,[21] was married but childless, so it was decided the orphans should go to London to live with him and his wife.

Stephen and his wife would have taught the children to read and write, and may even have sent them to school. The worst aspect of their new situation was that they had lost their community, their network of relatives and friends, and a sense of belonging to the town where the Wellers and the Walters had lived for generations. Stephen and his wife could not have replaced the wider security the children had had in Tonbridge.

The youngest child, Leonora, never quite emerges from the shadows. She went to London at five, and almost nothing is again heard of her until she died nearly forty-five years later. She doesn't seem to have been apprenticed in any trade, and she spent the rest of her life with connections of Stephen Austen. It has been suggested that she had some mental or physical disability, which would account for her being almost invisible.[22]

Her brother George, who was to become Jane Austen's father, was the luckiest of the three children. After four years in London he was brought back to Tonbridge to live with his aunt Betty's family and to attend Tonbridge School at the expense of his uncle Francis.[23] He had a benefactor he could depend on in his prosperous uncle; a surrogate mother and father in his aunt Betty and her husband; and companions in their children.[24] His father's brother Tom, the apothecary, still lived in the town, and had a son who was already at Tonbridge School.

George's elder sister was called Philadelphia, a name that might seem singular to us but was regularly if not commonly used in the eighteenth and nineteenth centuries. Phila, as she was usually called, was eleven and Leonora nine when their brother went back to Tonbridge to school. Four years later, in 1745, the fifteen-year-old Phila was apprenticed to a milliner in Covent Garden.[25]

Phila's apprenticeship indicates just how desperate her circumstances were. She had no benefactor to pay for her education and no mother like Elizabeth Weller to give her a clothes allowance and see that she was introduced to prospective husbands. Betty Austen had had £400; Phila had nothing. She had to prepare to earn her own bread. Her apprenticeship in Covent Garden would have provided glimpses of an even harsher side of London life. Covent Garden was a haunt of prostitutes, who often worked in brothels fronted by milliners' shops.[26]

Phila's aunt and uncle Payne and the Freeman cousins seem to have played some part in her London life. In later years Phila and her husband mention the Paynes and the Freemans in their letters in a way that indicates they maintained friendly contact with the families. Phila's husband wrote to one of the Freeman daughters that he would always feel a special obligation to her brother, John Cope Freeman, for his kindness to Phila in her earlier days.[27] Freeman was not much older than Phila and didn't marry until the mid 1750s, so it is unlikely he offered her a home. The exact nature of his kindness is never specified.

While Phila was learning sewing and hat-making so that one day she would be able to make a meagre living, her brother George was distinguishing himself as a clever and diligent pupil at Tonbridge School. In 1747 at sixteen he capped his early career by winning a scholarship to St John's College, Oxford. Up to now he had stood as more or less the adopted son of his uncle Francis, but his uncle finally married at the age of forty-nine and immediately produced a son and heir in the same year that George went to Oxford. This changed George's prospects, though his situation remained bright with possibilities and uncle Francis continued to treat him like a son.

Phila's life had no such promise. In 1750, the year she finished her apprenticeship, her uncle Stephen died. He had little money and felt himself honour-bound to leave it all to his widow. In his will he apologises for being unable to do anything for his relatives, evidently referring to his nieces.[28] His widow married again only a few months after his death, but she and her new husband agreed to let Leonora continue to live with them, even though Leonora wasn't her blood relative. Perhaps for a while Phila continued to live with them as well, but it must have been obvious to her that she would one day have to support herself and perhaps her sister too. The moment had come for her to act.

Marriage was the only practical solution to her problems. She was attractive and intelligent and, it appears, bold and daring as well. She had a strain of determination and a willingness to take risks that her gentle brother George lacked. Their grandmother Elizabeth Weller had had it, as did their enterprising and ambitious uncle Francis. Phila went out into the world to make her own fortune. Perhaps she created her opportunity herself, or perhaps she seized one that was offered.

She sailed for India in January 1752, a part of the cynically nicknamed 'fishing fleet', English women who went to find husbands among the eligible men who had gone out to make their fortunes but had few European women to choose wives from.[29] Phila must have known the value of her qualities and what they would procure for her. She was young and beautiful, her grandfather had been a baronet, and her uncle was a rich lawyer; that she had been brought up by a London bookseller and apprenticed to a Covent Garden milliner could be consigned to the past. In India she would be a far more attractive proposition as a wife than she was in England.

The venture took a lot of courage on Phila's own part. She knew from the Freemans' experience the danger of disease or shipwreck during such a journey. At its best the voyage was going to be long and uncomfortable, and probably lonely. She was leaving behind the few friends she had and going to a place where she was not likely to know anyone.

The more you think about Phila, the more mysterious she becomes, the more complex and ambiguous her motives seem. She may have been a mercenary young woman bent on marrying any rich man she could catch. She may have been the penniless, dutiful sister of a disabled girl and knew her only chance of being able to provide for her was to marry a man who would be able and willing to support her unfortunate sister. She may have gone to escape being dependent on relatives who supported her out of an onerous sense of obligation. She may have gone to escape spending the rest of her life making fine clothes for other people.

Whatever prompted her to take this course of action, she made the voyage and six months after she arrived she married twenty-nine-year-old Tysoe Hancock, an ambitious young surgeon whose aim was to get rich through business interests in India.[30] Tysoe's later expression of a debt of gratitude to John Cope Freeman may hint that Freeman paid Phila's way to India – an expensive undertaking.[31] With Phila's marriage to Tysoe Hancock, the venture could be counted a success.

Phila was to remain in India for more than ten years. In the early part of that time, her brother George was moving slowly if haltingly towards a settled place in the world. He was ordained in 1754 but had no clerical income except a curacy at Shipbourne in Kent, a position he combined with a stint of teaching as second master at Tonbridge School between 1754 and 1757. He then returned to Oxford where he was chaplain at St John's and junior proctor of the university – he was dubbed 'the handsome Proctor'.[32]

In 1761 a new benefactor emerged. Thomas Knight of Godmersham

Park in Kent gave George the rectorship of Steventon, one of the Knight estates in Hampshire. Knight's wife was descended from Jane Stringer, a sister of George Austen's grandfather John Austen. The gift to George may be a sign that uncle Francis, ambitious and knowing the futility of holding grudges, had been cultivating family ties, just as his mother Elizabeth Weller had desired. The gift of the Steventon living to George was the beginning of a close association between him and his Knight cousins, a relationship that continued in the friendship of George with the Knights' only son (named Thomas like his father), who was four years younger than George.

George had a living in hand at last, but he didn't strike out at once for Hampshire to take up the position at Steventon. He stayed on in Oxford for three more years and acted as tutor and guardian to George Hastings. The boy was the only child of Warren Hastings, who was later to achieve fame, power and wealth as the first Governor-General of Bengal.[33] How the child came to be put in George Austen's care is a mystery. What compounds the mystery is that the Austens had so many different possible connections with the Hastings family. It is speculated that George and Hastings knew each other in their youth; that the woman George was soon to marry knew Hastings in her youth (it is certainly a fact that her grandfather's will was witnessed by Hastings's grandfather); that Hastings's first wife was a friend of Phila Austen and had planned to travel with her to India but didn't go until later. All or none of these could have been the origin of the connection. The evidence is suggestive but not conclusive.

Many years later one of the Austen sons wrote to Warren Hastings:

> Your works of taste, both of the pencil & the pen were continually offered to my notice as objects of imitation & spurs to exertion. I shall never forget the delight which I experienced when on producing a translation of a well-known ode of Horace to my father's criticism, he favored me with a perusal of your manuscript and as a high mark of commendation said that he was sure Mr Hastings would have been pleased with the perusal of my humble essay.[34]

That George had such documents does make it look as if he and Hastings were friends in their youth, two clever boys talking about their work, advising each other, exchanging examples of what they had done. The papers were perhaps mementoes of a friendship. The connections that

Hastings's uncle and guardian had in Kent make it likely that the boys met each other there.[35]

The first certain link between the Austens and Warren Hastings came in early 1759 when Phila and Tysoe moved to Calcutta and became friends of Hastings and his wife.[36] Mary Hastings's second child, a daughter, had been born but soon died the autumn before, and Mary herself had never regained her strength. She died a few months after the Hancocks came to Calcutta.

Phila and Tysoe were still childless, a state often taken to indicate that they had a bad marriage. Tysoe, though, once wrote to Phila: 'I am certain nothing shortens a woman's days so much as her being married when too young', that is, by beginning to have children so young.[37] Perhaps they purposely waited until Phila was older and more acclimated to the conditions in India before they had a child. Hancock was a physician and so knew more about human physiology than most people. In December 1761 Phila had her first and only child, a girl they called Betsy after the daughter Warren Hastings had lost in infancy. Hastings was Betsy Hancock's godfather.

There were rumours that Phila had been Hastings's mistress. Lord Clive wrote to his wife that there was no doubt Phila had 'abandoned herself' to Hastings, but he makes no mention that Hastings was Betsy's father.[38] That seems to be a later assumption. Hastings himself never acknowledged paternity. A few months before Phila's daughter was born, Hastings sent his four-year-old son back to England and put him in the care of George Austen. This too may indicate that George knew Hastings before he went to India. Whatever the origin of George's connection with Warren Hastings, he was entrusted with the care and education of the boy.

Odd as such an arrangement seems now, it was not so unusual at the time. There was a long tradition of Oxford scholars taking responsibility for the care and education of a child. It was a way scholars had of making ends meet. The Hastings boy might have remained in George Austen's care for many more years, but in the autumn of 1764 the child died, only a few months after George had married Cassandra Leigh and taken up his duties as rector of Steventon in Hampshire.

2

Home

Cassandra Leigh was in an enviable position for a young woman of her time. She had the expectation of inheriting £3000, enough to protect her from dependence and penury, but not so much as to raise expectations of her marrying for wealth or rank. Her ordinariness gave her a kind of independence. She could remain single, or she could marry the man she chose. In accepting the poor country parson George Austen she exchanged security for matrimonial adventure. Her choice was not imprudent, but the marriage brought uncertainties that would have to be met with ingenuity and energy. Brisk, capable and intelligent, Cassandra probably found the challenge attractive.

Her early life had been stable and comfortable, free from the economic worries or the kind of upheaval and loss that George Austen had endured. Her father, Thomas Leigh, held the All Souls College living of Harpsden in Oxfordshire, where she had grown up in the elegant Queen Anne rectory with her sister, Jane, and their two brothers. In addition to the Harpsden living, her parents had a modest but not insignificant personal fortune of some £6000 to which Cassandra and her sister were co-heirs.[1]

George and Cassandra married on 26 April 1764 at Walcot church in Bath, where her family had been living since her father's retirement. She wore a smart and sensible red woollen dress that would serve her for several years to come – she was already anticipating certain deprivations that would come with married life. The newly-weds left immediately for Hampshire, where George took up his position as rector of Steventon.

Steventon parsonage was in a state of disrepair and not habitable, so George rented Deane parsonage, a couple of miles from Steventon. He only had an income of £100 a year and whatever the farm attached to the Steventon living yielded, but Cassandra's father had died a month before she married, and her mother soon came to live at Deane, where she no doubt made a substantial contribution to the household expenses. Cassandra's sister Jane was still unmarried and probably spent a lot of time at Deane too. Mrs Leigh also brought with her to the neighbourhood her youngest child, Thomas, who was mentally disabled. He didn't live at Deane but was placed with a family of labourers in a nearby village where his mother could visit him and see that he was well cared for.

The Deane family increased rapidly. The Austens' first child, a son, was born within a year of their marriage, and two more sons were born in the following two years. In January 1768 George's stepmother died and he at last came into his inheritance of about £1000 from his father. By midsummer Steventon parsonage had been repaired and refurbished, and the family moved to the house that was to be their home until George Austen's retirement more than thirty years later. Cassandra's mother died only a few months after the move to Steventon, and before the end of the year her sister Jane married Edward Cooper, a rich clergyman whose family had lived near Harpsden and had been lifelong friends of the Leighs.

With Mrs Leigh's death, Cassandra came into her inheritance and purchased £3350 in South Sea Securities. The investment yielded a supplement to the family income. The only further increase they could now look forward to was George's becoming rector of Deane, the living his uncle Francis had bought for him at about the time of his marriage. Deane didn't fall vacant until 1773, but the Austens managed to keep afloat, living a quiet, frugal but busy country life. If they were inordinately worried about their three sons' futures, they gave no sign of it other than prudently choosing a rich godfather for each child.

Susannah Walter, the wife of George's half-brother, William Walter, visited Steventon in the early summer of 1770 with her nine-year-old daughter Philadelphia, named for her aunt Hancock. For a few months following her return to Kent, Susannah corresponded with the Austens and kept their letters, which give us our only real glimpse of George and Cassandra in the early years of their marriage.

Temperamentally the Austens were not what Susannah was looking for as correspondents. They were too rational and philosophical, too unemotional, for her taste, and she was too sentimental and too much given to discontent for theirs. George replied to her first letter because Cassandra was in London with her sister Jane, who had just had her first child. Near the end of the letter George sends his love and tells Susannah that his sons are well, 'and what will surprise you, bear their mother's absence with great philosophy: as I doubt not they would mine and turn all their little affections towards those who were about them and good to them; this may not be a pleasing reflection to a fond parent, but is certainly wisely designed by Providence for the happiness of the child'.² George took a bemused, unsentimental view of children and delighted in the disparity between a parent's emotional expectation and the rational observation of the reality. He attributes the 'great philosophy' of his three, four and five year old sons to the design of Providence, but he and Cassandra, themselves so philosophical and so impatient with people who were not, had perhaps already taught the children to follow their example.

Susannah herself might have benefited from a lesson or two. She was a complainer. In her next letter she moaned about not having pleasant neighbours, and Cassandra, back home from London, replied briefly but not unsympathetically: 'Indeed my dear sister I do most sincerely pity your lonely situation, should have been most happy had fortune placed us in the same neighbourhood.'³ But fortune hadn't, so that was that.

Susannah held to her theme, saying she knew the Austens put off a visit to Kent because the Walters's neighbours were not worth meeting. This time Cassandra replied more bluntly:

> I wish my dear brother and sister Walter were not more than thirty instead of eighty miles from us, for believe me 'tis the distance, not the place you live in, which prevents my visiting you so often as I could wish. For your own sake I wish you were removed from the parsonage, as I think you would be happier any where else, but as to myself it is a matter of indifference. I know and care so very little about your neighbours, that they would never prevent my coming, as my visit would be to you, not to them.⁴

She set Susannah right: Susannah was attributing her own feeling about her neighbours to the Austens and, even worse, confusing reason with feeling. The truth of why the Austens did not go to visit the Walters in Kent was rational, not emotional. Kent was too far to go.

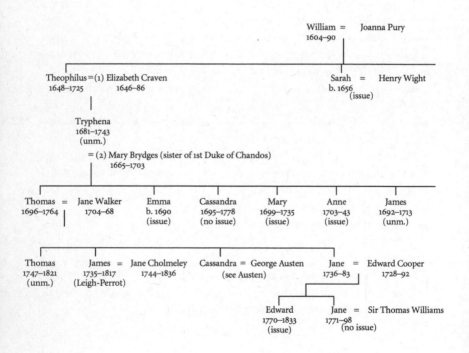

Leigh Family tree

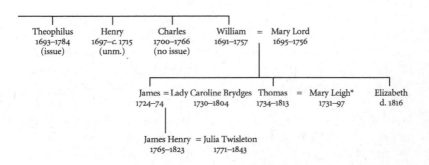

Martha   =   Henry Becke   Anne = Leonard Brandon
b. 1660   b. 1661
        (issue)   (issue)

Theophilus   Henry   Charles   William = Mary Lord
1693–1784   1697–c. 1715   1700–1766   1691–1757   1695–1756
(issue)   (unm.)   (no issue)

        James = Lady Caroline Brydges Thomas = Mary Leigh*   Elizabeth
        1724–74   1730–1804   1734–1813   1731–97   d. 1816

        James Henry = Julia Twisleton
        1765–1823   1771–1843

                        * Daughter of Theophilus Leigh (1693–1784)

In fact, on the rational side, Cassandra could have said a lot more: it wasn't just distance that kept them away from Kent; they had three small children, and she was pregnant with her fourth child; the Austens were relatively poor and George had a profession that demanded his time and energies. In the light of these facts, Cassandra's only mentioning distance seems almost delicate and reticent.

The Austens' own troubles at this time must have made Susannah's discontent with her home seem particularly trivial. In George's letter in July he mentions the difficulty he and his wife were facing: their four year old, little George, suffered from fits and was not developing normally. Susannah had asked how the child was, and George replied: 'I am much obliged to you for your kind wish of George's improvement. God knows only how far it will come to pass, but from the best judgement I can form at present, we must not be too sanguine on this head; be it as it may, we have this comfort, he cannot be a bad or a wicked child.'[5] Even on such an emotionally charged subject, George was philosophical and unsentimental, though tender.

A few months later Cassandra wrote that they had more or less given up hope that the boy would not be disabled: 'My poor little George is come to see me to-day, he seems pretty well, though he had a fit lately; it was near a twelvemonth since he had one before, so was in hopes they had left him, but must not flatter myself so now.'[6] She seems to imply that the boy was already living apart from the family, as he was to do for the rest of his life. He eventually lived with the same family as his mother's disabled brother and may have been in their care from the time he left Steventon. Not only was this a deep emotional loss to the Austens, it had financial implications as well. Little George must, as his godfather Tysoe Hancock later bluntly said, 'be provided for without the least hopes of his being able to assist himself'.[7] The Austens would have to find the money to pay for his keep.

Hancock was always worried about money; his chief personal concern was to make a fortune to leave to his own daughter, Betsy. He and his wife and daughter had returned to England in 1765, hoping to live on the wealth he had acquired in India, but after three years it was clear that England was more expensive than they had expected. In 1768 he went back to India to try to make more money, leaving Phila and Betsy in England, where they often visited the Austens at Steventon. Phila wrote regularly to him of the increase in the Austens' family, and Tysoe replied with growing disapproval and incomprehension. He could not understand how George and Cassandra could be, as it seemed to him, so irresponsible.

When Phila wrote that Cassandra had had her fourth son in 1771, Tysoe replied: 'That my brother & sister Austen are well, I heartily rejoice, but I cannot say that the news of the violently rapid increase of their family gives me so much pleasure.' [8] By the time he received this information, Cassandra was already pregnant again. She had her fifth child, a girl at last, in early January 1773, and Tysoe, tersely commented: 'I must own myself sorry to hear of your going to Steventon, & for the occasion of it: I fear George will find it easier to get a family than to provide for them.' [9] Tysoe was not yet fifty, but his health had been undermined by work and worry and the harsh climate in India; he didn't live to reply to the news that the Austens had had another son in 1774, and he died a month before their second daughter, named after her aunt Cooper, was born on 16 December 1775.[10] Jane Austen was the seventh of the Austens' eight children.

Jane was only about six months old when news of Tysoe Hancock's death reached Steventon,[11] and before she was two, her aunt Phila and fifteen-year-old cousin Betsy set out for the Continent where they eventually settled in France.[12] Phila and Betsy didn't re-enter Jane's life until 1786, at about the time of her eleventh birthday.

There had been talk about Phila and her daughter spending some time in France when Betsy was only seven or eight, long before Tysoe's death. He had thought it a good idea at the time because, he wrote to Phila, 'Betsy will soon be too old to risque her picking up the levity or follies of the French'.[13] Perhaps by 1777 Phila had forgotten this warning.

Not least of the reasons for their leaving England was that living abroad was less expensive. Tysoe had not made the great fortune he had dreamt of leaving his wife and daughter, and the failure had made him wretched at the end of his life. Whatever peace of mind he had on this score came from his friend Warren Hastings, who had given his goddaughter Betsy £10,000 in trust.[14] Tysoe worried because he thought his wife had no head for business and would find it difficult to live on the income from the trust.

He once wrote with almost tender regret to Phila: 'You know how incapable you are of managing such complicated affairs. Oh Phila, had a very few of those hours which were formerly spent in dissipations been employed in acquiring the necessary and most useful knowledge of Accounts, happy would it have been for us both.'[15] To make sure their daughter had the practical skills he thought her mother lacked, he insisted that Betsy have good instruction in mathematics as a part of her education: 'I must request you would get for her the best writing master to be procured by money and that she as soon as possible may begin to learn arithmetic. Her other accomplishments will be ornaments to her, but these are most absolutely necessary.'[16]

When Hancock died, his lawyer, John Woodman, wrote to Warren Hastings: 'I am sorry to find Mr Hancock's affairs are in so bad a situation: all his effects will not more than clear his debts here [in England].'[17] It seems both Woodman and Hastings miscalculated. Before Phila and Betsy left England for the Continent, Woodman paid about £3500 into Phila's bank account, and another £4800 was deposited in the form of a bill on the East India Company, evidently the settling of Tysoe's estate in India.[18] It is, of course, possible that Hastings himself provided this money, pretending that it had come from Hancock. Whatever the source of the money, Phila was now a rich widow and Betsy equally rich in her own right.

The Austens did not share the Hancocks' worldly ambitions, but when their last child, Charles, was born in 1779 they prudently asked George's rich cousin John Cope Freeman to be his godfather.[19] Freeman's only son had died three years before, so there was a fortune without an obvious heir.[20] George and Cassandra couldn't afford to ignore such a prospect. Freeman had inherited plantations and slaves in Jamaica from his father in 1734 and still owned them when he died in 1788.[21] The Austens seem to have held an anti-slavery position theoretically, but when it came to the possibility of their son's inheriting some of the tainted Freeman money they looked the other way.

Freeman lived in Hertfordshire, not Jamaica, but nevertheless the place was too far removed from the Austens for his godson Charles to have any reality to him. When Freeman died, he left his property to the son of his guardian, George Cure, who was not a blood relative. The connection must have been one of affection and gratitude, which the Austens would have respected.

The year Charles was born his eldest brother, James, left home. James was intelligent and hard-working, and when a place fell vacant for him at St John's in 1779, his parents sent him to Oxford at the age of only fourteen.[22] He had a Founder's Kin scholarship, open to him because he was descended through his mother's Perrot connection from the sister of the college's founder, Sir Thomas White. This association of Cassandra's family with Oxford was a particularly beneficial one for the Steventon Austens. James was being prepared to follow in his father's profession. He was intellectually and temperamentally suited to being a parson, and with the proper education he could take over his father's livings some day.

James had another prospect that originated with his mother's Perrot relatives. Mrs Austen's mother, Jane Walker, had been brought up by her maternal grandparents, almost as another sister to her Perrot aunts and uncles. It was almost certainly the marriage of her uncle Henry Perrot to Thomas Leigh's first cousin Martha Bourchier that brought Mrs Austen's parents together. Her brother, James Leigh-Perrot, for whom James Austen was named, had inherited a fortune from a Perrot uncle when he was still a boy, and had added Perrot to his name.

Leigh-Perrot had married in 1764 but in 1779 he and his wife were still childless, a fact the Austens must have noted with some satisfaction as the years passed. His parents took for granted that James would be his uncle's heir if Leigh-Perrot had no children.

The possibility marked James out as the potential benefactor to his brothers and sisters. But Providence, as the Austens would have called it, is full of surprises. James's younger brother Edward, the third son, was destined for the role. The same year that James went to Oxford, Thomas Knight, Mr Austen's cousin and son of the owner of the Steventon estate, called at the parsonage during his honeymoon. At the age of forty-four he had just married twenty-six-year-old Catherine Knatchbull. The Knights took an immediate liking to twelve-year-old Edward and invited him to accompany them on the rest of their wedding journey.[23] This incident has an inescapable air of oddness about it – as if the Knights already knew they would be childless and came to Steventon shopping, as it were, for a son. After this auspicious beginning, the Knights often invited Edward to Godmersham, their estate in Kent. They once sent their coachman to Hampshire with a pony for Edward to ride all the way back to Kent.[24]

Three of his brothers were at home when the pony was led up to the parsonage and presented to Edward. The youngest, Charles, was probably only a year or two old, but Frank was five or six, and at about this time became determined to have a pony of his own. It passed into family lore that at the age of seven the high-spirited and ingenious Frank managed to buy himself a pony for a little over a pound, rode to the hounds in a pink coat made from his mother's scarlet woollen wedding dress, and after two seasons sold the pony for a profit.[25] But it was Henry who in old age remembered the pony the Knights sent to Edward.[26] At nine or ten years old he would have seen more than the pony itself. He didn't want just the pony; he wanted the whole way of life it signified.

Henry was considered by his father the most intelligent of the boys and by his sister Jane the most amusing and charming. When Henry and Edward were children Mrs Austen remarked that Henry appeared to be the elder because he was so tall and Edward so small.[27] The clever and charming Henry must have felt a strong pang of jealousy, even a bitter sense of injustice, in seeing his brother chosen to be made rich. Perhaps it was when the pony was led up that Henry first felt stir in him the worldly ambition that was to be the great driving force of his life. He had something of the spark that had motivated his aunt Phila and his great uncle Francis; he had a sense that he was meant to be rich.

Edward spent more and more time at Godmersham, and Mr Austen worried that his son was falling behind in his studies. But the shrewd Mrs Austen perceived that this was the moment when learning had to give way to money. She advised her husband to let the boy go to his cousins.[28] It was a brilliant move. Old Mr Knight died in 1780, and two or three years later his still childless son and daughter-in-law formally adopted Edward and made him their heir. The Knights had the highest regard for all the Austens; although they adopted Edward, Thomas Knight left his estates, if Edward died without children, to the eldest surviving Austen son. This virtually ensured that one of the boys would come into the Knight fortune. In effect, Thomas Knight left his estates to the Steventon Austens.[29]

At a stroke, James's possible inheritance from his uncle Leigh-Perrot became less important, at least as far as the good of the Steventon family was concerned. The Knights were much richer than the Leigh-Perrots; Edward would be the making of his whole family. The turn of events was invigorating. Henry, the family planned, would follow James to Oxford in the course of time, would be ordained, and Edward would purchase a living for him.

Little is known of Jane's own life before 1783, but we can reconstruct something of life at Steventon. In 1773, two years before Jane was born, George Austen began to take boarding pupils as a means of increasing the family income. It was a good way to make money while beginning to educate James. Mr Austen taught the boys, and Mrs Austen acted as housekeeper, adviser and mother to the pupils as well as to her own children.

On the side of formal instruction, Mr Austen is said to have had considerable talent as a teacher. Frank later remembered that his father 'joined to an unusual extent of classical learning and a highly cultivated taste for literature in general, a remarkable suavity of temper and gentleness of manners'.[30] Mrs Austen's genius was of a different kind. She was capable, energetic and sensible. She had a facility for composing impromptu verse, a lively talent she used to cajole the boys and keep them amused.

When she was a small child, her uncle Theophilus Leigh, the Master of Balliol College, Oxford, had called her 'the poet of the family',[31] and a few surviving poems written to or for the Steventon pupils give a sprightly picture of the part she played in their lives. When Gilbert East kept making excuses to delay his return to Steventon and his studies, Mrs Austen sent him a letter in verse to urge him to come back. She begins the poem with a cheerful expression of concern:

> Your Steventon Friends
> Are at their wits ends
> To know what has become of Squire East;
> They very much fear
> He'll never come here
> Having left them nine weeks at least.[32]

After six more verses relating what the pupils and family at Steventon had been doing both in work and play, she comes to the point with a compliment and a question:

> That you dance very well
> All beholders can tell,
> For lightly and nimbly you tread;
> But pray, is it meet
> To indulge thus your feet
> And neglect all the while your poor head? [33]

Another poem is a petition ostensibly from two of the boys to her husband to ask him to do something about a creaking weathercock on the house that kept them awake at night and left them too tired to study in the day:

> Dear Sir, We beseech and intreat and request
> You'd remove a sad nuisance that breaks our night's rest
> That creaking old weathercock over our heads
> Will scarcely permit us to sleep in our beds.
> It whines and it groans and makes such a noise
> That it greatly disturbs two unfortunate boys
> Who hope you will not be displeased when they say
> If they don't sleep by night they can't study by day. [34]

This kind of easy, humorous approach to the problems of the boys, whether a reluctance to study or a hesitation to explain why they could not study, must have made her popular with the pupils. But at least one boy, Frank Stuart, felt slighted because she had written no verses for him. Her response was a poem about why he did not inspire her, for Mrs Austen was no more inclined to indulge the little jealousies of a pupil than she was the moaning of her sister-in-law Walter. She briskly told the boy what was required to inspire her muse:

> Ah! Why Friend Frank
> D'ye look so blank,
> So wondrous discontented?
> Each lucky hit,
> Each stroke of wit,
> Are by those looks prevented.

The Cheerful Muse
Does here refuse
To lend her kind assistance;
She cannot bear
A serious air,
So wisely keeps her distance.
Yet I must write
This very night,
Or you will look still graver;
And I shall be
Reproached by Thee
That rhyming goes by favour.
But oh dismiss
A thought like this,
Which does me such injustice;
I mind always
That rule which says
'Serve that Man first who first is'.
And now, my Friend,
I pray unbend
That brow so long contracted;
And never break
(For your own sake)
The following law enacted.
I here decree
That you nor he
Shall ever be offended;
Or e're be wont
To take affront
Where no affront's intended.[35]

She is a bit more gentle with Master Stuart than she was with Mrs Walter, and the last lines are a kind of apology, but there is still the sense that Stuart, like Mrs Walter, needs to be less emotional and more rational. If Stuart wanted an amusing poem, he would have to be cheerful and good-humoured himself.

Mrs Austen was happily engaged with the pupils, including her own sons, and there is no reason to suppose she was any less interested in her daughters. Nevertheless, with so many to attend to, she probably had less time to give to every individual than each thought deserved. With a house full of noisy, toiling, demanding boys, Mrs Austen may sometimes have had trouble finding the time to teach her daughters. This might explain in part why Mr and Mrs Austen decided to send the girls away from home to receive more regular and systematic instruction in the spring of 1783.

The plan seems to have originated with Mrs Austen's sister and brother-in-law, Jane and Edward Cooper. The Coopers had two children, a son and a daughter, named Edward and Jane after their parents. Their daughter was twelve and, like her cousins Cassandra and Jane Austen, had up to now been educated at home.

Dr Cooper had a widowed sister who lived in Oxford and was willing to undertake the instruction of her niece Jane Cooper as well as the two Austen girls. There is no indication that economic circumstances forced her to take in pupils – she had inherited £6000 from her mother, a sum that would yield a very good income for a childless widow.[36] Perhaps Mrs Cawley thought – or her brother thought – that the activity of teaching and caring for the girls would be as beneficial to the teacher as to the pupils. A childless woman with time and money and energy needed a project.

There was another aspect to the situation that the Austens, flushed with the recent providential good fortune of their son Edward, would not have overlooked: a childless widow with £6000 might take a fancy to one of the girls and decide to make her the heir to that fortune. The possibility was fairly remote – after all, Jane Cooper was the obvious choice to inherit since she was Mrs Cawley's niece – but then Dr Cooper was a rich man and already able to provide his daughter with a handsome dowry. The Austens had nothing to lose by sending the girls to Mrs Cawley. They would get more instruction than they received in the busy Steventon household and they would have the company of their cousin, whom they adored. The plan seemed to offer definite benefits to everyone involved and to have the possibility of even greater ones if Mrs Cawley became attached to one or both of the Austen girls. It must have looked like a very sensible arrangement to the parents, but thirty years later Jane Austen gives a hint as to what her feelings were when she was sent away to Mrs Cawley. She was not happy to leave her family.

In 1813, only a few months after she had finished writing *Mansfield Park*, Jane recognised that the situation of her own childhood was about to be repeated with her brother Charles's daughter Cassy. Charles, a naval officer, and his family were living on board his ship at Sheerness, but Cassy was often made seasick by the winter storms. Jane's sister Cassandra suggested that Charles and his wife send the child to stay with her aunts, but Cassy did not want to go, and Jane wrote to Cassandra concerning the plan that 'the cheif, indeed the only difficulty with Mama [Charles' wife] is a very reasonable one, the Child's being very unwilling to leave them. When it was mentioned to her, she did not like the idea of it at all'.[37] Jane knew that the word 'reasonable' held powerful sway over her sister.

But for Cassandra feelings did not weigh much in the balance; she judged by the commonsense convenience to Cassy and her parents. Jane knew her sister's tenacity, and when she heard a few weeks later that Charles and his family were going to spend Christmas with his mother and sisters, Jane urged Cassandra, 'do not force poor Cass to stay if she hates it'.[38]

Jane was doing what no one did for her when she was a child – she insisted that the girl's own feelings should take precedence over any rational or practical considerations. The child Jane Austen must have thought her own feelings should settle the question of her going to Mrs Cawley's; when she was nearly forty in 1813, she still felt she had been right and was even prepared to disagree with her sister, to whose judgement she almost always deferred. In his memoir of his aunt Jane Austen, James Edward Austen-Leigh remarks on Jane's deference to her sister: 'Something of this feeling always remained; and even in the maturity of her powers, and in the enjoyment of increasing success, she would still speak of Cassandra as of one wiser and better than herself.'[39] Jane was insistent because she felt strongly about the matter.

In 1783 her own parents had not considered her being unwilling to leave them a 'reasonable' difficulty. The reasonable thing was for Jane to go to Mrs Cawley's. Mrs Cawley was not just the sister of Mrs Austen's brother-in-law, she was a life-long acquaintance, having grown up with Mrs Austen in the neighbourhood of Harpsden. Moreover, James was in Oxford and would be able to keep an eye on his sisters. True, Jane was very young to be going away to school, even to such a casual arrangement as Mrs Cawley's, but sometimes pupils even younger than seven were sent to Steventon. Jane would become better educated; she might even become an heiress, in a modest way.

We don't know what it was like at Mrs Cawley's, but it was not home and has the air of being somewhat haphazard and unsettled as a school. After only a few months, Mrs Cawley moved with the girls to Southampton, where in September there was an outbreak in the town of 'putrid fever' – probably typhus. The Austen sisters both fell ill, but Mrs Cawley didn't inform their parents. Jane Cooper, though, wrote to her mother, and Mrs Cooper and Mrs Austen hurried to Southampton to see about their daughters.[40]

Cassandra and Jane recovered, but their aunt Cooper came down with the fever and died in October, leaving poor twelve-year-old Jane Cooper with the knowledge that she had been the unwitting instrument of her own mother's death because she had raised the alarm in Southampton. Jane Cooper now remained at home with her bereaved father, and Jane Austen and Cassandra were back at Steventon.

Mrs Cawley apparently moved back to Oxford, making her reason for having gone to Southampton in the first place all the more obscure. She died in Oxford in the autumn of 1787 and left her money to her brother, as in retrospect might have been predicted. She asked to be buried in the Cooper family vault at Henley, though her husband was buried in Oxford.[41]

Jane soon discovered a new pleasure at home, a friendship with Anne Lefroy at neighbouring Ashe parsonage. Anne was not a playmate, a little girl of Jane's age. She was the thirty-four-year-old wife of the rector, George Lefroy. They had come to live at Ashe with their two young children in May while Jane and Cassandra were with Mrs Cawley. The Lefroys' daughter was four years younger than Jane, and though Jane was fond of Lucy it was the mother who became her valued friend. Mrs Lefroy was an ideal that can be discerned behind the faults and

imperfections of all of Jane Austen's heroines. Jane expressed this ideal
in a sketch of Mrs Lefroy's character in a poem she wrote after her
friend's death many years later:

> I see her here with all her smiles benign
>   Her looks of eager love, her accents sweet,
> That voice and countenance almost divine.
>   Expression, harmony, alike complete.
> Listen! It is not sound alone, 'tis sense,
>   'Tis genius, taste and tenderness of soul.
> 'Tis genuine warmth of heart without pretense,
>   And purity of mind that crowns the whole.[42]

In Jane's eyes Anne Lefroy embodied a harmony and balance of sense
and sensibility, intellect and heart, reason and feeling. This is too vague
and generalised for us to form a clear picture of Mrs Lefroy, but one
thing is quite specific: she singled out the child Jane as an object of
particular interest – 'her partial favour from my earliest years', as Jane
says in her poem. [43] Mrs Lefroy's 'partiality' was not just flattering; it
was an important affirmation to a child who still lacked confidence and
self-assurance. And they shared a love of literature.

Anne's brother Egerton Brydges remarked in his memoirs: 'I remember Jane Austen, the novelist, a little child; she was very intimate with
Mrs Lefroy and much encouraged by her.' [44] Anne's great passion was
for poetry, and it was perhaps she more than the novel-reading Austens
who was responsible for Jane's cultivation of her own love of poetry.
Brydges wrote that his sister 'had an exquisite taste for poetry, and could
almost repeat the chief of English poets by heart, especially Milton,
Pope, Collins, Gray and the poetical passages of Shakespeare; and she
composed easy verses herself with great facility'.[45] Brydges thought
highly enough of his sister's work to get two of her poems published
before she was married.

In *The Poetical Register and Repository of Fugitive Poetry*, there appear two poems by a 'Miss Brydges'. In his 'Advertisement' to the
third edition, what we would call a preface or introduction, the editor
remarks: 'To S. E. Brydges, Esq. [the editor] is also indebted for
much valuable assistance. The poems of Miss Brydges and Dr Beauvoir
were furnished by that gentleman.' [46] In one of her poems, the

author refers to herself as Anna (rather than Anne) to meet metrical requirements.

Both poems confirm the idea of the author given by Jane Austen in her own poem about Mrs Lefroy – but the first poem is a work of sense not sensibility, and reveals a certain wit:

On Seeing Some School-Boys in the Green at Canterbury with Drums, Fifes, etc

O warriors here a fancied train,
  With drums and fifes advance,
While, like their streamers, light and vain,
  Their youthful spirits dance!

Perhaps 'mid this fantastic band
  Some future Wolfe may tread,
When Time has nerv'd the infant hand,
  And Youth its roses shed.

Yon tiny elf, on stilts upborne,
  A giant stalks the green,
While by those props that raise his form,
  His childish folly's seen:

'Tis thus, when rais'd by wealth or birth,
  To fill a lofty sphere,
The idle coxcomb's want of worth,
  More plainly must appear.[47]

This detached, amused, well-observed vignette reveals a play of mind that Jane Austen would have liked, with its wry satirical view of masculine grandiosity and pretension apparent even in little boys. Jane must have seen a lot of that among her brothers and her father's pupils.

But the second poem reveals another, and less detached and less ironic side of the feminine mind. The work is pedestrian and does not really tell us much more about the writer than Jane Austen's own poem on Mrs Lefroy. The first two stanzas give sufficient sense of Anne Lefroy in a less playful mode:

Poetical Epistle to Miss K. B.
Aug. 1776

From rural scenes, where peace and quiet dwell,
Where no beaux flatter, and where shines no belle,
Where books and work our harmless hours employ,
And a calm ramble is our highest joy;
What can my friend expect? I strive in vain:
No lively thoughts can all my efforts gain.
Yet still one truth these stupid lines may prove,
How much my Kitty shares her Anna's love!
When musing o'er the lonely scenes I stray,
Or to fair Denton bend my pensive way;
The mirthful scenes, that lately charm'd our eyes,
Lovely and gay at Fancy's call arise;
Again I weave the dance to music's sound;
Again I gaily trip the giddy round:
Thoughtless and blythe I join the jocund train,
Or smiling listen to soft flattery's strain.[48]

It is not the quality that matters here, but rather what the poem tells us about Anne Lefroy. She was willing to reveal her feelings, to show herself without the armour of self-protective irony. With her friend, Jane could also let down her guard, forget the need to conceal the acute feelings that might leave her open to ridicule by her witty mother and teasing elder brothers. As Mrs Austen's sharp, comic verse shows, at Steventon feelings were treated philosophically, sardonically, and with an acerbic scepticism. Mrs Lefroy was warmer, more at ease with feelings. Much as Jane was attached to her family, she needed a place outside that satirical household, even away from her adored sister, who was so perfectly rational and controlled. Her affinity with Mrs Lefroy provided her with that place, and she found there a companion in feeling who was also a person of sense.

Perhaps she was first attracted to Ashe because Mrs Lefroy gave her the attention that in the busy, chaotic Steventon household her parents had little time for. Jane enjoyed the liveliness and fun at home, tree-climbing and rolling down the grassy slope behind the parsonage, the whoops and shouts of her father's pupils at play. But Ashe was a different kind of place and offered a different kind of pleasure. The parsonage was an elegant gentleman's residence, both in its appearance and in its atmosphere, very different from the rough, somewhat shambling and rambunctious place Steventon was. At Ashe Jane discovered quieter pleasures, peacefulness and order, and a friend who had the freedom and inclination to take an interest in her, a bright and affectionate child who craved a little special attention.

Her flourishing friendship with Mrs Lefroy was interrupted in the spring of 1785 when the Austens decided to send Jane and Cassandra away to school again – this time to a real school. The plan probably again originated with Dr Cooper. His son Edward was at Eton, and he perhaps thought his daughter would be happier at school with her cousins than alone at the rectory with a grieving father. He chose the Abbey School at Reading because the year after his wife's death he had taken the living at Sonning, a village near the town. He would be able to see his daughter and nieces often and entertain them at the parsonage now and then as an outing from school.

The Abbey School was no high-powered academic establishment but was said to be a comfortable and easy-going place.[49] The headmistress was Sarah La Tournelle, born Hackitt, who assumed the French name to give cachet to the school. She was a warm, slightly eccentric lady with a cork leg.[50] The girls must have been intrigued and full of speculations about this strange appendage. How did she lose her real leg? Would she float in water?

Mrs La Tournelle loved the theatre and was particularly fond of gossip about actors.[51] Perhaps it was from her that Jane began to acquire her wide knowledge of plays, which enters her fiction in her mastery of the dramatic scene and the economical dynamic of the narrative. The only allusion in her letters that Jane makes to her schooldays is to quote a favourite saying of the pupils: 'I could die of laughter at it.'[52] She and Cassandra remained at the Abbey School for a year and a half.

When they returned home at Christmas 1786, Steventon must have seemed almost empty to Jane and Cassandra. Henry and Charles were the only two boys still at home. Frank had left in April to attend the Royal Naval Academy in Portsmouth. The sturdy and enterprising twelve year old was preparing to become a sailor. He was expected home for a short visit during the Christmas holidays.[53] James and Edward had both gone abroad, though James's travels were less extensive and on a much more modest scale than his brother's.

The Knights had decided a Grand Tour would be more in keeping with Edward's talents and expectations than a stint at a university. During this time he had his portrait painted in Rome. What we see in the picture is a slightly foppish and disdainful young milord. Edward was now a potentially rich young man, heir to Godmersham Park. But the painter depicted the stereotype of his position in life, not Edward himself.

Edward spent the month of August 1786 in Switzerland and kept a journal of his impressions and adventures, a small volume bound in cardboard with the title written on the spine and the cover in the author's hand.[54] It does not read like a journal you write for yourself – it is much more like a letter, written with a recipient in mind. He probably sent it back to England for the amusement of his family and the Knights. Perhaps Jane read it when she got home from the Abbey School. Edward is the first of her brothers whose voice we hear, and in it ring distinctly characteristic notes of Jane's famous style. After Jane, Edward was the most talented writer in the family, based on the evidence we have, and she must have appreciated his skill and learned from him.

Edward's style is informal and conversational, the flow of his sentences natural and unaffected. At his best, he is playful and, like Jane, enjoyed giving a comic turn to an otherwise pedestrian observation by dropping in an unexpected word or phrase: 'Walked in town in the morning, which is by far the neatest I ever saw, and kept constantly well cleaned by a set of malefactors who chained two and two are condemned for a certain number of years, sometimes for life, daily to clean the streets and remove whatever rubbish may offend the eyes or the nose.' [55]

He describes a not unusual night's accommodation during his rambles in Switzerland: 'We had the comfort however of having a longer sleep than usual, which not withstanding the badness of the beds, the closeness of the room, and the quantity of the fleas, we most of us took occasion to profit of.' [56] He could also laugh at the discomfort he brought on himself. 'I continued my walk a few hundred yards farther to a large heap of snow, being curious to make a snowball in August. I paid [for] my curiosity by getting perfectly wet in the feet and then went contented back and found dinner already served.' [57] He conjures a scene with deft assurance and gives it a humorous turn:

> By way of dinner we found some excellent curds and whey of goats milk and tolerable bread, which we eat in an open part of the hut that served as a pigsty and at that moment a fine old sow was lapping up her whey in one corner whilst we with two or three dirty Germans were lapping up ours in the other … After having dined in our pigsty we took a nap in the open air.[58]

His comments are not just straightforwardly comic. He could direct his irony against his readers. He takes a bit of wicked delight in debunking what he knew must be his family's idea of their rich son's Grand Tour. He eats swill in a pigsty with a sow and sleeps in a stifling room on a bad bed infested with fleas. So much for his coddled and luxurious life abroad.

Evidence of Edward's talent only survives in his journal but is a slight foretaste of Jane's gift, a gift that in her was to develop into genius. Soon after she came home to Steventon at Christmas 1786, she began to write.

3

Scenes

The Christmas holiday of 1786 promised a lot of excitement: Phila Hancock and her daughter were about to reappear on the scene for the first time since they had gone to live in France in 1777. Betsy was now twenty-five and had transformed herself into a French countess, Eliza de Feuillide. She had married Jean Capot, Comte de Feuillide, in 1781, and in the early summer of 1786 set out for England because her husband wanted their child to be born there as a compliment to his wife, at least that was her story.[1] The baby was, however, born in Calais in June and named Hastings after Eliza's childless godfather and benefactor, Warren Hastings. They eventually continued on to London, and just before Christmas Eliza and her mother arrived at Steventon with the fat, fair baby and a gift for Jane, whose eleventh birthday was on 16 December. The present was a set of books in French called *L'ami des enfans* and is dated 18 December 1786 in each volume.[2] One volume is inscribed: 'Pour dear Jane Austen' in what appears to be her aunt's hand. The affectation of mixing French and English catches something of both the women's style – the fashionable French '*pour*' and the affectionate and familiar English 'dear'.

Jane was entranced, and was probably surprised that she was. Put another way, she was surprised that her glamorous cousin seemed entranced with her. A few years later, James Austen wrote a story about a rich and worldly woman (educated in France) who visits her poor cousins at their country parsonage. The narrator, Cecilia, one of the parson's daughters, confesses: 'I could not look forward without fear and trembling to the arrival of my Great Cousin, whom, with the levity of youth, I declared I was sure I would never like.'[3] Then she describes what happened when her cousin arrived: 'For the elegance of her address, the complacency of her smile, and the easy politeness of her manner ... operated so effectively in her favour, that before she had been in the house three days, I gave it as my opinion, that she was the sweetest woman in the world.'4 This sounds close to what we know of Jane and Eliza.

Jane later said that, at the age of ten or eleven, she was shy, awkward, reserved, and uncomfortable with strangers. She lacked confidence and, in her own phrase, 'ready civility'.5 Such a child must have felt trepidation at meeting a woman of the great world – a countess, rich, fashionable and foreign. But, like James's Cecilia, all Jane's wariness at the prospect of meeting her cousin was groundless. Eliza was relaxed, friendly, affectionate and lively, ready to talk to everybody, and to be interested in everything. She charmed Jane by being attentive to her, by taking the trouble to put her at ease and to make her feel that she herself was amusing and charming.

Eliza fitted comfortably into the Steventon family circle, entering into their spirited conversations and playing for them every day – the Austens had borrowed a piano for her.6 The family prized agreeable manners, but they looked deeper, and in Eliza's relationship with her mother they soon saw the strength of her affections. Their cousin Philadelphia Walter remarked in a letter to her brother around this time that Eliza 'has many amiable qualities, such as the highest duty, love and respect for her mother: for whom there is not any sacrifice she would not make, & certainly contributes entirely to her happiness'.7 The Austens too would have noticed this and seen it as a sign of Eliza's warm and loving nature.

Philadelphia, who had visited Steventon with her mother in 1770, was now grown up and had become Eliza's intimate friend. She was called Phylly in childhood and later sometimes Phillida, but the formal name, not a diminutive, suits her charmless character and distinguishes her from her adventurous aunt. Philadelphia was actually a few months older than Eliza, but Eliza was far beyond her in experience and sophistication. Nevertheless they had been friends since childhood and had corresponded during Eliza's years abroad. Philadelphia carefully numbered and kept Eliza's letters all her life. She worshipped her cousin, even though Eliza showed off to her, shocked her prim notions, and sometimes tried to bully her. Eliza provided her with a lot of vicarious thrills, which Philadelphia thoroughly enjoyed while pretending to be prissily censorious.

On New Year's Eve 1786, Mrs Austen wrote to Philadelphia, who

had taken over her mother's letter-writing duties, and commented that
Eliza had 'grown quite lively, when a child we used to think her too
grave'.[8] Time or France, or a combination of the two, had changed Eliza
– for the better in the Austens' view. They valued cheerfulness and
vivacity, and were unimpressed by titles and worldly show. After all,
people with titles, real titles (English ones) were not uncommon in Mrs
Austen's family – her grandmother Leigh had been the sister of the
Duke of Chandos. It was Eliza's personal attributes, not the social
elevation acquired through marriage, that attracted the admiration of
the Austens.

Two portraits of Eliza survive. In the earlier she appears a sweet,
pretty girl with large dark eyes – a hint of her childhood gravity caught
by the miniaturist. She is static and tranquil, and the painter conveys
that his subject was short. There is no sign of the olive skin ('the native
brown of my complexion', as Eliza herself wrote),[9] and even less in the
second picture, which is probably closer to the woman Jane Austen met
at Christmas 1786. This picture shows a more mature woman with an
expression that reveals a strange blend of pride and sadness.

The first and strongest impression the real Eliza made was that she
was playful and unaffected. She made it her business to be agreeable
to everyone, and Jane was not the only member of the family who was
captivated by her. So was Henry, who was clever, lively and affectionate
– very like Eliza. Jane associated his given name with all she admired
in a man, as far as charm and manners went. Once she met a Henry
who didn't fulfil these expectations, and she wrote to Cassandra, 'They
say his name is Henry. A proof how unequally the gifts of Fortune are
bestowed. I have seen many a John & Thomas much more agreeable'.[10]

Henry had a special place at Steventon that Christmas. He was the
only young man for Eliza to flirt with. Frank and Charles were too
young even for her. Henry was not yet sixteen but was tall and good-
looking, and his height already gave him the appearance of being a
young man, so he was an acceptable target for Eliza. Flirtation was one
of Eliza's great pleasures – she called it 'trade'![11]

Henry became Eliza's acknowledged favourite and the following April
went to stay in London at her house in Orchard Street.[12] Happily
unencumbered by her husband for a time, Eliza had established a

fashionable social life and went about in a carriage marked with a
coronet.13 Henry was as dazzled as he had been by Edward's pony.
Through Eliza he had his own taste of the great world.

While Henry was gallivanting around London, Jane was at home and
beginning to write. Watching Henry and Eliza flirt had made Jane aware,
perhaps for the first time, of the puzzling matter of sexual attraction.
It wasn't love that was in the air at Steventon at Christmas 1786, it was
sex. The eleven-year-old didn't know quite what to make of it, but she
knew it was there and knew it was real. The attraction of a young man
and an older woman found its way into her story 'Jack & Alice'.

Jane wrote her early pieces for the amusement of her family and friends,
and she put in shared jokes, teasing jibes, and allusions to real events
in their lives. She made Eliza one of the charmed inner circle of readers
by introducing a motif in 'Jack & Alice' (a 'novel' possibly written in
1787) that would immediately call her cousin to mind.14

Eliza's letters to Philadelphia Walter often mention height. She
admired tall people, especially young men: that she herself was short
was one of the charms of her theory and a key to what she claimed was
her own disposition. It is Henry Austen's height that she most frequently
notes in her letters to Philadelphia Walter. She remarked when he was
seventeen that he was 'at present taller than his father'.15 A year later,
'I hear that Henry is taller than ever',16 and four years later, 'Henry is
now rather more than six foot high, I believe'.17 It seems almost like a
code.

Eliza's harping on height may account for Jane's mentioning several
times in 'Jack & Alice' that Mr and Mrs Jones are 'tall and very
passionate', and showing that, though short, Sukey Simpson is also
passionate – she feels such passionate rage that she murders someone.
There seems to be a private, teasing joke here but it remains obscure.
In later work Austen was also to bring in height in connection with
characters clearly associated with Eliza and sometimes gives the name
of Susan – Sukey is a diminutive of Susan – to Eliza figures.

Less obscure than the joke about height and passion in 'Jack & Alice'
is Eliza's connection with the theme of sexual attraction. The centre of
the story is the outrageously handsome Charles Adams: '[He] was an
amiable, accomplished and bewitching young man; of so dazzling a

beauty that none but eagles could look him in the face.' [18] 'Bewitching' was an eighteenth century code-word for having sex appeal. All of the women in the story are mad about Charles, but the narrator is quick to say that Mrs Jones does not fall in love with him because 'though very tall and passionate [she] was too fond of her husband to think of such a thing';[19] and that the widowed Lady Williams resists his allure because she was 'too sensible, to fall in love with one so much her junior'.[20] The narrator (not to be confused with the author) makes conventional assumptions about Mrs Jones and Lady Williams, but Jane had formed her own opinion and overturns the idea that a 'sensible' woman is immune to the sexual attractions of a good-looking young man.

At the end of the story she insouciantly has the older titled woman marry the bewitching Charles Adams. The reader is left to decide whether this is an example of a sensible woman doing a foolish thing, or whether the narrator was wrong in the first place to call Lady Williams sensible. The reader is even free to ask if it really is foolish for a woman to fall in love with a man much younger than herself.

Even at eleven years old, Jane had perceived that Eliza was strongly attracted to Henry, however sensible she might be: if she were free, she might even marry him. Nevertheless the possibility was so remote that it could be made into a joke. Eliza wasn't free. She was a married woman, and that settled the matter. Jane felt at liberty to laugh at the infatuation of her brother and their cousin.

Eliza and her mother were coming to Steventon again for Christmas in 1787. By the autumn a plan was underway to put on plays at the parsonage during the holidays. The Austens had amused themselves with home theatricals in the past, and before she left France Eliza had been invited to stay with friends who had had a theatre built for acting parties.[21] Once Eliza and her cousins discovered this mutual enthusiasm, the project began to take shape. They would fit up the barn as a theatre and the troupe would perform *Which is the Man?* by Hannah Cowley and *Bon Ton* by David Garrick. Eliza saw the two plays in Tunbridge Wells in September and chose them for the Steventon performance.[22]

The theme of both plays is the conflict between the laissez-faire French attitude to love and marriage and the more sober and sentimental

English one. Eliza took the French view. She once wrote to Philadelphia Walter in anticipation of going to a wedding: 'I never was but at one wedding in my life & that appeared a very stupid business to me.'²³ The only wedding she had been to was of course her own.

When she saw *Bon Ton* and *Which is the Man?* in Tunbridge Wells, Philadelphia was with her, and Eliza admitted (so Philadelphia reported to her brother) that 'for her husband she professes a large share of respect, esteem and the highest opinion of his merits, but confesses that love is not of the number on her side, though still very violent on his'.²⁴ Eliza enjoyed being the object of 'violent' love but was too cool and sensible to be ensnared herself. Although both plays come down on the side of English values, the French attitude gets a thorough airing, mainly through the characters of Miss Tittup and Lady Bell Bloomer, the parts Eliza had chosen for herself. To play these roles would not require much acting skill from Eliza; they would just allow her to be herself on stage.

Miss Tittup in *Bon Ton* is a wily flirt with a cynical view of love and marriage that she has picked up abroad. 'What a great revolution in this family, in the space of fifteen months!' Miss Tittup exclaims; 'we went out of England, a very awkward, regular, good English family! but half a year in France, and a winter passed in the warmer climate of Italy, has ripened our minds to every refinement of ease, dissipation and pleasure.'²⁵ Having learned her lesson well, she is now going to marry a man who is about to become her cousin's lover; she herself is set to become the mistress of her cousin's husband.

Of marriage she declares: 'We must marry, you know, because other people of fashion marry; but I should think very meanly of myself, if after I was married, I should feel the least concern at all about my husband.'²⁶ If Eliza shared these views, she probably kept them to herself at Steventon – or perhaps the Austens just laughed them off as French notions, which Eliza might affect but couldn't seriously believe.

Lady Bell Bloomer, Eliza's part in *Which is the Man?*, is a widow who has lived in France and professes to hold the cynical French view of love and marriage. Her values are put to the test when she has to decide who to pick for her second husband – a rich, dissolute fool, Lord Sparkle, or a charming young army officer.

Lady Bell's sensible friend, Mr Fitzherbert, says of her: 'She conceals a fine understanding under apparent giddiness; and a most sensible heart beneath an air of indifference.'[27] Not a bad sketch of how Eliza herself wanted to be perceived. Mr Fitzherbert knows Lady Bell better than she knows herself; she claims that love is only an exercise of power motivated by vanity. But when she suddenly feels jealousy, she knows she really is in love: 'I had persuaded myself [my heart] knew no passion but the desire of conquest; that it knew no motive to admiration but vanity.'[28] Perhaps beneath Eliza's cynical pose she wished she could have such a revelation. In any case she could fancy herself a rich widow choosing her next husband for love. She would be splendid in the part and was busy lining up the other members of their company.

When they were in Tunbridge Wells together, Eliza and Philadelphia had talked about private theatricals, and Philadelphia had declared she could never act. By mid November the allotting of parts had shown the Steventon troupe needed women, and Eliza tried to persuade Philadelphia to join them. Marshalling all her power and charm, Eliza wrote to her cousin, reminding her of how long and how keenly she had looked forward to the theatricals and what a disappointment it would be to her to return to France without having indulged in the pleasure of acting. For good measure she threw in that it might be many years before she had another chance to spend Christmas with Philadelphia and that, moreover, this occasion would be a good opportunity for Philadelphia to flirt with their cousin James. (Eliza had a hidden motive for wanting James out of *her* way.) She called on Philadelphia, 'if you love me',[29] to put off all other plans and come to Steventon. But Eliza pleaded in vain. Philadelphia wanted to join the party, but she couldn't bring herself to act.[30] Her refusal prompts one of the few times we get a glimpse of Eliza out of temper.

Eliza could be peevish if she didn't get her way, and her response to Philadelphia's letter of refusal is tersely disagreeable; the acting party was too important to Eliza for her to indulge Philadelphia:

> You wish to know the exact time which we should be satisfied with & therefore I proceed to acquaint you that a fortnight from New Year's Day would do, provided however you could bring yourself to act, for my aunt Austen declares 'She has not room for any *idle young* people'.[31]

That Mrs Austen actually said this is by no means certain, but Eliza's meaning is clear: if Philadelphia would not act she was not welcome at Steventon. It sounds as if Eliza was trying to force Philadelphia into agreeing to act. Philadelphia would not give in; she didn't go to Hampshire for the holiday.

With no other cousins to recruit for the troupe (seventeen-year-old Edward Cooper and his sixteen-year-old sister, Jane, were already included), the party had to look beyond the family for actors. For the past year and a half Egerton Brydges, Anne Lefroy's brother, had been living at Deane parsonage with his wife and his sister Charlotte. The young women would provide the much needed females for the company and roles could be found for Egerton himself. He later published a poem originally written as a prologue 'Intended to have been spoken in the character of Violante, at a private Theatre, in Hampshire, 1787'.[32]

Although inviting the Brydges family to join the theatricals solved one problem, it seems to have created another. Egerton's writing leaves no doubt that sharp, dry humour did not attract him. He fancied he was a poet – or at least had the soul of a poet – but the distinction he achieved was as a bibliographer and editor, about which work he has this to say in his autobiography: 'These were unworthy pursuits ... they overlaid the fire of my bosom ... they suppressed in me that self-confidence without which nothing great can be done, and bound my enthusiastic spirits in chains. The fire smouldered within and made me discontented and unhappy.'[33] The man who wrote this would have wanted to do plays with high drama and overblown emotions, not drawing-room comedy with stylish wit. Ranting would have been his acting style. Neither *Bon Ton* nor *Which is the Man?* could have satisfied his sense of what real acting was, so the group had to cast around for plays that would have something for everyone's taste.

They settled on a very different play from those Eliza had favoured: Susannah Centlivre's *The Wonder! A Woman Keeps a Secret.* The author designated the play as comedy (it has a happy ending) but today we would call it melodrama – and a pretty feeble one at that. *Bon Ton* and *Which is the Man?* have a sophisticated naughtiness and witty erotic titillation, but *The Wonder!* contains coarse conversations about sex, and crudely open, though usually farcical, sexual situations. Some cuts would certainly have been made for the Steventon performances. But there was plenty of action and bombast to satisfy Egerton. In *The Wonder!* the main female role of Violante gave Eliza a chance to play an independent-minded woman, though without the elegance of Bell Bloomer or the daring of Miss Tittup. The real question was who would get to play her lover – James or Henry?

Eliza's flirtatious ways were creating emotional havoc at Steventon. James too had been smitten. He must have felt – and his feelings must have been very muddled – that as the eldest brother the right to flirt with Eliza belonged to him. Henry, though, had no intention of giving way to him. Henry's being only sixteen would have masked Eliza's behaviour and provided a blind to what was really going on – her flirting with him was meaningless; she was just larking around enjoying Henry's puppyish infatuation. If she had encouraged the twenty-three-year-old James, though, the whole scene would have taken on a different, rather suspect, look. Just two weeks before Christmas James had been ordained a clergyman and should have understood that his pursuing a married woman was unjustifiable. Nevertheless, he was determined to play Felix and to taste in play-acting what it would be like to be Eliza's lover. All the rational control of emotions the Austens were supposed to practise went out the window.

James may have insisted that Henry was not old enough to play Felix, but Henry might have countered that he was too young to play one of the fathers; and he was certainly not right for the role of the coarse and buffoonish Colonel Britton. It would have been interesting to hear how the Austen boys argued a question so charged with emotion but meant to be a straightforward matter of who was best suited for the role. In the end Henry got the part, and he and Eliza began rehearsals of their love scenes. Acting the parts meant they embraced and touched; Henry even got to kiss Eliza's hand.

James had to endure the jealousy aroused by watching it all and knowing a covert romance was going on under the guise of acting. He probably tried to console himself by turning his attentions to Egerton Brydges's sister Charlotte. He is known to have been in love with her at some point during the time she lived in the neighbourhood: he wrote swooning romantic verse to her, including a sonnet that ends:

> Teach me not then to bear a load of pain,
> But teach me Sweet Enchantress how to die.[34]

James was of a decidedly passionate disposition; of course he was tall.

There are two ways of looking at what went on during the theatricals: the French way – a married woman was seducing her sixteen-year-old cousin; and the English way – two young men were making fools of themselves over their married cousin. Jane took the English view, and the rest of the family probably did too. In their eyes Henry was a callow, affected youth with a sentimental crush on his cousin, a married woman ten years his senior. James should have known better – where, after all, could a romance with Eliza lead? She was married, and common sense indicated the foolishness of such an attachment. The family probably took no more notice of James and Henry's fascination with Eliza than they did of Jane's. Or if they did it was to ridicule the young men.

After the theatricals, Jane wrote a 'novel' that she called 'Henry & Eliza' in which a scene echoes *The Wonder!* The character Eliza throws her clothes out the window of her prison cell to cushion the fall of her children when she throws them out. This incident calls to mind the scene in *The Wonder!* when Isabella jumps out a window and is caught in the arms of a man who happens to be passing – and who, of course, later marries her. Austen's scene is absurd but perhaps at least as plausible as the incident it satirises.

More generally, the story is a spoof on the theme of the foundling heroine and has nothing to do with Jane's brother and cousin. There is no hint of a romance between a woman and a younger man this time; the linking of the two names is itself the joke. Austen felt at liberty to tease Henry and Eliza. There was no reason for secrecy. Everybody knew Henry was making a fool of himself. Austen dedicated 'Henry & Eliza' to Jane Cooper, with whom she had joked about Eliza and Henry's flirtation during the rehearsals of *The Wonder!*

It was more than twenty years before Austen returned to the theatricals with the acting episode in *Mansfield Park*, but she connected the Steventon and Mansfield theatricals by calling two of the characters in her novel Mr Yates and Mr Norris, the names of real actors who took roles in the London productions of *The Wonder!* and *The Chances* – the latter performed at Steventon in July 1788. [35] What Austen created in *Mansfield*

Park is probably, as James's son James Edward Austen-Leigh later said, a pretty accurate reflection of 'some of the incidents and feelings' Jane recollected of the Steventon theatricals.[36]

The summer after the theatricals, the Austens finally did what Susannah Walter had begged them to do nearly twenty years before. They went to Kent. But they did not stay with the Walters. They were the guests of Mr Austen's benefactor, uncle Francis, who was ninety that year. In spite of the celebratory aspect of the visit, it was also a time to pay a sympathy call on the Walters. Earlier in the year the Walters had heard that one of their sons, William, had died in Jamaica, at the age of thirty-seven. As a young man, William had gone out to Jamaica where his cousins Sir George Hampson and John Cope Freeman had interests. He had been joined by his younger brother, who had died after four years in Jamaica.[37] One purpose of the Austens' visit to Kent was to pay their respects to the Walters, who had now lost two sons.

It was not a propitious time for Jane to meet her cousin Philadelphia. The Walters' mourning inevitably cast a shadow of solemnity over the visit, and Jane already had other reasons for being apprehensive about meeting her cousin. She had a pretty good idea of Philadelphia's character, and what she had heard was not promising. Philadelphia had refused to act with the party at Steventon and had hinted that her religious scruples made her doubt it was right to indulge in such an amusement at Christmas. Jane might have laughed with Eliza at someone so strict and high-minded, but she did not want to be judged by her. The prospect of meeting Philadelphia made Jane self-conscious and ill at ease.

But it was not Philadelphia's principles that Jane had reason to be apprehensive about; it was her emotions. Jane didn't know how jealous of her the twenty-seven-year-old Philadelphia was. Eliza had told Philadelphia about their Steventon cousins, had praised and complimented them, had said that Jane adored her. In Philadelphia's eyes, Jane was a rival for Eliza's affections.

At their first meeting Jane was quiet and subdued, and Philadelphia was quick to find fault with the girl's appearance and manners. She wrote to her brother that she liked Cassandra, but Jane 'is very like her brother Henry, not at all pretty & very prim, unlike a girl of twelve'.[38] Jane sensed her cousin's disapproval and when they met again a few days later she tried to be more open, less reserved. But it was no good. Philadelphia had made up her mind even before she met Jane that she was not going to see anything to admire in the child. After the second visit she praised Cassandra (who she thought resembled her) but dismissed Jane: 'Jane is whimsical & affected.' [39] Of course when she next saw or wrote to Eliza, she criticised Jane's person and manners. Eliza later refers obliquely to Philadelphia's negative opinion:

> Cassandra & Jane are both very much grown (the latter is now taller than myself) and greatly improved as well in manners as in person, both of which are now much more formed than when you saw them. They are I think equally sensible, and both so to a degree seldom met with, but still my heart gives the preference to Jane.[40]

This was not what Philadelphia wanted to hear. Eliza's words must have rankled.

Jane never forgot the impression Philadelphia had made on her. Many years later when Cassandra wrote to her about how low-keyed the Christmas celebrations were in their brother Edward's family, Jane dryly remarked: 'Your Christmas Gaieties are really quite surprising; I think they would satisfy even Miss Walter herself.' [41]

Jane was soon diverted from the unpleasantness of the time spent in Philadelphia's company. On the Austens' return journey to Hampshire from Kent, they dined with Eliza and Mrs Hancock in Orchard Street. This was probably Jane's first visit to London and the first time she had seen Eliza at home in her own world, especially invigorating after Philadelphia with her cold manner.

London and Eliza were a potent combination. The effect on twelve-year-old Jane is reflected in 'The Beautifull Cassandra', a story that has a unique place in Austen's early work because it is the only time she writes about herself and reveals her own feelings. The emotions of the 'novel' are not romantic – romantic feelings are mocked by having the heroine fall in love with a bonnet: 'When Cassandra had attained her sixteenth year, she was lovely and amiable and chancing to fall in love with an elegant Bonnet her mother had just completed bespoke by the

Countess of ___ she placed it on her gentle head and walked from her mother's shop to make her fortune.' [42]

Jane Austen writes about the impulse to seize for yourself the possessions and pleasures of the world. London represented all that Jane's country values and country upbringing told her she should resist and deplore. But when she actually experienced 'the Metropolis' (as Eliza would say), dined in elegance in Orchard Street, went out in Eliza's carriage, was given treats by Eliza, Jane had no instinct to resist or condemn this way of life; on the contrary, she wanted it for herself.

Before Jane was born, her mother had said of London, ''tis a sad place, I would not live in it on any account: one has not time to do one's duty either to God or man'.[43] At twelve Jane found she did not share her mother's sentiments. A whirl through London with Eliza banished a sensible, rational belief in duty, and Jane felt the urge to give in to her impulses without regard for God or man. Once the exhilaration had passed, she must have been almost shocked by what she had discovered about herself. She understood the meaning and causes of the experience. She knew what her feelings were and she laughed at them while actually celebrating them.

'The Beautifull Cassandra' is the only early story in which Austen creates an intimacy, even a collusion, between a character and readers rather than between author and readers. She keeps us with Cassandra and in her; there is no pulling back and looking at the heroine with amused superiority. Few of Austen's other early characters are as satisfied with their own actions as Cassandra is, and those who end up with what they want are viewed with ironic detachment. Happy endings are usually spoofs on happy endings. But the beautiful Cassandra expresses genuine satisfaction: she has done what she wanted to do and has got away with it. At the end of the story, back at home in the arms of her mother, Cassandra gives a secret smile and whispers to herself, 'This was a day well spent'.[44]

What Cassandra had done during the day was steal a bonnet from her mother's shop and set out to have adventures on the streets of London. She eats six ices in a shop, refuses to pay (because she has no money), knocks down the shopkeeper, and runs away. She goes joy riding in a hackney-coach, and when the driver demands the fare, 'she placed her bonnet on his head and ran away'.[45] So much for love.

Jane felt the seductiveness of Eliza's life – the bonnet, the carriage, the treats – and she wanted it all. Up to now Jane had admired her cousin for her liveliness, charm and intelligence, and had loved her for returning her admiration and affection. Now another connection was formed: Eliza mirrored Jane's desire for freedom, pleasure, possessions; and she showed that a woman could have these. The clever child went straight to the difference between Eliza and herself: Eliza was rich, she was poor.

Someone with less imagination and insight would have begun such a wish-fulfilment fantasy by lining her heroine's pockets, but Jane was too clever and had too stubborn a streak of realism to be self-indulgent to her fictional self. To get what she wants, the beautiful Cassandra has to steal, assault and brazen it out. Her blithe disregard for the possible consequences of her acts shows how strong a desire drives the girl. It was natural to covet what Eliza had, and lucky Eliza had the means to procure what she wanted without resorting to crime. Jane had discovered the London maxim that 'everything is to be got with money', but in the world of the imagination she could get it all without 'Pewter', as one of her nephews later called money. [46]

4

The Good Apprentice

At about the time Jane went to Kent and London, seventeen-year-old Henry went up to Oxford to begin his studies at St John's. Founder's Kin scholars were limited to six, and Henry had been waiting for a couple of years for a vacancy to occur. The opening put an end to a scheme he and Eliza had had for him to accompany her back to France. Philadelphia Walter was inspired to make a remark that is almost humorous: 'Henry Austen', she wrote to her brother, 'is sadly mortified at one of the Fellows of St John's choosing to marry or die.' [1]

In late August, Eliza went to Oxford to say goodbye to Henry and James before she left England. Writing to Philadelphia about the visit, she mentions James only in passing, but praises Henry enthusiastically, saying Philadelphia would not even recognise him now 'with his hair powdered and dressed in a very *tonish* style'. [2] At seventeen Henry was becoming fashionable, a bit of a dandy – just what Eliza would admire. 'Oh! what a Henry', as Jane later exclaimed. [3]

How much of his posing was done to impress Eliza, and how much was an expression of his own wish to be worldly and smart, even he probably did not know. His family must have laughed at his affectations, just as they made fun of his being moonstruck by Eliza. He was the younger son of a poor country parson – his imposing height and wearing powder in his fashionably styled hair notwithstanding. With maturity, his family trusted, would come his understanding and acceptance of this fact. They took the prudent view that he should settle for a simple life as a country parson, a life within his reach.

In what he wrote during his first year and a half at Oxford, Henry seems to have agreed with them. Perhaps he was trying to convince himself that his family was right. He contributed eight pieces to the *Loiterer*, a weekly paper that his brother James published from the end of January 1789 to March 1790. Each issue consists of a single work –

either an essay, or a short story in the form of a letter-memoir. In addition to Henry's eight contributions, James wrote thirty of the sixty issues, and the rest are probably by other Oxford friends. Just over half the numbers are essays; the others are short stories. Although James announced in the first issue that 'this kind of colloquial writing bears the nearest resemblance to conversation', [4] the *Loiterer* style tends to be self-conscious and affected, lacking the relaxed informality of a conversational voice such as Edward's journal. The most interesting *Loiterer* pieces are those that allude to Eliza de Feuillide.

Even though she had returned to France, she was still on Henry's mind. In his first piece, published as the *Loiterer* for 3 March 1789, Henry wrote as 'H. Homely', a middle-aged clergyman, telling how his frivolous Oxford life – lazy, self-indulgent and spendthrift – was redeemed when, after squandering his money and getting into debt, he became a country curate. He fell in with a set of good people, reformed his life, and married the sister of the squire who was his patron. This is pretty standard and uninspired stuff, characteristic of the *Loiterer*.

The unexpected detail in the story is the gratuitous information that the squire's sister was older than Homely. Henry gives himself a chance to insist that he and his cousin might have married and lived happily in spite of their age difference (if Eliza were not already married):

> My wife was to be sure a few years older than myself. But though the good natured world may therefore put an unfavourable opinion on the motives of her regard for me, I can only say that fifteen years of the tenderest attention and uninterrupted contentment on both sides convinced me too well, what a friend I had lost at the end of them.[5]

His family is sarcastically alluded to as 'the good natured world', and one of them was quick to respond to his jibe.

The next issue of the *Loiterer* is an essay attributed to James, but incorporated into the essay is a letter signed 'Sophia Sentiment'. The letter refers to Henry's story, specifically to the part about Homely's marrying an older woman. Sophia Sentiment complains that the paper contains no subjects interesting to female readers and tweaks Henry for writing a story without love or a young lady in it:

> As for your last paper, the story was good enough, but there was no love, and no lady in it, at least no young lady; and I wonder how you could be

guilty of such an omission, especially when it could have been so easily avoided. Instead of retiring to Yorkshire, he might have fled into France, and there, you know, you might have made him fall in love with a French Paysanne, who might have turned out to be some great person.[6]

It has been suggested that the Sophia Sentiment letter was written by the thirteen-year-old Jane Austen.

The voice does sound like hers, and the quickness and inventiveness of the letter are characteristic of Jane. The writer has picked up from Henry's story the detail of the older woman and cunningly spun another fantasy suggested by Eliza, this one deriving from her French connection. Whoever wrote the Sophia Sentiment letter certainly understood that Eliza was the origin of Henry's comment about Homely's marriage.

The hints H. Homely and Sophia Sentiment give of Eliza led James to another set of associations. The next issue of the *Loiterer*, on 17 March, describes the differences between the French and the English and concludes by contrasting the qualities of French and English women. The theme of French versus English values and manners becomes a recurring motif in the *Loiterer*, though the type James represents as characteristically French is sometimes identified as a London type. Twenty years later Jane Austen was to give some of these 'French' qualities to Mary Crawford in *Mansfield Park*, a novel that has connections to Eliza de Feuillide and to themes found in the *Loiterer*.

In the winter of 1788–89 Eliza was *la princesse lointaine* in Henry's imagination, and he enjoyed adoring her, far away and unobtainable; but between March and the end of the summer circumstances changed, and he began to see Eliza in a different light. As early as February Eliza and her mother were planning to return to England from Paris in June for about a month. They arrived on 7 July, just one week before the fall of the Bastille on 14 July, signalling the beginning of the French Revolution.[7] Eliza and Phila and three-year-old Hastings remained in England.

Eliza's return threw Henry into confusion. He thought she was pursuing him. In September he writes as 'Rusticus', a rich but (as the name suggests) inexperienced country bumpkin. Rusticus's aggressive and sophisticated cousin Louisa, a woman older than him, is trying to lure him into marriage. (Her younger sister is named Betsy.) The story is meant to be a farce in the mode of Jane's early work, but Henry lacked his sister's sharp intelligence and stylish mastery of the material. Her stories are driven by talent and high spirits; the energy of 'Rusticus' comes from Henry's feeling of panic.

Henry muddles the real and the fictional and as a result loses control of his story. He starts out writing a comic account of Rusticus trying to elude Louisa, but he lapses into an almost whining apology for being attracted to her: 'Such civilities [flirtatious attentions] from a fine woman (for indeed, Mr Loiterer, she is still a fine woman) could not fail of pleasing me, the more particularly as I had been but little used to the attractions of unreserved, yet delicate freedom.'[8] This is not Rusticus and Louisa; it is Henry and Eliza. The phrase 'fine woman' fits Eliza but not Louisa, larded with make-up and trimmed with hanks of false hair. Saying Louisa behaves with 'unreserved, yet delicate freedom' is even more out of kilter: she is presented as a buffoonish figure of low comedy.

Rusticus is scared Louisa will lure him into marriage, but it was Eliza herself, not marriage, that Henry was anxious to escape. At the end of the story, Rusticus asks Mr Loiterer for advice. How can he get away from Louisa? The reply is unequivocal: 'Fly the country at once.'[9] Henry probably wrote the advice himself.

Henry could not follow the advice. He was an Oxford undergraduate, he had no money of his own, and his father had little to give him. His only plausible way of escape was to break with Eliza and to conquer his feelings by reason. A few months later, Henry wrote a long story implying that he had escaped. The story was published in two parts in the *Loiterer*, on 19 and 26 December. The narrator is called Aurelius, alluding to the great rationalist Marcus Aurelius, appropriate to a story that purports to show the victory of reason over passion, of prudence and virtue over unbridled emotion.

Aurelius is an old man recounting an episode from his youth when he fell under the spell of the Marquise de la V___ in Paris. Although he claims that reason induced him to leave the seductive Marquise, the story tells a different tale. He is driven away by jealousy and anger. He rejects the Marquise when he realises that he is just another in a succession of lovers whom she uses for her own amusement and pleasure. Love is a game of power and manipulation to her. She isn't condemned so much for her moral character as for not really being in love with Aurelius. She is denounced for her vanity, but there is a strong and lingering impression that Aurelius's withdrawal has more to do with the wound to his own vanity than to his abhorrence of some never quite stipulated depravity in the Marquise.

Aurelius is able to escape by leaving Paris to continue his Grand Tour in Italy. He soon persuades himself that he was never in love with the Marquise, that she was not even attractive and charming: 'Whenever I attempted to trace the progress of my error, and to recount the sum of her attractions, it could not but increase my astonishment at having so long been charmed by so weak a spell.' [10] This is not reason; it's denial. He later hears that the Marquise calls him 'Le Garcon Anglois, sans foi and sans coeur'.[11] The English youth without faith and without heart. This has an authentic ring. Perhaps it was Eliza's cool taunt when Henry accused her of trying to make him jealous and of not really caring for him. However muddled, contradictory and unconvincing Henry's story is, one point is clear. Under the guise of fiction Henry was saying that he had come to his senses and was no longer in love with Eliza.

We don't know how much Jane knew about the unfolding of her brother's relationship with Eliza, but we can be sure that she read the *Loiterer*. 'Rusticus' might have given her her first inkling that Henry's flirtation with Eliza was no longer a joke and that he wanted to extricate himself from the situation. And on reading 'Aurelius' she would have perceived, with relief, that he had done so. Jane did not reveal her own thoughts about Henry's situation for several months, but James responded to his brother immediately with a story of his own, published in the *Loiterer* on 23 and 30 January 1790.[12]

Henry had written three times about the relationship of a young man and an older woman. James takes the pattern but makes a significant change. He writes about a girl who falls under the influence of her cousin, a rich and sophisticated older woman educated in France. The cousin persuades the girl to marry for money rather than for love. Henry had had his say about the dangers of sexual entanglement; James wanted to highlight a different aspect of the situation. He writes about the attraction of money and position. He announces his theme with an epigraph from the now little-read poet George Lyttelton:

> Yet may you rather feel that virtuous pain,
> Than sell your violated charms for gain;
> Than wed the Wretch whom you despise, or hate,
> For the vain Glare of useless wealth, or state;
> The most abandoned Prostitutes are they
> Who not to Love, but Avarice, fall prey;
> Nor aught avails the specious name of Wife,
> A maid, so wedded, is a *Whore for Life*.[13]

This is strong stuff and a bold warning, even though it refers to a *woman* who marries for money, to the charming and ambitious Henry.

Henry's Rusticus and Aurelius are both rich – money plays no part in the power Louisa and the Marquise have over them, but James's narrator, Cecilia, is the daughter of a poor country parson. She is captivated by her cousin's wealth and charm and begins to think the way to be happy is to become rich herself. The cousin proclaims 'that it was a pity so Fine a Girl as [Cecilia] should be buried in the country', and takes Cecilia with her to London, introduces her to the great world, and finds a rich man for Cecilia to marry.[14] Cecilia acquiesces to her cousin's judgement and marries Sir Harry Thoroughbred, a baronet and thought to be rich. But he turns out to be dissipated and nearly bankrupt. Cecilia has been duped, and she has to live with the consequences of having been guided by her cousin. After Cecilia's husband dies, she is left almost penniless, but when the cousin dies she bequeaths nothing to Cecilia.

It is the death of the cousin that is most significant on the biographical level of the story. The cousin's failure to leave money to Cecilia reveals a completely new aspect of the situation. The cousin had treated Cecilia almost as an adopted daughter, and Cecilia had expected to be provided for. There is no hint that Eliza was looking for a rich wife for Henry, but circumstances were such that he might well have thought Eliza would make him her heir or might even adopt him.

Eliza's child, Hastings, was not normal. The fat, fair baby Mrs Austen had referred to at the end of 1786 looked healthy, but two years later he was still unable to walk or talk. Philadelphia Walter told her brother that Hastings had fits – perhaps epileptic convulsions – and that the family all feared 'his faculties are hurt'.[15] She speculated that he was like the Austens' son George, whose disabilities were first manifested in his being subject to fits. Eliza continued to insist that Hastings could recover, but it was clear to everyone else that the boy would never be able to take an active part as his parents' son and heir.

Eliza couldn't marry Henry because she was already married, but she had singled him out as her favourite from their first meeting. She might well decide to choose her first cousin as her heir, might even adopt him as the Knights had Edward. The idea was not utterly improbable; after all, Mrs Knight was only fourteen years older than Edward, hardly old enough to have been his mother. James, though, seems to be warning Henry not to count on Eliza's money. Henry's weakness was not just his passion for Eliza; he was succumbing to the fantasy that she would make him rich. Perhaps he was ashamed to admit that the money was more important to him than Eliza herself.

In his own stories Henry had blamed Louisa and the Marquise for taking advantage of the heroes' innocence and inexperience, but in James's story the older woman is not deceitful and duplicitous. She is frank about her intentions and her values. She doesn't mean to hurt or dupe Cecilia; she believes her influence is good and that her advice is in the girl's best interest. She has no notion that her values are corrupt, and she thinks Cecilia is sensible to adopt those values. The cousin is mistaken but she has no malicious intent. This makes both the character and the story more complex than anything Henry had written. And it brings us closer to a sense of Eliza's true self. Eliza liked being a rich countess, liked the pleasures her wealth and status brought her. That she wished that people she cared about were in the same position was generous, not wicked.

James does not let Cecilia off the hook by blaming the cousin. Cecilia is held responsible for her own actions. James's story is an attempt to get Henry to face an aspect of the real situation that he might prefer to forget – his desire for wealth. There is a lot of truth in what James wrote. And even more if you put his 'Cecilia' and Henry's 'Aurelius' together. The obvious implication is that in exchange for the possibility of becoming Eliza's heir, Henry would have, in some sense, to play her lover. That was the crux of his dilemma. Henry said no more in his work in the *Loiterer* about his relationship with Eliza or his expectations in connection to his cousin.

At the beginning of 1790 Jane had just turned fourteen, and she soon made clear whom she blamed for all these complications in Henry's life. She could not deny that Henry might have a mercenary motive, but she defended him anyway.

In 'Love and Freindship', dated 13 June 1790, the rich widow Phillipa (a name chiming with that of Eliza's mother) marries a younger man who is identified only as a 'fortune-hunter'. The reference seems more off-hand and inconsequential than the marriage of Lady Williams and Charles Adams in 'Jack & Alice', but Jane knew it would be noticed. She did not have to belabour her point. In one neatly turned clause she puts all the blame on Phillipa and exculpates the young fortune-hunter. Phillipa is 'a ridiculous old Woman, whose folly in marrying so young a Man ought to be punished'. [16] The mercenary young man is apparently blameless. As in Henry's stories, it is all the woman's fault. With mock solemnity Jane audaciously dedicated 'Love and Freindship' to Eliza: 'To Madame La Comtesse De Feuillide This Novel is inscribed by Her obliged Humble Servant The Author.' [17]

The title is linked to both Eliza and Henry. Eliza had written it on the back of a miniature portrait of herself. Henry uses the phrase in the *Loiterer* of 1 August 1789. But perhaps most significantly it occurs in Garrick's *Bon Ton*, a play Eliza had acted in at Steventon, possibly in the spring of 1788. The phrase comes near the beginning in a speech made by Miss Tittup, the part Eliza took, so she would have had the lines by heart and could hardly have failed to understand the allusion: 'Pooh, pooh', says Miss Tittup, 'Love and Friendship are very fine names to be sure, but they are mere visiting acquaintances; we know their names indeed, talk of 'em sometimes, and let 'em knock at our door, but we never let 'em in, you know.' [18] Whether Jane was distancing *herself* from Eliza or was hinting that Eliza never let love and friendship in is ambiguous. Jane already had an elegant economy of method and might well have intended both. Below the title of the story, Jane provided an epigraph: 'Deceived in Freindship & Betrayed in Love'.[19] The tag fits with the title of the story, but it is more appropriate to how Jane and Henry felt about their relationships with Eliza than to anything that happens in the novel. James's Cecilia story had been meant for Henry, but 'Love and Freindship' is a warning to Eliza herself to leave Henry alone. It had its effect.

Eliza must have read 'Love and Freindship' since it was dedicated to her, was indeed written for her to read, and she probably read the *Loiterer* as well. A rupture between Henry and Eliza as well as between Jane and her cousin apparently followed. Eliza, who was no fool, had understood both what Henry was saying in the *Loiterer* and Jane in 'Love and Freindship'. For the next two years a veil of silence falls over Eliza's relationship with both her cousins. There are no letters from 1790, but in those Eliza wrote between 1791 and October 1792, all to Philadelphia Walter, she often passes on news about the Austen family – Edward, James, Charles and Cassandra. She writes of 'the sisters' but does not once refer to Jane by name. She makes no allusion to Henry at all. Henry and Jane, Eliza's acknowledged favourites since Christmas 1786, suddenly disappear from the scene. Eliza later told Philadelphia Walter: 'Never will the year 1791 be effaced from my memory for from the first month of its commencement to the present period my feelings have constantly been exposed to some fresh trial.' [20] The defection of Jane and Henry was one of Eliza's lesser worries.

On nearly every front her life was troubled. She could not go home to France because of the political situation, and her husband was unable to join her in England. He was embroiled in the Revolution, at one point going to Turin where the 'Princes of the Blood' had gathered to plan a strategy for seizing back power from the revolutionaries. [21] He knew the situation in France was too volatile for his family to leave the safety of England. The boy Hastings required special care. In England Eliza could provide a familiar, safe and stable environment; and she had confidence in her doctors. She was still insisting that with proper care her son would become strong and able. She and Phila took him to Margate for a sea-bathing cure in late 1790, and Eliza said he was much improved.

It may have been at Margate that Phila first became aware of a swelling in her breast. By the spring of 1791 the seriousness of the ailment was acknowledged. Eliza wrote from London to her aunt Austen, informing the family of her mother's condition. Phila was dying. Her impending death was the worst blow to Eliza. Phila was her daughter's best friend and had been her lifelong constant companion. Now Eliza had to look on while her beloved mother suffered great pain as the cancer took its course. The London house became a sombre place, and Eliza's social life and freedom of movement were curtailed. There is no indication that she visited Steventon or Oxford during her mother's final illness.

It is difficult to pinpoint when 'Lesley Castle' was written. Jane copied it into *Volume the Second* between 'Love and Friendship' (June 1790) and 'A History of England' (November 1791), so its place indicates it was written in the interval. But the ten letters that make up this unfinished 'novel' are dated the first months of 1792 – perhaps the year the story was transcribed, not composed. 'Lesley Castle' has links with the Eliza stories in the *Loiterer* and with Jane's own fictional treatment of her cousin.

Her brothers' *Loiterer* stories are shaped by the conflict of moral dichotomies – passion versus reason, town versus country values, but in 'Lesley Castle' Austen rejects that form. 'Aurelius' and 'Cecilia' are illustrative moral arguments, giving them a tendentious, even self-righteous tone. 'Lesley Castle' has no argument; it is a picture of what Jane takes to be Eliza's world; and it is identified as such by the presence of not one but two characters that suggest Eliza herself.

The deceitful, manipulative and amoral Louisa Lesley derives from Henry's Marquise and has the given name of the pursuing cousin in 'Rusticus'. (The Marquise has no given name.) She duped the Lesley son into thinking her sweet and good-humoured; he married her, they had a child, and then Louisa abandoned husband and daughter to run off with her lover. In place of Henry's meandering sentences and over-blown language, Jane captures Louisa with epigrammatic succinctness: 'Never was there a sweeter face, a finer form, or a less amiable Heart than Louisa owned!' [22]

The other Eliza figure is Louisa's stepmother-in-law, Lady Lesley. She is called Susan, a name shared with Sukey Simpson, the character Jane used in 'Jack & Alice' to make a joke about Eliza's preoccupation with height. Lady Lesley looks like Eliza: 'She is short, and extremely well-made; is naturally pale, but rouges a good deal; has fine eyes, and fine teeth, as she will take care to let you know as soon as she sees you, and is altogether very pretty.' [23] In manners and disposition Susan Lesley is probably closer to the woman Jane knew than is Henry's wicked Marquise: 'She is remarkably good-tempered when she has her own way, and very lively when she is not out of humour.' [24] Eliza's letters are generally cheerful and pleasant, but her sharpness when Philadelphia Walter refused to act in the theatricals shows how coolly disagreeable she could be when she did not get her own way.

Austen peoples the world of 'Lesley Castle' with an array of the self-obsessed, those always governed by self-interest. Every member of the Lesley family is a variation of Lady Lesley and Louisa. All are callous and self-absorbed. Their feelings are solipsistic and shallow. Louisa's husband is said to be devastated when she abandons him and their child, but he goes off to Paris, soon decides it is rather pleasant to be single again, and abandons the child, just as Louisa did. His father and stepmother, Sir George and Lady Lesley, are careless, spendthrift pleasure-seekers, and make no pretence to being anything else. His sisters Margaret and Mathilda (Aurelius's wife is named Mathilda) pretend to be concerned for others, but their motive is self-serving – all they want is a way out of dreary and isolated Lesley Castle and a chance to have some fun.

The Lutterell sisters in 'Lesley Castle' seem different from the Lesley crew, but what gives them pleasure is no less selfish and makes them no less heedless of the feelings of others. When Eloisa's fiancé is killed in a riding accident the day before their wedding, her sister Charlotte is wholly preoccupied with what will become of the food she has prepared for the wedding feast. Charlotte is a comic grotesque in her obsession with food; she can think of nothing else:

> Indeed, my dear Friend, I never remember suffering any vexation equal to what I experienced on last Monday when my Sister came running to me in the Store-room with her face as White as a Whipt syllabub, and told me that Hervey had been thrown from his Horse, had fractured his Scull and was pronounced by his Surgeon to be in the most emminent Danger. 'Good God! (said I) you dont say so? Why what in the name of Heaven will become of all the Victuals? We will never be able to eat it while it is good.[25]

Amusing as this is, the purpose is to show how an obsession is an extension of the self and blunts natural feeling for others.

Charlotte's sister, grieving Eloisa (a name twinning her with Louisa), does feel her loss in the death of her fiancé, but soon begins to enjoy her suffering so much that it becomes a compulsive, masochistic pleasure. Her grief ceases to be a natural feeling and becomes cultivated sensation. Eloisa is a more sophisticated creation than Louisa because Louisa is conscious of her duplicity, while Eloisa does not quite realise that her pain has become self-gratification, that the mask of sorrow conceals her pleasure.

The variations Austen plays on the theme of self-interest are so subtly done that 'Lesley Castle' has been said to have no unifying theme to hold the plotless story together. But the story is far more than a clever interweaving of jokes and character sketches. It conjures the world that Henry located in France and James in London. Jane knew better. The denizens of 'Lesley Castle' exist everywhere from Perthshire in the north to Sussex in the south, from a village in the east to a watering-place in the west. Austen takes a steady look at their world and laughs, as if it is hardly worth serious consideration. But she called Henry's particular attention to her story. She dedicated 'Lesley Castle' to him.

Once 'Lesley Castle' was out of the way, Jane moved on to other, less intense projects. In the spring of 1791, at about the time Eliza told the Austens that Phila was seriously ill, Edward Austen became engaged to Elizabeth Bridges, two of whose sisters, Fanny and Sophia, also married in that year. Fanny married first, and then Elizabeth and Sophia had a double wedding on 27 December. Jane celebrated the occasion by writing 'The Three Sisters', which she dedicated to Edward. The three sisters in the 'novel' aren't called Fanny, Sophia and Elizabeth. That would have been too obvious. One is called Sophia, and she has a friend named Fanny. The name of Edward's fiancée, Elizabeth, is conspicuously omitted from the story altogether. The title of the 'novel' and the inclusion of the names Sophia and Fanny were enough to make the story an appropriate wedding present for Edward. There are probably other allusive jokes that are lost to us.

On 26 November, a month before Edward married, Jane completed 'The History of England', a spoof of history books. It consists of humorous sketches of British monarchs from Henry IV to Charles I. Even here Austen finds an opportunity to connect her work with her family. When she mentions Sir Francis Drake, she pauses to compliment her brother, another Francis:

> Yet great as [Drake] was, & justly celebrated as a Sailor, I cannot help foreseeing that he will be equalled in this or the next Century by one who

though now but young, already promises to answer all the ardent & sanguine expectations of his Relations & Freinds, amongst whom I may class the amiable Lady to whom this work is dedicated, & my no less amiable Self.[26]

Frank had left the Royal Naval Academy and at the end of 1788 sailed as a midshipman for the British East Indies (of which India was the centre), where he remained until 1793. Charles followed Frank to the Academy in July of the year Jane wrote 'The History of England'; with his departure her brothers had all left home.

Early in 1792 Jane dashed off the last of the 'novels' in her juvenile work. She called it 'Evelyn', the name of the village where the story is set. Like 'Lesley Castle', the only other piece among the early fiction to take its title from a place, the village of Evelyn stands for a set of values characteristic of its inhabitants. The people of Evelyn, an inversion of the characters in 'Lesley Castle', are amiable, sympathetic and unselfish; their exaggerated generosity and hospitality make them as comically ridiculous as the characters in 'Lesley Castle' are in their callous selfishness.

'Evelyn' is dedicated to Mary Lloyd, who with her widowed mother and elder sister Martha had been living at Deane parsonage since 1789. The hyperbolic graciousness of the Webb family in the story seems to be Jane's unsentimental, satirical way of thanking the Lloyds for their kindness to her at Deane.

Jane had dedicated 'Frederic & Elfrida', the first piece in *Volume the First*, to Mary's sister Martha. Martha was ten years older than Jane, but they had become intimate friends. Jane had an affinity with older women. Her closest friends were always considerably older than she was. Jane was not so attached to Martha's sister Mary; but from what we know of Mary's brusque ways, she was quite capable of complaining that Jane had never dedicated anything to her, thus prodding Jane into writing 'Evelyn'.

The Lloyds were about to leave Deane because James Austen was getting married at the end of March and would bring his bride to live there, where he was to be his father's curate. In 'Evelyn' Mr Gower asks the Webbs to give him their house, which they agree to do at literally a moment's notice – probably a joke referring to the Lloyds giving up Deane to James.

At the end of March 1792 James married Anne Mathew, the daughter of General Mathew and Lady Jane Bertie, daughter of the Duke of Ancaster. (James had a weakness for high-born women.) The connection with the Mathew family provided the Austens with an influential tie. General Mathew's niece was married to Admiral James Gambier, a Lord of the Admiralty, who was to be instrumental in securing the advancement in the navy of both Frank and Charles Austen.

A few months after she wrote 'Evelyn', Jane Austen made her first attempt to write a realistic (evidently full-length) novel. She preserved the unfinished 'Catharine' in *Volume the Third* and dated it August 1792 on its last page. Not least among the qualities that distinguish 'Catharine' as a more mature work than its predecessors is the absence of 'messages' to her known readers. 'Catharine' was written for the unknown audience, the reading public, and it was also written for Jane Austen herself. However much she shared Henry's confusion of feelings about Eliza, it was Henry's situation she saw in the *Loiterer* stories and addressed in 'Love and Freindship' and 'Lesley Castle'. But at sixteen Jane was already looking at her own life, both what was and what might have been, and this was the material she drew on for 'Catharine'. The novel is not autobiographical – Austen is never autobiographical in the crude sense of recording what happened to her or to people she knew. But a real situation was sometimes her starting point and developed in her imagination as something quite separate from the 'real'.

'Catharine' has two such identifiable situations. The heroine is a girl whose judgement has not yet been tested and who is only just beginning to grapple with the confusing and conflicting emotions of becoming a woman. Her first challenge comes in the person of a dazzlingly charming stranger, Edward Stanley. Although we only have their initial encounter and Catharine's instantaneous infatuation with the bewitching young man, it appears the novel was to develop along the lines of all of Austen's mature novels: Catharine is captivated by Stanley, the false hero; she misjudges his true character; she will meet the true hero, eventually recognise her mistaken perception of Stanley, and will marry the true hero.

Jane seems to have begun with her own experience with Eliza: she was charmed; she was blind to her cousin's true character; and she was subsequently disillusioned. It is a neat paradigm that lends itself to many possibilities of development. Jane transformed the experience into a romantic plot. There may be some vestige of Eliza in Edward Stanley – he bursts upon the scene from France, a delightful and anarchic presence. Eliza already had so deep a place in Jane's imagination that she had become a prototype that could be used for both male and female characters. Henry Austen later wrote that his sister 'drew from nature ... never from individuals'.[27] Perhaps Edward Stanley is an example of what he meant. Characters may evoke Eliza but none is ever quite Eliza the real individual.

The subplot of 'Catharine' concerning the Wynne family seems to come even more explicitly from life, this time from the history of George Austen and his sisters. The Wynnes are left orphaned and penniless, dependent on their relatives. The brother, like George Austen, has no means for providing for his sisters. Mary Wynne, like Leonora Austen, lives on the margin of a family of relatives. Cecilia Wynne, like Phila Austen, goes to India and marries there. In the fragment it is Cecilia's situation that receives most attention.

On the surface, Cecilia's story appears to be a straightforward recounting of Phila's, and biographers have usually taken it as such. Jane, though, knew only the sophisticated and elegant middle-aged woman her aunt became, and she may have had no more information about the feelings and motives of the young Phila than we do. What 'Catharine' reveals is Jane Austen's almost appalled interest in what Phila had done. It seems likely that the feelings given to Cecilia are those Jane thought she herself would have had in such circumstances. Phila continues to elude us.

There is, though, evidence to show that Mr Lascelles, Cecilia's husband, is *not* a portrait of Tysoe Hancock. Lascelles is described as a man 'whose disposition was not amiable and whose manners were unpleasing'.[28] He is twenty years older than Cecilia. Until recently Tysoe was believed to have been twenty years older than Phila, and from that mistaken information the rest of the character of Mr Lascelles was taken to be Tysoe's. His letters were read as supporting this assumption. The facts are rather different.

Tysoe was under thirty when he married Phila, and he had had the charm and polish of a dandy. Near the end of his life, he thanked his wife for intending to embroider a waistcoat for him but warned that 'if there be the least finery in it, I shall never put it on. It is fully sufficient to have been a coxcomb in my younger years'.[29] His letters, all written from India during the last years of his life, are anxious and fretful – 'gloomy' is the word he himself used – because he feared that he was never going to make a great fortune to leave his wife and daughter. The private worries that he confided to his wife, however, he concealed from the world.

When Philip Dormer Stanhope, the son of Phila's cousin Margaretta Freeman, went to India in 1774, he praised Tysoe, 'whose general knowledge of mankind renders him a most agreeable companion, and who though upwards of fifty years of age still retains all the fire and pleasantry of youth'.[30] After Tysoe died, Stanhope paid him further tribute: 'I believe no man ever lived more generally beloved, or died more universally regretted. In unaffected character and real integrity of heart he was not inferior to Mr Hastings.'[31] It is hard to square these descriptions with Cecilia's husband, and the obvious conclusion is that Austen never intended Lascelles to be a portrait of her uncle. Jane Austen was not writing to record family history.

It might seem callous of her to have taken such an easily recognisable situation from her family and to have presented the husband as so disagreeable. Jane was not, though, thinking of the real man (whom she never knew) but of the demands of her fiction. When the frivolous and unthinking Camilla Stanley says that Cecilia Wynne was lucky to go to India – it was a pleasant and exciting adventure – Catharine replies:

> 'But do you call it lucky, for a Girl of Genius & Feeling to be sent in quest of a Husband to Bengal, to be married there to a Man of whose Disposition she has no opportunity of judging till her Judgement is of no use to her, who may be a Tyrant, or a Fool or both for what she knows to the Contrary. Do you call *that* fortunate?'[32]

To show in the novel what a cruel destiny this might be for a woman, Austen had to make Cecilia's marriage unhappy and her husband an unpleasant man. For a marriage made in those circumstances to be any better was a matter of luck, not to be reckoned on.

Jane Austen's own situation at sixteen was neither that of Catharine (who seems to have an independent fortune) nor of the Wynne sisters (penniless orphans). Jane had no money of her own and could expect little from her parents, but she had a home with her parents, her brother Edward was rich, James had the expectation of inheriting uncle Leigh-Perrot's fortune, Henry had talents and education he meant to put to good use, and Frank and Charles had embarked on their naval careers. With such brothers, Jane felt as secure and well provided for at sixteen as she would have been if she had had £3000. Her penetrating imagination, though, told her that things could easily have been different. She could have found herself in the same situation as the Wynne sisters. In 'Catharine' she is imagining what might have happened to her, not what did happen to her aunt Phila.

With all of the Austen children (except Charles) now more or less educated and grown up, Jane took a hard look at her own parents' way of providing for the children. Like the Wynnes, the Austens believed they could make up for the lack of money by giving their children a good education and depending on rich and influential relatives to help. The idea about education must have come down in the family from Elizabeth Weller and her sons. When Camilla Stanley says it was lucky the Wynnes had only four children for relatives to provide for and wonders what might have happened if Parson Wynne had had ten children, Catharine complacently replies: 'He would have given them all a good Education and have left them all equally poor.'[33] Catharine thinks the Wynnes were right to hold that education was enough. The dependence on education is so sound and sensible today that we may overlook how frankly limited it was, especially for girls, in the eighteenth century. Jane Austen at sixteen saw that the solution to the problem of not having money was not so simple.

Even the Wynne sons don't seem to gain much benefit from being well-educated. The younger is still at school, but the elder, educated to be a parson, is forced to go into the army. He cannot get a clerical living unless someone buys him one (as uncle Francis had for George Austen) or gives him one (as Thomas Knight had). An education was no substitute for money and influence.

The education of Cecilia and Mary Wynne is of no more use than their brother's. No mention is made of the one option their education would have given to Cecilia and Mary: to become governesses. Austen's own personal conviction was that nothing could be worse than being a governess. She studiously avoided the subject until she wrote *Emma* in

1814, twenty years after 'Catharine'. The governess in *Mansfield Park* is only a name in the narrative, a nobody. Why Austen held being a governess in such dread is never explained, but when Jane Fairfax in *Emma* speaks of applying to an agency to find a post, she refers grimly to 'Offices for the sale – not quite of human flesh – but of human intellect'.[34] To be a governess was to be a slave. Austen doesn't go so far in her letters as to confirm that she shared Jane Fairfax's opinion, but once when her brother Edward hired a governess for his daughters, Jane remarked: 'Poor creature! I pity her, though they *are* my neices.'[35]

Whatever advantages Jane Austen thought a good education gave a woman, it was not as preparation for being a governess. Did she, like Catharine, think the Wynne parents were right, or is Catharine's earnest approval another indication of her good-natured but naive optimism? Is Austen using her fiction to challenge the validity of her own parents' philosophy? She never again in her work returned to the theme of formal education for women. Education in her novels means learning from experience; and it is in this broader sense that Catharine Percival suited Austen's imaginative needs.

Academic education for women could not, Jane Austen saw, within the structure of society as she knew it, compensate for lack of money. Her grandparents, the Harpsden Leighs, had accepted this fact. One of Jane's nieces acknowledged, almost apologetically, that her grandmother Austen had had little formal education: 'The education of my Grandmother had not been, for a person in her station of life, much attended to; but whatever she had the opportunity of learning, there was quickness of apprehension, & a retentive memory to make the most of.'[36] Cassandra Leigh was, however, one of the fortunate, a woman with enough money to be free to decide her own destiny. In the Wynne subplot of 'Catharine', Austen must have seen that placing women without money too close to the centre of a novel would constrict the imaginative possibilities, and was too dark and unyielding in its implications.

She was already exploring the position of women of her own class who had no money of their own. She was one of them herself. Catharine blames Cecilia's troubles on her relatives. She – and perhaps Jane Austen herself – sees an alternative to the Wynne girls' circumstances: the rich relatives should have given Cecilia and Mary enough money to enable them to live in modest independence. It is a generous view, a nice thought, but it is a naively idealistic one.

The will of John Austen of Horsmonden was stark proof that relatives, even one as close as a grandfather, could not be counted on to be generous or just or fair. In 'Catharine' the relatives salve their conscience – and congratulate themselves on their generosity – by paying for Cecilia to go to India and by allowing her sister Mary to live almost as a servant on the margin of the family. Bad as Mary's lot is, Catharine thinks it better than Cecilia's, because Mary is still nominally free; she has the possibility of making a change for the better. Cecilia's fate is sealed: she has to endure a marriage to a man she does not like or respect. All that can save Cecilia is the death of her husband. Jane had written herself into a corner, had put her character in a position that took away her freedom and left her dependent on chance.

In August 1792 Jane abandoned writing 'Catharine'. But she must have known that she had taken her first step into the territory she would explore in her mature work. The date suggests another possible reason for her not persevering with the novel. At about that time, Eliza de Feuillide reappeared at Steventon.

Just before Phila Hancock died in February, Eliza's husband had finally managed to come to England, but by the summer he was forced to return home because the revolutionary government threatened to confiscate his property if he stayed away any longer. Eliza now found herself alone for the first time in her life. She made plans for a long stay with the Austens at Steventon. In mid July she told Philadelphia Walter to write to her after the beginning of August at Steventon, where she intended to remain for the rest of the year.[37]

When Eliza arrived, Henry and Jane were the only two of the younger generation at home. Cassandra was at Rowling in Kent with Edward and his wife, who were expecting their first child. James and his wife, Anne Mathew, who was also pregnant, were living at Deane parsonage, but outside the immediate family circle. Frank was still in the East Indies, and Charles at the Royal Naval Academy. Jane, Henry and Eliza were again thrown into an intimacy, an uncomfortable intimacy for Jane. During the theatricals, the twelve-year-old Jane had been a merry and willing spectator, but now she was nearly seventeen and understood the implications of the relationship between her brother and their cousin.

Why did Henry again put himself in the position of being in such close and constant contact with Eliza? Perhaps his resolve was weakening, or perhaps he thought he was now strong enough to meet his cousin without being too much attracted. He was no longer the naive and inexperienced boy who had been infatuated with her; he had spent four years at Oxford, was a well-educated twenty-one year old, more self-controlled and wiser in the ways of the world. But if Henry thought he was ready to put to the test the rationality he had claimed for himself as Aurelius, he had miscalculated.

A lot happened between Eliza's arrival at Steventon and her finally writing to Philadelphia in late October. She refers to the past trouble between herself and Henry, and is able to report that a rapprochement has taken place:

> [Henry] is ... much improved, and is certainly endowed with uncommon abilities, which indeed seem to have been bestowed, though in a different way upon each member of this family. As to the coolness which you know had taken place between H. & myself, it has now ceased, in consequence of due acknowledgements on his part, and we are at present on very proper relation-like terms.[38]

Philadelphia had stayed with Eliza several times during Mrs Hancock's illness, and had evidently heard Eliza's own version of the breach with Henry.

Eliza presents the resumption of their relationship as her own decision to readmit an improved – even penitent – Henry into her favour. Since Eliza's letters to Philadelphia all through 1791 and as late as June and July of 1792 make no mention of Henry, it seems the reconciliation took place at Steventon between August and October. What Eliza wrote about Henry in October is innocuous enough, but her postscript to the letter sounds as if she is treating Henry as a clandestine lover and Philadelphia as her confidante: 'Pray do not neglect burning this.' [39] Only her mention of Henry could have been a reason for wanting the letter destroyed.

Eliza's letter contains a surprising revelation about Henry's character, something very much at odds with the picture of him as the innocent and open young man who never kept anything to himself. During Eliza's visit it came out that Henry was to be a clergyman. He had never revealed this piece of information to her. After writing to Philadelphia about Henry's improvement and their reconciliation, Eliza adds tersely: 'You know that his family design him for the church.'[40] Her wording suggests that his intended profession had never been mentioned to her before but was so generally known that it would come as no surprise to Philadelphia. Eliza's ignorance is odd because she had known Henry quite intimately for six years. Perhaps Henry's silence was a kind of deceit; or perhaps he was silent because he himself doubted he would ever be a clergyman. Eliza opposed Henry's becoming a parson. To have a beau who was still at Oxford had a certain cachet for a married woman; but for a rich and elegant countess to take a parson as a lover would have been humiliating. This was not the part Eliza had in mind for Henry. Nor, perhaps, was it really the part Henry had in mind for himself.

Along with the other contributors to the *Loiterer*, Henry had championed the good, the desirability of the quiet life of a country clergyman. But there were obstacles in his own nature to his embracing this life. He was ambitious, confident, energetic and optimistic. He did not worry about how he would get on in the world; he took for granted that, given the opportunity, he would. Henry wanted a profession that would give him scope and reward for the exercise of his talents, that would enable him to rise quickly in the world through his own enterprise, activity and charm. He doesn't seem to have had any particular profession in mind; but he was not sure the church was the place for him. His family was too practical and prudent to have encouraged this line of thought. They saw him as a bit unsteady. In Eliza he found an ally, someone who agreed with him that he was made for better things.

In the intimacy of their threesome during those last weeks of late summer 1792, Jane must have seen and heard a lot to disturb her. Henry was again in thrall to Eliza and she had the power, foreseen by James in 'Cecilia', to influence the future course of Henry's life. Eliza's discovery that the family intended Henry to be a parson opened a new aspect to their relationship. It was now more than a matter of an illicit love affair.

Henry would not have been the first young man to sow wild oats. A liaison with a married woman, though hardly in keeping with the family's moral values, was not likely to affect him for the rest of his life. His choice of profession would. Eliza might persuade him to abandon the plan to become a clergyman in order to pursue his worldly ambitions. That was the real danger. Jane knew Henry's weaknesses and feared that Eliza would find him receptive to her arguments. There was a legal barrier to their marrying; there was a moral barrier to their becoming lovers; but the only barrier to Henry's rejecting the profession of clergyman was his own judgement.

Jane must have been happy when her cousin Jane Cooper appeared on the scene, even though the cause of her coming was a sad event. Jane Cooper's father had died on 27 August, not long after he and his daughter returned from a holiday on the Isle of Wight. They had gone there early in July, and Jane had soon met Captain Thomas Williams. By the end of July, she and Williams were engaged and the date for their wedding set. Her father's death led to a postponement of the wedding, and she went to stay with the Austens until December, when she would be married at Steventon. Her presence in the meantime created space for Jane Austen, a little respite from being a fifth – and unwilling – wheel to Henry and Eliza's coach.

To celebrate Jane Cooper's marriage, Jane Austen wrote 'A Collection of Letters' as she had 'The Three Sisters' for Edward's, but 'A Collection of Letters' is a more disjointed work. There is no continuous narrative line or unifying theme, nothing so inventive as the comic variation on the idea of the three husband-hunting sisters. It is, as the title indicates, several unconnected letters. One of the characters in the second letter is named Jane, and the third letter is signed Maria Williams, the surname Jane Cooper was soon to take. This is very perfunctory, far from the cleverness of 'The Three Sisters'. Something was constricting the play of Austen's imagination. Jane Cooper and Thomas Williams were married on 11 December. Jane Austen was one of the witnesses, and by the new year Eliza had presumably gone to wherever she chose to spend the rest of the winter.

The link between Henry and Eliza in 1793 and 1794 is an unexpected one. Both their lives became inextricably bound up with the consequences of the French Revolution. It had already caused the exile of Eliza, her mother and her son to England; then Feuillide's forced return to France to prevent his property from being confiscated. There was worse to come. On 21 January 1793, Louis XVI was guillotined. The king's execution had dangerous implications for Eliza's husband as an aristocrat with royalist connections. In February France declared war on Britain, and Henry was presented with the opportunity to advance his own ambitions. He became an officer in the Oxford Militia. It must have appeared a lucky chance to try the role of soldier without having to commit himself to the profession. He could get a taste of military life and see how it suited him, before purchasing a commission in the regular army. Henry's becoming a soldier might be a sign that Eliza's influence was prevailing; but his own ambitions were an important factor in his taking this first step away from a career in the church.

Henry's joining the Militia may have increased Jane's agitation, for 1793 was the least fruitful year in terms of composition since she had begun writing in 1787. She wrote no stories, only slight, miscellaneous pieces cobbled together to celebrate an occasion. 'Scraps' is dedicated to her first niece, Fanny, Edward's first child, born on 23 January, and 'Detached Pieces', dated 2 June 1793, and dedicated to James's first child, Anna, born on 15 April. This may be the first indication we have of Jane's difficulty in writing when her emotional equilibrium was upset.

Jane Austen celebrated her eighteenth birthday on 16 December 1793. By that time she had completed all of the fiction she was to preserve as *Volume the First*, *Volume the Second*, and *Volume the Third*. Not one of the eleven pieces that are thought to have been written between 1787 and 1789 stands out as the very first thing she wrote. Everything is from the hand of a confident and controlled stylist. The work shows sophisticated literary technique, so sophisticated that it is a temptation to say it wasn't mastered but came to her naturally. There is little awkward groping about as she tried to find her way.

The first part of her writing career was over. She was no longer the precocious girl who wrote for the entertainment of her family and friends. She was a young woman of immense talent, brilliant gifts, potential genius. Yet, if she had never written anything else, these three volumes might at best have been handed down in the family from generation to generation, preserved as a curiosity, the work of a remote spinster ancestor.

Inside the cover of *Volume the Third*, her father wrote: 'Effusions of Fancy by a very Young Lady consisting of Tales in a Style entirely new.'[41] This was Jane Austen's first review, and it was a very shrewd one. She had mastered her style and it was completely original. Her skill must have owed a lot, as has often been remarked, to the depth and discernment of her reading, seeing what writers before her had done and learning to do it as well or better herself, and adding something uniquely her own.

What distinguishes the girl Jane Austen as much as her polished and controlled style is the refinement of her intellect. By the time she was eleven, she was a formidable rationalist. Immense though the influence of earlier writers, especially the great prose writers of the eighteenth century, was on Jane Austen, there was a more profound influence: her own family. From their conversation she learned logic, a keen sense of cause and effect, a firm grasp of probability, and a quick penetration into human motivation. These were the tools with which she judged the books she read and the people she observed. The Austens' minds by habit – and probably by inclination – were trained to spot logical and emotional inconsistencies. This is revealed everywhere in Jane's writing and is overtly celebrated in *Pride and Prejudice* in the characters of Mr Bennet and his daughter Elizabeth, both separately and in their collusive view of the world. Jane Austen shared this way of looking at things with her whole family.

Eliza de Feuillide did not find her place in their circle because she was rich, beautiful and a countess, or even because of her warmth, liveliness and cheerfulness. She was very much one of them because she could meet them in the acuteness of her perceptions and in her ability to give form to her ideas and observations with wit, style and discernment. When caught out herself, she could be mocked and teased, as she was by Jane in 'Jack & Alice'; and she didn't slink off to nurse her wounded feelings and self-esteem. As outsiders reading the Austens' letters, Edward's journal or the *Loiterer*, we can take a pure pleasure in the workings of their minds. The scenes we glimpse at Steventon seem exciting and invigorating, as they no doubt were, but this is not the whole picture. The Austens could be formidable, even threatening. If you were an Eliza de Feuillide, you might be able to hold your own, quick to laugh at them and quick to laugh at yourself. Someone like

Philadelphia Walter, with her jealousies, her moaning, her primness and her supercilious self-regard, would not have fared so well.

Jane's rigorous family probably did a lot to make her strong, but it also made her closed and cautious and defensive. She honed her intellect early and quickly, the most brilliant pupil among seven very clever students. But the family was also a school for feelings, a far more difficult subject for Jane because hers were as acute as her intellect. Showing your feelings was a risky business in the Austen family and generally held in deep suspicion. You might be accused of what Jane more than once calls 'a parade of feeling', which carried the automatic suspicion that the emotions were spurious; or you might be laughed at for sentimentality or self-indulgence. Even if your feelings were authentic and to you quite 'reasonable', you might be dismissed as being over-sensitive merely because the others didn't feel what you felt. Jane could not help what she felt in the way that she could help what she thought – it is easier to change your mind than your feelings. She feared her feelings could be as 'wrong' as her ideas – or would be perceived so by her family. By the age of eleven, she had worked out one thing: to protect herself she had to conceal her feelings. She might not be able to avoid the pain of disappointment and rejection, of wounds to her pride, vanity, and self-esteem, but she could, by concealment, avoid the humiliation of exposure.

Her will to write must have been very strong because it involved the risk of disclosure. Writing could be a means of showing off her talent, of getting praise and attention – and indeed of getting even. But laughing at writers was a popular pastime at Steventon. Although Jane took the risk, she devised elaborate strategies for dissociating herself from what she wrote. She commits herself to hardly a single feeling in her stories. She transformed the need to conceal herself into an aesthetic problem and solved it successfully at an early age. Whether this was the working of her precocious intellect or the instinct of genius even she probably could not have said.

The problem of the emotional content of the stories was very elegantly and, it appears, easily solved. Austen holds up to ridicule the feelings, especially the romantic feelings, of all the characters. Even the feelings that prompt the 'beautifull Cassandra' are treated with a high-spirited nonchalance that undercuts the sense of their authenticity. In the juvenile stories emotion, like stupidity, is something to be laughed at, made the butt of jokes. The child Jane Austen was sure of her intellect but had no confidence in the validity of her emotions.

Between the ages of eleven and eighteen, she wrote twenty-two works of fiction (counting 'A History of England') but only in 'Catharine' are there feelings that have to be taken seriously. That this omission does not damage the pieces is one of their most ingenious aspects. The stories are so amusing, so energetic, that we are distracted from the absence of any real emotional dimension. Jane's personal struggle to gain control and understanding of her own emotions – muddled, conflicting, contradictory, and elusive – is not enacted in her work and only hinted at in her treating feeling as the object of ridicule.

At the end of 1793, this is what Jane Austen had accomplished, this is how far she had come, this is who she was. She had every reason to congratulate herself on her achievement over the past seven years.

5

History

'Catharine', the last substantial piece of fiction she wrote during her apprenticeship, points so directly to the six novels Jane Austen was later to publish that we would expect her next work of fiction to be a natural progression from that unfinished work. But it was not the natural bent of her imagination that she followed; she was diverted from that course by an urgent personal preoccupation.

Eliza de Feuillide's visit to Steventon in the autumn of 1792 had returned her to a central place in Austen's imagination. And an event early in 1794 made Jane's need to express her view of Eliza yet again a matter of pressing necessity: Eliza's husband was tried by the revolutionary government in Paris for attempted bribery and the suborning of witnesses; he was guillotined on the same day he was found guilty, 22 February 1794, coincidentally the anniversary of the marriage of Eliza's parents.[1]

Jane's fears in the autumn of 1792 had been contained by one simple fact: Eliza was married. A year and a half later Eliza was free and could offer more than encouragement to Henry's ambitions. They could marry and she could provide the financial backing for him to have a fashionable career, promising the kind of life that she led and that he was so strongly attracted to. Jane's 'beautifull Cassandra' has to knock down the pastry-cook and run away without paying, has to thrust her stolen bonnet on the hackney-coach driver's head and again run away without paying, but Henry could satisfy his longings simply by marrying the rich and beautiful Eliza.

In the winter of 1794 Eliza was still rich in her own right, though whatever remained of the Feuillide fortune was lost with his execution. Eliza's own fortune was safe, thanks to her uncle George Austen. Warren Hastings had named him as a trustee of Eliza's £10,000, and he had been instrumental in the refusal to release her capital for her husband to invest in France when they married. Mr Austen had not approved of her marriage, because he saw in it the danger of her giving up her religion as well as her country.[2] Now rich, widowed and with a French title, Eliza's time to play Lady Bell Bloomer, the role she had designated for herself in *Which is the Man?* back in 1787, had come at last. With Henry already a charming young army officer, the parts for her life imitating Cowley's play were filling up nicely. She only needed a Lord Sparkle to complete the triangle.

Austen had implied in 'Lesley Castle' that Eliza was governed by self-interest, but perhaps it was the perfectly understandable and for-givable self-interest of someone in love. Maybe Eliza had always loved Henry and now wanted to marry him because she loved him and thought he would make her happy. She had done perfectly well, it is true, without her husband during her exile in England, but at that time her emotional needs were fulfilled by her mother. Phila's death must have left a far larger gap than the count's did, though we know little about her marriage except her claim in 1787 that her husband was still passionately in love with her. After Feuillide's death Eliza had no one, but she kept insisting to Philadelphia Walter how independent she was. Her pursuit of Henry, however, casts some doubt on her determination to remain single.

Materially, Eliza had the most to bestow in a marriage to Henry. She was rich, he poor; she had connections in the great world and moved in exalted (or semi-exalted) circles. What was in it for Eliza? A young and handsome husband – Henry was generally considered the best-looking of the Austen sons. Although there is no portrait of him in his youth, if he was handsomer than Charles he was very good-looking indeed. Maybe more important to Eliza was her later claim that Henry knew and accepted that he must always let her have her own way. Perhaps Eliza needed to be married, and marriage to Henry entailed the least risk of ending up under a husband's thumb.

Had they been different people, Henry and Eliza could have settled happily in a country parsonage with an income well supplemented by her money. Jane wanted to believe Henry would have been satisfied with such a life, but she did not think Eliza would. She believed marriage to Eliza would mean Henry's giving up the church to lead a life of fashion in London.

In her ruminations, Jane might even have found herself wishing Henry would just have a fling with Eliza, become her lover for a while. At this point a love affair may have looked preferable to a marriage. Jane appreciated such contradictions – that in this case the immoral act would be more desirable than the moral one. Of course it did not have to be one or the other. Cassandra with her starched notions would have been quick to point out that Henry's right course was to reject Eliza both as mistress and wife.

The most striking thing about Henry's situation is that the roles were reversed from what we tend to think of as the usual order of things. Eliza was the 'masculine' figure with the money to buy herself the spouse she wanted; Henry was the 'feminine' figure, poor but with looks and charm for sale. This intriguing inversion would have made a good basis for a story, but Jane Austen could not or would not tell it. Instead, she wrote an epistolary novel, *Lady Susan*.

Lady Susan is thought to have been written in 1793 or 1794. Whether Jane had begun to plan it before the execution of Eliza's husband, or had even already begun to write it, is not known. It certainly addresses the change that Feuillide's death brought to Henry's situation. The novel is the culmination of the sequence of didactic, persuading, even coercive stories that Henry wrote advising and defending himself in the *Loiterer*, and that James and Jane wrote in response, trying to convince Henry to sever his connection with Eliza. Taken together these stories form a fictional history of Henry's relationship with Eliza, but as James had perceived in his Cecila story, Jane's own history with Eliza was at the beginning parallel to Henry's. And *Lady Susan* is obliquely, even covertly, as much about Jane's relationship with Eliza as it is overtly about Henry's.

Jane's immediate concern was for her brother, but she herself was troubled by Eliza. It appears that once Jane perceived the faults in Eliza's character, she withdrew from the intimate friendship that they had established – not so difficult because Eliza was such an irregular correspondent and was taken up with Henry, not Jane. It seems simple: the child Jane had made a mistake, had misjudged, and had come to see that she had been wrong. But Jane was appalled by her error, even, it almost seems, ashamed of herself. The first hint of this came in 'Lesley Castle' when she allowed her own relationship with Eliza into her fiction for the first time. There is no intrinsic need in the story for Charlotte Lutterell to give an account of her friendship with Lady Lesley; it seems to be there for no other reason but Jane's own need to say something about her relationship with Eliza. And her account is a lie:

> Perhaps you may flatter me so far as to be surprised that one of whom I speak with so little affection should be my particular friend; but to tell you the truth, our freindship arose rather from Caprice on her side than Esteem on mine. We spent two or three days together with a Lady in Berkshire with whom we both happened to be connected. During our visit, the Weather being remarkably bad, and our party particularly stupid, she was so good as to conceive a violent partiality for me, which very soon settled in a downright Freindship, and ended in an established correspondence. She is probably by this time as tired of me, as I am of her; but as she is too polite and I am too civil to say so, our letters are still as frequent and affectionate as ever, and our Attachment as firm and sincere as when it first commenced.[3]

Jane apologises for *appearing* to be Eliza's friend. The light irony of the early part of the passage becomes heavy with the final clause of the last sentence. The meaning in terms of Jane's relationship with Eliza is pointed: I have never really been her friend, and she has never really cared for me. But this was not true; whatever Eliza's feelings for Jane were, Jane without doubt had adored Eliza. Soon after she met Eliza, she had written the affectionately teasing 'Jack & Alice'; and a year later she wrote 'Henry & Eliza', in which the heroine 'Eliza' is the focus of attention. Even though the character has nothing to do with Eliza de Feuillide, the name is a compliment and is meant to flatter her. Now Jane wanted to deny that Eliza had ever amused her, inspired her, excited her.

She must have recalled 'Jack & Alice' and 'Henry & Eliza' with something like distaste, even with self-reproach. She had been swept away by her delight in Eliza, had been flattered by the attention Eliza had shown her. She had taken the whole business of the flirtation of Henry and Eliza so lightly that she had made jokes about it. She had even let the widowed Lady Williams marry the dazzling Charles Adams in 'Jack & Alice'. Now she was angry with herself for having, she believed, been duped by Eliza. She didn't want to laugh at the prescience she had shown in the earlier stories; she wanted to undo it. In the contours of its plot, *Lady Susan* does just that. It is a wish-fulfilment fantasy in two senses: it shows the young man undeceived by the wicked Lady Susan; but it also insists that the author was never taken in by Eliza.

The plot is very simple: Lady Susan, a widow, forces her company on her brother-in-law and his wife, Mr and Mrs Vernon, and proceeds to try to lure Mrs Vernon's brother Reginald, an innocent young man twelve years her junior, into falling in love with her. Her design is to make Reginald marry her. Reginald's sister is unable to do anything but stand by in a state of anxiety as he is drawn into the trap. In the end Reginald discovers Susan's true moral character when he meets Mrs Manwaring, the wife of the man Lady Susan is having an adulterous affair with.

By writing *Lady Susan* Austen herself takes the role of Mrs Manwaring, the revealer of Susan's true nature. Mrs Manwaring has the facts, and as Susan's friend Alicia says: 'Facts are such horrid things!'[4] Susan is a spendthrift and an adventuress and is only interested in Reginald because he is his rich father's heir; she is a heartless mother, not just indifferent to her daughter but maliciously cruel; she likes to cause people pain and she delights in making fools of them. She is sexually amoral and thinks nothing of destroying a marriage; she is perfectly conscious that she is wicked and cynical but feels no guilt or remorse.

There is no evidence that any of this was true of Eliza, and strong indications that most of it is false. Eliza was rich, not Henry, and she was sensible with her money. Philadelphia Walter told her brother that Eliza never bought anything on credit, never contracted a debt, and 'never touched a card'.[5] Eliza was too shrewd to risk her money at the card-table. She was a good mother to her poor son, saw that he was well cared for and kept him with her until he died in 1801 at the age of fifteen. About her sex life we only know that she was a flirt. How far she was prepared to go in her flirtations is a matter of conjecture. Jane was ready to assume Eliza was a libertine.

Eliza was a much more subtle and interesting person than Lady Susan. She did not consider herself wicked and unscrupulous. She saw herself as lively, clever, flirtatious and independent, qualities she was proud to possess. Of course she always wanted her own way, and she was lucky in that she usually succeeded. As the letters she wrote to the priggish Philadelphia Walter show, she had little sense that her ideas and values were really different from those of other people. She admitted what other people concealed.

In *Lady Susan*, Austen pretends to be just to Eliza's charm; Mrs Vernon gives the fullest description of Susan's social powers:

> Her address to me was so gentle, frank & even affectionate, that if I had not known how much she has always disliked me for marrying Mr Vernon, & that we had never met before, I should have imagined her an attached friend. One is apt I believe to connect assurance of manner with coquetry & to expect that an impudent address will necessarily attend an impudent mind; at least I was myself prepared for an improper degree of confidence in Lady Susan; but her Countenance is absolutely sweet, & her voice & manner winningly mild. I am sorry it is so, for what is this but Deceit? Unfortunately one knows her all too well. She is clever & agreable, has all that knowledge of the world which makes conversation easy, & talks very well, with a happy command of Language, which is too often used I believe to make Black appear White.[6]

This is a good beginning, and the reader is set to see all this directly, not at one remove. But Austen keeps us at a distance. It is as if she doesn't trust the reader, she is afraid we too will be taken in by Susan. But we have a right to form our own opinion, even to be duped. Being duped is, after all, central to the experience of knowing Lady Susan.

Austen as determinedly manipulates the reader as she does the character of Susan. We are manoeuvred into a corner with the first two letters of the forty-one that make up the body of the novel. In the first letter Susan writes to the Vernons as a grieving widow begging for the consolation and support of her late husband's family. In the second, to her friend Alicia, she reveals her contempt for the Vernons and her plan to exploit their good nature. From this point the reader is in the same position as the author: we know the truth about Susan. We cannot be fooled by her. We are not even given the chance to feel the contrast, described by Mrs Vernon, between what Susan seems to be and what we know she is. We see her bad side directly in her letters to Alicia; but her power to charm is always filtered through another character, thus making it impossible for the reader to feel the direct effect of her spell.

In all her work before *Lady Susan*, Austen had given her characters the freedom to be seen directly being themselves and had given readers the freedom to form their own judgement. This gives even the slightest and most unfinished of her work a special quality: There is room to move around, and neither readers nor the characters is pinned down.

But in *Lady Susan* everyone is locked into a narrow space – Susan, readers, even Jane Austen herself.

The style of the novel is so clear, concise and elegant that we may at first be unaware of how constricted it is. But when we reach the narrative conclusion everything changes. Austen liberates herself and in doing so she liberates readers and characters too:

> Frederica was therefore fixed in the family of her Uncle & Aunt, till such time as Reginald De Courcy could be talked, flattered & finessed into an affection for her – which, allowing leisure for the conquest of his attachment to her Mother, for his abjuring all future attachments & detesting the Sex, might be reasonably looked for in the course of a Twelvemonth. Three Months might have done it in general, but Reginald's feelings were no less lasting than lively.
>
> Whether Lady Susan was, or was not happy in her second Choice – I do not see how it can ever be ascertained – for who would take her assurance of it, on either side of the question? The World must judge from Probability. She had nothing against her, but her Husband, & her Conscience.
>
> Sir James may seem to have drawn an harder Lot than mere Folly merited. I leave him therefore to all the Pity that anybody can give him. For myself, I confess that *I* can pity only Miss Manwaring, who coming to Town & putting herself to an expence in Cloathes, which impoverished her for two years, on purpose to secure him, was defrauded of her due by a Woman ten years older than herself.[7]

When you reach these paragraphs, the effect is startling. You feel you have been let out of a narrow space into a wider, more capacious place. Then you realise it was Jane Austen who had first been liberated: she could speak as herself again.

In this narrative conclusion, even the good and the sympathetic characters, the well-meaning and tender-hearted, are good-humouredly mocked. The playfulness and warmth of style have returned. The language is fluid, easy, confident and natural. We can laugh at Reginald's susceptibility to the influence of others and at the changeability of human affections. Lady Susan's nature becomes a subject for wit rather than condemnation. Austen almost shrugs at Susan's faults.

Above all, in the final paragraphs, Austen explicitly separates herself from the reader, acknowledging the possibility of different values, different opinions, different ways of looking at things. We may take the high-minded view and give our pity to Sir James for the disparity between his faults (his weakness and stupidity) and his punishment (his being finessed into marriage by Lady Susan). But Austen exults in her own freedom to reserve her pity for the girl who has squandered two years' allowance on her clothes in the hopes of captivating the man she lost to an older woman.

The corollary to this shift was a change in Jane's perception of her responsibility to Henry. Because Mrs Vernon's motives are good and disinterested, it seems a pity that she has no power over her brother. But however well-intentioned Mrs Vernon may be, Reginald is a grown-up man and must in the end take his chances like everyone else. At the very centre of Mrs Vernon's goodwill and unselfish concern for her brother lies a wish to impose her will on him, and that in itself is wrong.

Jane thought she knew what was good for Henry, knew what kind of life would be best for him – what profession, what kind of wife, what style of living. But she had to respect Henry's right to make his own destiny, to choose his own profession, his wife, the way he lived – however mistaken he might be. Telling herself she was trying to counter-act the bad influence of Eliza justified nothing. This was not solely a matter of high principles; it was a matter of common sense. In *Lady Susan* Austen has Susan remark: 'I have never yet found that the advice of a Sister could prevent a young Man's being in love if he chose it.'[8] Jane did not want this to be true, but she knew it was.

Jane Austen had reached what she would call the 'interesting' part of her own life. She turned eighteen at the end of 1793. She had gone to balls and parties in the Steventon neighbourhood, but now she began to go further afield. Her parents contrived in the most discreet and delicate way a little 'season' for their daughters. The time had come for Jane and Cassandra to be seen in the marriage marketplace.

Around Jane's eighteenth birthday, she and Cassandra had gone to Southampton to visit cousins. The town had a good supply of naval officers and, being a fashionable watering-place, drew an assortment of young men from the country as well. Jane later recalled going to a ball there in December 1793. The year before, Cassandra had been sent to Kent to be seen by the eligible young men in her brother Edward's neighbourhood, but by the time she and Jane went to Southampton, it was all for Jane's benefit. Cassandra had become engaged to the Rev Thomas Fowle, a former pupil of Mr Austen and a nephew of their friend Mrs Lloyd, who was the sister of Tom's mother. He was twenty-eight and the rector of Allington in Wiltshire. He and Cassandra could not marry yet because his income was too small to support a wife and the children that would almost inevitably follow the marriage.

In the summer of 1794, Jane and Cassandra went to a place they had probably never visited before, Adlestrop Park in Gloucestershire, the Leigh family estate for more than a century. Mrs Austen's father Thomas Leigh had grown up there. Thomas's eldest brother, William, had begun restoration of the house in about 1750 with the construction of a Gothic front, the architectural feature afterwards usually shown in engravings of the house. His son continued the project in the late 1750s and early 1760s, rebuilding and enlarging most of the house.[9] When he died in 1774, the place was inherited by his nine-year-old son James, who in 1794 was twenty-nine and lived there with his wife Julia and their three-year-old son, Chandos. Probably also there was James's mother, Lady Caroline Brydges, the daughter of the 2nd Duke of Chandos, a man who in his youth was summed up in a remark by George II: 'There is my Lord Carnavon [the future duke's courtesy title], a hot-headed, passionate, half-witted coxcomb.'[10] So much for family glory. He had ended by taking as his third wife a woman he reputedly bought from her husband, an ostler at the Pelican Inn in Newbury.[11]

Whether Jane knew this detail of the family history is doubtful but not impossible. She certainly would have heard something of the history of the Adlestrop Leighs from her mother before she visited the place. Once there she would have learned a lot more. Jane and Cassandra did not stay at the great house but at the parsonage with their mother's cousins, another Thomas Leigh and his wife Mary, who were themselves first cousins. The Leighs were already known to the Austen girls. They sometimes visited Steventon and had once stopped to see Jane and Cassandra at the Abbey School. The couple, now aged about sixty, lived at Adlestrop rectory, just a stone's throw from the great house, with Thomas's spinster sister Elizabeth, Cassandra's godmother. Mary Leigh had recently written a history of the Leigh family, which Jane is likely to have read during her stay.[12] Mrs Leigh could no doubt have provided more intimate details that were not recorded in the book.

Mary Leigh also wrote novels, although though none has survived.[13] In her history there is a novelistic impulse to include domestic detail and anecdote. She not only recorded the achievements of the men of the family but sketched the stories of the women, which would have been of particular interest to Jane Austen.

The strongest evidence that Jane read Mary Leigh's history comes from the virtuoso opening paragraph of *Mansfield Park* recounting the history of the three Ward sisters. It is derived from the story of the three sisters of Jane's great grandfather Theophilus Leigh, and is given in Mary Leigh's manuscript. The eldest, Sarah, married Henry Wight, a match the family approved and celebrated; her youngest sister, Anne, was married respectably but not spectacularly to Leonard Brandon, a merchant of the Turkey Company; the middle girl, Martha, fell in love with Henry Becke of no specified profession and 'eloped at night from a high balcony in the front part of the house'.[14] Mrs Becke suffered much, had numerous children, and lived in 'low circumstances'.[15] Jane made up her own details and transformed the Leigh sisters into the Ward sisters of Huntingdon – Lady Bertram, Mrs Norris and the hapless Mrs Price.

Mary Leigh adds in her account that 'Mr Theophilus Leigh arriving early the next morning [after his sister's elopement], met his good father walking and smoking his pipe composedly, "See Son," (said he) "the Cage door is open; no wonder the bird is fled"'.[16] This sharp little scene and the old man's enigmatic utterance stuck in Jane Austen's mind and re-emerged in the images of prisons and cages in *Mansfield Park*, the spiked iron gates, the locks and keys, and Maria Bertram quoting Sterne, 'I cannot get out the starling said'.[17]

Jane Austen felt free to use the story of the Leigh sisters because it had occurred more than a century before and was unlikely to be recognised. She was more circumspect about drawing on the stories of her great-grandfather Theophilus's own daughters, but she did later take something from Leigh history for *Persuasion*, and there may even be a hint of it in *Emma*.

Theophilus had five daughters, one from his first marriage and four from his second. His eldest, the splendidly named Tryphena, was twenty-five when her stepmother died after giving birth to her twelfth child in thirteen years of marriage. Tryphena was handsome and rich – she had inherited a fortune from her mother, Elizabeth Craven [18] – but she chose not to marry, remaining instead as mistress of Adlestrop and mother to her half brothers and sisters, who ranged in age from new-born to twelve at the time of their mother's death. According to Mary Leigh's account, Tryphena ultimately fell under the influence of her maid, 'the harpy Abigail',[19] and went off with her to Painswick near Gloucester. She died, however, at Barnsley Park, the home of her stepmother's nieces, Cassandra and Martha Perrot, in 1743, and is buried in the Barnsley parish church.

Tryphena's four half-sisters had little or no money of their own (their mother Mary Brydges had brought little to her marriage) and were dependent on whatever their father might have after his sons were provided for. Unfortunately, they had five brothers, in addition to the eldest who would inherit the family estate, who had to be educated and set up in professions. As his daughters came of marriageable age, Theophilus Leigh was approaching the age of seventy, and he looked to his brother-in-law James Brydges to find husbands for the girls. Brydges had become immensely rich as paymaster to the armies of the Duke of Marlborough, a post that is reputed to have brought him £600,000 and in 1719 he was made Duke of Chandos. [20]

Brydges had a wide circle of eligible friends, no daughters of his own to marry off, and is said to have been prepared to give each of his Leigh nieces a dowry of £3000 if they married the men he chose.[21] It sounds like a fairy tale, offering everything Betty Austen and her niece Phila lacked. But not all of the Leigh girls were willing to be Cinderellas.

Mary Leigh was frank about the drawback to uncle Brydges's generous scheme: '[He] regarded Fortune and Character, more than Person and age' in choosing husbands for his nieces. [22] His candidate satisfied the first girl, Emma; she went to the duke's house, was presented with a rich clergyman, the Rev. Peter Waldo, and married him at Westminster Abbey in 1712.[23] This must have seemed to bode well for the whole project.

But the second sister, Cassandra, was not so compliant. 'An elderly rich County Gentleman', writes Mary Leigh, 'was pitched upon for the pretty Cassandra.' [24] Cassandra declined the match, earning herself the reputation of being a rebel. She informed her father that she was engaged to her first cousin, Captain Thomas Wight, but Theophilus would not agree to the marriage. The only mark against Thomas seems to have been that he was the youngest son in his family and had no money of his own.

Cassandra was adamant in her choice, though she was not so wilful as to marry without her father's consent. (Or perhaps the dire consequences of her aunt Becke's elopement made Cassandra think twice.) She settled down to be a patient, dutiful daughter and to wait and see what would happen. She might never marry Thomas Wight, but she would not marry anyone else.

Perhaps Theophilus thought his mistake had been in waiting until Cassandra was eighteen to send her to her uncle, so he sent his third daughter, Mary, to the duke when she was only sixteen, before she had time to fall in love with some penniless cousin. Mary may have been more yielding and less demanding than Cassandra; or perhaps her uncle's choice suited her. At seventeen she married Sir Hungerford Hoskyns, twenty years her senior.[25]

The youngest girl, Anne, was her father's favourite, but when he tried to send her to the duke at sixteen she refused outright even to go. She was romantic and independent of spirit (though not of fortune) and had no intention, on principle, of marrying a man someone else chose for her.[26] She was not in love with anyone; she simply disliked the whole situation at her uncle's house, and was having none of it. She stayed at Adlestrop with Tryphena and Cassandra until their father died, aged seventy-seven in 1725.

The historian Mary Leigh does not mention Theophilus's will but she must have known its contents. He left a token sum of £20 to his two married daughters, and to Tryphena her grandmother Craven's silver and pictures. Anne received £1500, even though she had refused to oblige him by going to the duke. The recalcitrant Cassandra was left only £1000 outright and would receive another £500 'if she does not marry Thomas Wight, youngest son of my sister Sarah Wight'.[27]

Soon after her father's death, Anne married her sister Mary's brother-in-law, the Rev. John Hoskyns, a match it seems no one objected to.[28] Theophilus had delayed but did not prevent the marriage of Cassandra to Thomas Wight. In 1728 they were married at St Peter's, Cornhill, London, and lived in Essex.[29]

Cassandra is said to have been the favourite of her brothers and sisters, and she was next in age to Jane Austen's grandfather. It was probably she (and not James Brydges's second wife and co-matchmaker, his first cousin Cassandra Willoughby), that Jane's mother was named for. Cassandra Wight lived until 1778 and was godmother to the Austens' son Edward. After her husband's death in 1747 she lived in Oxford with her brother the Master of Balliol. Mary Leigh was the Master's daughter and so would have known her aunt well.

Mary Leigh's history recounts another story similar to that of Cassandra and Thomas Wight. Cassandra's brother William had a sister-in-law, Elizabeth Lord, who fell in love with a soldier named Thomas Wentworth; Elizabeth's mother forbade the marriage but the couple were wed secretly. The story ended happily. Elizabeth's mother became reconciled to the marriage, and Thomas Wentworth rose to the rank of lieutenant-general. After Wentworth died, his widow lived at Adlestrop and was much loved by her nieces and nephews.[30]

Austen found a lot of material in the Leigh history to stimulate her imagination, and she used some of it in her later novels. We find Theophilus's three sisters in the Ward sisters of *Mansfield Park*, and the refusal of Cassandra and Anne to marry rich men in Fanny Price's rejection of Henry Crawford. Tryphena's independent fortune and her attachment to her ageing father may have contributed something to Emma Woodhouse, as did Anne Leigh's marrying her brother-in-law. Cassandra's long and determined fidelity to Thomas Wight lies at the centre of *Persuasion*, and another part of the Leigh history perhaps provided a hint for Sir Walter Elliot's situation. After Theophilus Leigh's death it was discovered that Adlestrop was encumbered with debt. The heir rented out the estates and went to live abroad on a small stipend until the debts were cleared.

Most significant, though, is probably the general situation and characters of the women in the Leigh family. Jane had tried in 'Catharine' to explore Phila Austen's plight, but it was too dark and offered no space for the Wynne sisters to determine their own destinies. The Leighs provide the profile of the mature Austen heroine: they had enough money to prevent them from being forced by circumstances to marry (with the exception of Emma, the Austen heroines have about £1500 – even Fanny Price, if we can trust Sir Thomas Bertram, has 'the provision of a gentlewoman').[31] And like the Leigh girls, Jane Austen's heroines all have a solid sense of their own worth and their right to live by their own feelings and principles. Jane of course knew such women herself – her mother was one, as were Anne Lefroy, Jane Cooper and her friends the Bigg sisters. The histories of Theophilus Leigh's daughters, though, seem to have clarified for Jane Austen the common denominator all her heroines would share: good sense and right feeling in making judgements, and enough money to prevent their fearing destitution.

No record exists of the Gloucestershire visit, though Jane later refers to it, and her cousin Thomas recorded giving Jane and Cassandra a small gift of money. The impact of the visit does not, though, go unacknowledged. By 1794 Jane's habit of using names to allude to her sources of inspiration was well established, and the network of Leigh and Brydges connections receives a tribute in her use of some of their names in every novel: Brandon, Middleton and Willoughby in *Sense and Sensibility*; Bennet and Bingley in *Pride and Prejudice*; Tilney in *Northanger Abbey*; Ross in *Mansfield Park*; Woodhouse, Knightley, and Fairfax in *Emma*; Wentworth, Carteret and Dalrymple in *Persuasion*; even in the unfinished work we find Musgrave in *The Watsons* and Brereton in *Sanditon*.

Only a few of these names appear in Mary Leigh's manuscript history – Brandon, Ross, Wentworth and Tilney – but others Austen would have seen on memorial tablets and graves and would have heard talked of in the family. The Leighs and Brydgeses were distinguished families and tended to marry within their sphere. Many of them turn up in Sir Walter Elliot's book of books, the baronetage and the peerage, and Jane Austen's awareness of some of the more remote connections through marriage of her own family suggests she was almost as familiar with the book as Sir Walter.

The purpose of Jane's visit to Gloucestershire had been a discreet trawl through the marriage market. She did not find a husband there, but she found wealth in a different form, a form very much to her own purpose as a novelist. Less than a year passed before she began writing 'Elinor and Marianne', the first version of *Sense and Sensibility*. She continued using the Gloucestershire material for the rest of her life.

From Adlestrop, Jane and Cassandra went to Kent to stay with Edward and his family at Rowling. There Jane did meet a man she found attractive. She later joked that she had once doted on the dark-eyed Edward Taylor of Bifrons, and she rejoiced when she heard that he might marry his cousin because the match would insure that his beautiful eyes would pass to another generation.[32] The visit to Kent seems to have been the end of the concerted effort to show Jane off to eligible men.

Early in May 1795 James Austen's wife Anne Mathew died. Although her death was sudden, she had never been in good health. James's grief caused his romantic disposition to become melancholic. He was so disturbed by his two-year-old daughter, Anna, asking for her mother that he sent the child to Steventon to be cared for by her grandmother and aunts – another reason Jane and Cassandra stayed at home for the rest of the year.[33]

Jane was not idle. She spent the year writing 'Elinor and Marianne', which Cassandra said later had something of the same characters and story as *Sense and Sensibility*, Austen's first published novel.[34] The manuscript of 'Elinor and Marianne' has not survived, but judging from *Sense and Sensibility* the core of the novel derives from the abstract problem Henry had sketched, oversimplified and somewhat muddled, in his 'Aurelius' story – the old and abiding theme so central to Austen family thinking: the conflict between reason and passion.

Tempting as it is to take Elinor and Marianne as deriving from Cassandra and Jane themselves, it is probably closer to the truth to see them as conflicting sides of Jane Austen's own nature. She is harder on Marianne Dashwood than on any of her other heroines, perhaps because she knew her own stronger inclination was emotional. Jane had to struggle to be rational about her own feelings. But she tried to have a stoical Elinor side too.

Jane had more space in her novel than Henry had in 'Aurelius' to elaborate the complexities of the theme of reason versus passion, and she imagined a resolution more plausible than Aurelius's claim that he had reasoned himself out of love with the Marquise. Marianne does not reason herself out of love with Willoughby, but gives free rein to her emotions. In indulging the physical manifestations of her grief – not eating or sleeping, wandering about in the rain and refusing to change her wet clothes – Marianne brings on a near-fatal illness. Thwarted passion finds its consummation in the body as certainly as fulfilled passion would have done. Marianne's recovery is not the triumph of reason over feeling; it is her physical being that saves her. She is young and strong; her body is victorious, not her rational principles, whatever lessons she says she has drawn from her experience.

One aspect of Austen's treatment of the theme does accord with Henry's. Marianne, like Aurelius, learns her lesson about the dangers of passion and marries someone for whom she feels rational affection. But Jane does not commit herself wholeheartedly on the question of passion. The passion of Marianne and Willoughby is not itself inherently bad. It is Willoughby's general moral character and Marianne's unthinking self-indulgence that are bad. Willoughby is not a novelistic seducer; Marianne contributes her own share of erotic energy to their relationship. Jane Austen never shows women as passive victims of sexual seduction. Marianne Dashwood, Lydia Bennet, Maria Bertram and Mrs Clay all *think* they know what they are doing.

By 1795 Jane had seen the strength of sexual passion from the outside in observing the relationship of Henry and Eliza, but she herself had not yet experienced the full force of it for herself. Intense as her own infatuation with Eliza had been, it had lacked the dimension of sexual passion that made Henry's connection with Eliza so much stronger and more complicated than her own. How Eliza's being a widow would affect her relationship with Henry still remained to be seen.

In mid 1795 Cassandra had been engaged to Tom Fowle for about two years, but no lucrative living had presented itself to enable them to marry. Sometime during the year Lord Craven, the cousin of Tom's mother, Jane Craven, asked Tom to accompany him as chaplain on a voyage to the West Indies. Craven was a man of wealth and influence with rewards to bestow on those who served him. Tom believed that if he accepted the chaplaincy, Craven would present him with a living on their return to England.[35]

The decision required boldness and courage. Fowle would face the dangers and hardships of the long sea voyage, of diseases on the ship and in the hot climate of the West Indies. He decided to take the risks, and in the autumn accepted Craven's offer. He made his will in October and was to sail early in the new year of 1796. At Christmas Cassandra went to Kintbury in Berkshire, where Tom's family lived, for a farewell visit to her fiancé before his departure. She did not return to

Steventon when Tom left Kintbury but stayed on, perhaps to keep herself busy and distracted. Two of Jane's letters to her sister during this time have survived.

These two letters are high-spirited, entertaining and diverting, just what would have helped distract Cassandra from an inevitable tendency to be in low spirits, considering her situation. The recurring subject is a stranger who had come to the Steventon neighbourhood for a visit. Like Cassandra's fiancé, the young man's name was Tom – Tom Lefroy.

6

Love and Art

Jane Austen and Tom Lefroy met during the Christmas season of 1795. He had come to Hampshire to visit his uncle and aunt, George and Anne Lefroy, before going to London to study law. He was the eldest son of George Lefroy's brother Anthony, who had had a career in the army in Ireland, married Anne Gardiner, the daughter of a Limerick squire, and had settled there with his large family. Tom was handsome and clever – everything but rich.[1]

Jane described him, with some restraint, as 'a very gentlemanlike, good-looking, pleasant young man'.[2] A miniature painted of him at about this time confirms that he was handsome, though his humorous mouth was a bit too small. He had large eyes and a lively expression with just a hint of shyness in it. You can see the attraction: it is a witty, mobile face. But it is immature, the face of a boy.

Christmas was a time of balls, and Tom and Jane met at four balls during his stay at Ashe. Their attraction seems to have been immediate. Jane implies as much in a letter to Cassandra when she remarks that their friend Elizabeth Bigg and her swain William Heathcote 'do not know how to be particular', but that she herself had set an example for them: 'I flatter myself, however, that they will profit by the three successive lessons which I have given them.'[3] She says in the same letter that she and Tom had met at the last three balls, so their flirtation, their being 'particular', had begun at their first meeting.

Jane's teasing admission – really, a boast – was not the first Cassandra had heard about her sister's flirtation with Tom, and she had evidently written to Jane warning her to be more restrained in her behaviour. Jane laughed it off: 'Imagine to yourself everything most profligate and shocking in the way of dancing and sitting down together.'[4] She was in high spirits and even a scolding from Cassandra (if in fact it was serious) could not dampen her mood.

Everyone seems to have noticed the pointed attentions Tom and Jane were paying each other at the balls. One young man even took the trouble to draw Tom's picture and presented it to Jane 'without a Sigh' – proof, according to her, that the artist himself was not harbouring a secret preference for her. [5] At Ashe the Lefroys teased Tom about Jane, and when a few days before the third ball (which was at Manydown, the home of the Bigg-Withers, on Tom's twentieth birthday) Jane called on Mrs Lefroy, Tom had run away because 'he is so excessively laughed at about me at Ashe'.[6] He made amends by coming to Steventon to see Jane the day after the Manydown ball.

The call at Steventon may have given Jane her first glimpse of Tom outside a ballroom, and she declared to Cassandra that she had discovered his only fault: his morning coat was white. She had an explanation for this lapse of taste: 'He is a very great admirer of Tom Jones', she told Cassandra, 'and therefore wears the same coloured clothes, I imagine, which *he* did when he was wounded.'[7] This is the only concrete detail Jane gives about Tom Lefroy, and she makes the most of it. She and Tom had talked about books, and his admiration of *Tom Jones* and his choice of coats become Jane's means of hinting to Cassandra that Tom was in love. In *Tom Jones* Fielding plays with being wounded as a metaphor for being in love: 'It was some time before she discovered, that the gentleman who had given him this wound was the very same person from whom her heart had received a wound.'[8]

Tom's coat had seized Jane's imagination, and in her next letter to Cassandra she mentions it again. Mrs Lefroy was giving a ball at Ashe, apparently an encouragement to the romance between her friend and her nephew. 'I look forward with great impatience to it, as I rather expect to receive an offer from my friend in the course of the evening. I shall refuse him, however, unless he promises to give away his white Coat.'[9]

Jane could not keep away from the subject of Tom, and later in the same letter she declares, apropos of nothing: 'I mean to confine myself in future to Mr Tom Lefroy', and then undercut this confession by adding, 'for whom I donot care sixpence.'[10] She didn't finish this letter until the morning of the Ashe ball, and she wrote picturing herself as the heroine of a sentimental novel: 'At length the Day is come on which I am to flirt my last with Tom Lefroy, & when you receive this it will be over. My tears flow as I write, at the melancholy idea.' [11] Jane makes fun of herself as a romantic heroine but in doing so she stakes her claim to the role.

That Tom Lefroy delighted her is obvious, and that she savoured the excitement of the romance is indisputable. But at this point it is hard to make out just how serious her feelings for Tom were. She might easily have been using the flirtation as epistolary capital. It gave her something lively and amusing to write about, and Jane was particularly aware that at this time Cassandra needed to receive entertaining and diverting letters. We might suppose that Jane was mining her flirtation with Tom Lefroy for just the kind of happy chat that would take Cassandra's mind off her own worries about Tom Fowle. But there is a sign that Jane was not just generating a sparkling and playful adventure for the sake of amusing her sister.

After the Manydown ball Jane wrote that she had been 'very much disappointed at not seeing Charles Fowle of the party'.[12] Charles was Tom Fowle's brother, and he had been expected to attend the ball. It was natural enough that Jane wanted to see him and get first-hand news of Christmas at Kintbury, of Tom's departure to join Lord Craven, and of course Charles's impression of how Cassandra was bearing the strain of parting. But Jane had another reason for being disappointed that Charles had not come. Later in her letter she returns to Charles and explains why she had been disappointed by his absence: 'I wish Charles had been at Manydown, because he would have given you some description of my friend, and I think you must be impatient to hear something about him.' [13] This is the most serious remark in these two letters to Cassandra. Tom Lefroy was not just the stuff of ephemeral jokes. Jane wanted Cassandra to hear more about him, was eager for someone to confirm and elaborate what she had written about Tom, someone who could answer Cassandra's questions about him. She was confident that anyone who met Tom Lefroy would carry away a good impression of him. And she knew that, in spite of all the lightness and levity of what she had written to Cassandra, her sister understood this was just the way Jane had chosen to express being in love. Jane wanted Tom Lefroy to be made more real to Cassandra.

We do not know what happened at the Ashe ball. Tom Lefroy left Hampshire for London a day or two later, and Cassandra returned from

Kintbury to ask Jane herself all the questions she had been storing up. Jane must by then have been ready to give a more sober account of what had occurred in Cassandra's absence. Cassandra was the only person she would have spoken to openly about her feelings for Tom Lefroy.

Six months later Jane's brother Edward came to Hampshire and Jane returned to Kent with him, along with their brother Frank, who was back from the East Indies. They spent the first night at Staines and then continued on to London, where they again broke their journey. They stayed in Cork Street, where Tom Lefroy was living with his great-uncle, Benjamin Langlois, while he was studying law.

Although Langlois was the uncle of the Austens' Hampshire neigh-bours, there is something a little unusual in the young Austens staying at his house. Yet the friendship of the Steventon Austens and the Ashe Lefroys might explain the invitation, especially if Mrs Lefroy had pro-posed and arranged it. Jane wrote to Cassandra from Cork Street, the shortest among her known letters to her sister. She does not say they are staying with Langlois – Cassandra would have known that – but Jane's reticence in giving particulars is itself significant.

Cork Street is short and in those days had houses only on the west side – on the opposite side were gardens attached to the houses facing Old Burlington Street. Benjamin Langlois was the only rate-payer in Cork Street that the Austens have a known connection with. Nor does any house in the street seem to have been a hotel. Jane heads her letter 'Cork Street'; but if they had been staying at a hotel she would have given its name, rather than that of the street. For the Austens to have stayed there by chance at this particular time, in the very street where Tom Lefroy was living, would have been a strange coincidence.[14] There is no direct proof that they stayed with Langlois and his nephew, but it looks as though they did.

Jane's letter from London is excited but vague, even cryptic. She doesn't mention Tom at all but says her brothers have gone out and 'We are to be at Astley's to night, which I am glad of'.[15] Astley's was an equestrian circus, which might well have been amusing – why not say 'which will be amusing' or 'which I look forward to'? The phrase Jane uses sounds a little odd. It implies a wish not to be at home in the evening, or even a wish for some kind of public diversion, not just pleasure for its own sake.

Jane had probably met uncle Benjamin before because he sometimes visited the George Lefroys at Ashe, but in London he appeared as Tom's benefactor. Egerton Brydges described Benjamin Langlois as 'a good and benevolent old man with much diplomatic experience, but fatiguingly ceremonious, with abilities not much above the common'.[16] Overly formal, and not very intelligent. Someone Jane would have enjoyed laughing at if nothing important were at stake – a Mr Collins or a Lady Catherine de Bourgh. Certainly not someone who would put a clever and reserved young woman at ease. Small wonder Jane was glad to have the distraction of the bustle and excitement of a circus that evening. To pass the time at home under the restraint of uncle Benjamin's formal fussing about and the close observation of Frank and Edward would have been heavy going for any lovers.

Uncle Benjamin might appear to be a rather comic figure, but in the Lefroy family he was a man to be taken seriously because he controlled the money. His sister was the mother of George and Anthony Lefroy; and, since their father had not been able to do anything for the boys financially, they were dependent on their uncle. He was generous to his nephews and was prepared to continue helping, provided they made prudent, advantageous marriages. In short, his generosity had the same strings attached to it as had that of James Brydges when he was finding husbands for his Leigh nieces at the beginning of the century. In marrying Anne Brydges (no relation to James Brydges), who had money of her own and came from a prominent Kent family, George Lefroy had satisfied uncle Benjamin and was rewarded with a gift of the rectorship of Ashe.[17]

Tom's father Anthony had taken a great risk. He had married a woman who had no money – and money counted a lot to uncle Benjamin. Anthony knew his uncle had another weakness – he was interested only in males of the family line. Anthony thought all would be well as soon as he produced a son. In the meantime, to conceal his imprudence, he kept his marriage a secret from his uncle. But over the next ten years, his wife produced five daughters.[18]

At long last, in early January 1776, Tom was born, saving his family's fortune by guaranteeing their place in uncle Benjamin's good graces.

All was now revealed to Langlois, and he forgave all because Tom was the first male of his generation, the first great-nephew. Uncle Benjamin doted on him, paid for his education, planned his future, and brought him to London to study law.[19] What his matrimonial plans for his nephew were is never hinted.

Jane was penniless, a strong mark against her. Her family, though, had illustrious connections to the short-lived glories of the dukes of Chandos and the more solid and enduring Leighs of Adlestrop Park. In the present generation Edward had great wealth and a place in the landed gentry of Kent, and James expected to inherit the Perrot family fortune. Perhaps everyone thought Edward's money and position and James's expectations from his uncle, along with Jane's personal qualities, would make uncle Benjamin overlook the fact that she had no money of her own. Jane seems to have thought their meeting a success.

In her first letter to Jane in Kent, Cassandra wanted to know what had happened in London, and Jane apologised for her previous letter. 'I am sorry that you found such a conciseness in the strains of my first letter. I must endeavour to make you amends for it, when we meet, by some elaborate details, which I shall shortly begin composing.' [20] In other words: you have to wait to hear it in person. Cassandra was at home, where she was expected to read out some if not all of each of Jane's letters. If Cassandra had picked up even a hint that things had not gone well in London, she would not have pressed Jane for information. She would never have asked Jane to write something painful just to satisfy her own curiosity.

Jane didn't write about her own romance, but she had no such scruples about writing of Henry's. He was there when she arrived in Kent but was about to return to his regiment at Great Yarmouth. More than two years had passed since the death of Eliza's husband, but she and Henry had not married. He was, though, still in the army and on the look-out for a regular commission. In January Jane had told Cassandra:

> Henry is still hankering after the Regulars, and as his project of purchasing the adjutancy of the Oxfordshire is now over, he has got a scheme in his head about getting a lieutenancy and adjutancy in the 86th, a new-raised regiment, which he fancies will be ordered to the Cape of Good Hope. I heartily hope that he will, as usual, be disappointed in this scheme.[21]

Eliza, however, no longer seemed a factor in his decisions concerning his profession. By the end of the summer he was in love with someone else.

His courtship of Mary Pearson, the daughter of Sir Richard Pearson, an officer of the Greenwich Hospital, was well advanced when Jane was in Kent, and she devoted some energy to promoting the match. She met Mary Pearson and they became friendly enough for Jane to invite her to go back to Steventon with her when she returned to Hampshire. Jane warned her family that they might be disappointed by Mary's appearance:

> If Miss Pearson should return with me, pray be careful not to expect too much Beauty. I will not pretend to say that on a *first veiw*, she quite answered the opinion I had formed of her. My Mother I am sure will be disappointed, if she does not take great care. From what I remember of her picture, it is no great resemblance.[22]

Mary went to Steventon with Jane, and Eliza wrote to Philadelphia Walter, early in November, with ill-concealed jealousy about Henry's engagement:

> I hear [Henry's] late intended is a most intolerable flirt, & reckoned to give herself great airs. The person who mentioned this to me says she is a pretty wicked looking girl with bright black eyes which pierce through & through. No wonder this poor young man's heart could not withstand them.[23]

Jane's own feelings in the autumn of 1796 must have been very different from Eliza's. She was herself in love, and Henry was safely engaged to a suitable girl: everything was going to be all right.[24]

Jane's joy overflowed into her writing, indeed became her writing. A creative energy was released, and she began writing 'First Impressions', the first version of *Pride and Prejudice*, soon after she returned to Steventon. The novel is as closely linked to Tom Lefroy as some of Austen's early work is to Eliza de Feuillide and other members of the Austen family circle – and in much the same way.

Jane's imagination was struck by the early uncertainty of Tom's parents. They married in the expectation of having a son, but five daughters arrived in the first ten years. Austen transformed the pressure exerted by uncle Benjamin into an entail, the legal demand for a son.

There she stopped. It is a brilliant situation. Without a son, no money; and five girls to provide for by finding them husbands. We know what Austen's imagination did with the subject.

In the novel she gives clues to its origin. The name Bennet comes from Tom Lefroy's favourite novel, *Tom Jones*.[25] Perhaps Jane noticed the name Bennet in the first place – it is only mentioned once in the novel – because of its connection with the Leigh family. Two of Theophilus's daughters married sons of Sir Bennet Hoskyns, whose wife was the daughter of Sir John Bingley. The name does double duty, referring not only to Fielding's novel but also to the Leighs. Less obscurely, Austen calls the fourth Bennet daughter Kitty, the name of Tom's fourth sister. Truncating the Lefroy family after the birth of their fifth daughter and giving them an entailed estate rather than a difficult uncle provided all the camouflage Jane needed to conceal the origin of her story – the Lefroys' eldest daughter had died in infancy and they had had six more children after Tom.

Jane's joy in her love for Tom Lefroy informs the whole of *Pride and Prejudice*, but Tom himself perhaps provided a more specific inspiration. Jane Austen was not the Elizabeth Bennet we sometimes like to assume. The creator of Elizabeth Bennet had an indisputable genius, but she herself did not possess Elizabeth's spontaneous wit and charm. Jane certainly did not see herself as a Lizzy. But she *did* see Tom Lefroy that way. She had discovered when she wrote the fragment 'Catharine' the trick of changing the gender of her prototype – making Eliza de Feuillide into Edward Stanley. The lesson now served her well. By an imaginative squint she created a woman who might have been Tom's sister, a woman with his charm and liveliness and intelligence transformed into a feminine mode. Austen hints this by making Elizabeth, like Tom Lefroy, the child of a Miss Gardiner.

The essentially diffident, sometimes stiff and self-conscious person Jane herself was has far more affinity with Darcy. Many years later Frank Austen wrote to an American admirer of his sister's work that 'though [Jane was] rather reserved to strangers so as to have been by some accused of hautiness of manner, yet in the company of those she loved the native benevolence of her heart and kindness of her disposition were forcibly displayed'.[26] This sketch of Jane Austen almost exactly coincides with her picture of Darcy in the novel.

Pride and Prejudice is famous for its style, for the sharpness, precision and balance of its sentences. It is one of the great examples of the rational, almost mathematical, eighteenth-century English style both in prose and poetry. Its beauty, clarity and rhythms call up comparisons with Mozart's music. Like Mozart, Jane Austen was incapable of being ponderous. What is most striking and mysterious about the style of *Pride and Prejudice* is Austen's using the most restrained and controlled style to convey the most intense vitality and passion. The style itself embodies what the story and the characters tell us: reason is the servant of passion; reason may procure a kind of happiness, but without passion there can be no joy.

Pride and Prejudice celebrates passion, though it glances at its pitfalls. Lydia's passion for Wickham is unremarkable, what today we would call a simple case of raging hormones; there seems little reason in Lydia to overcome her animal spirits. But reason alone is no guarantor of happiness. Charlotte Lucas, who is as rational as Lydia is passionate, is Lydia's foil in the novel, and it is impossible to say who makes the better match. Lydia would certainly have been far more miserable with Mr Collins than she could ever be with Wickham, and you suspect that had Charlotte been Mrs Wickham she might have discovered a dimension of pleasure she never knew existed.

Mr Bennet's romantic history reveals more about the comparative powers of passion and reason. In him we are shown how impervious passion is to sense and reason. As a young man, he saw the pretty and lively Miss Gardiner, and lost his head – a good example of just what that phrase means. Darcy himself ungallantly admits in his first proposal to Elizabeth that he has been overwhelmed by his passion for her: 'In vain have I struggled. It will not do. My feelings will not be repressed. You must allow me to tell you how ardently I admire and love you.' [27] He goes on to enumerate all that his judgement has counselled against the match. That Elizabeth is in every way superior to her mother is not so much a sign of the superiority of Darcy's judgement to Mr Bennet's as a stroke of good luck for Darcy.

However much Austen's reticence and control of style may suggest otherwise, passion is the centre of Jane Austen's novels. The primacy of passion links *Pride and Prejudice* to the three novels of her later career. Fanny Price and Anne Elliot stake everything on passion, and reject marriage to men for whom they feel no passion. Emma Wood-house only becomes aware of her passion for Mr Knightley near the end of the novel, but her indifference to Frank Churchill, for all his charm and attractiveness, comes from her not having such feelings for him. The heroines may validate their passion in a rational way by their respect for their lovers' moral character, and these qualities may be – like their social and financial positions – desirable in prudent, practical ways, but passion is always the animating factor in the heroines' decision to marry.

Jane Austen is not taking a philosophical position in the feeling versus reason debate and arguing that feeling is better than reason; she is portraying in her novels what her own experience had told her was true. In what is perhaps her least passionate novel, *Northanger Abbey*, she was to state this most directly when Mrs Morland talks to her daughter about the Tilneys, and the narrator remarks that 'there are some situations of the human mind in which sense has very little power; and Catherine's feelings contradicted almost every position her mother advanced'.[28]

The energetic intensity of *Pride and Prejudice* attests to the effect that falling in love had on Jane Austen. It is an irrepressibly happy novel. Between October 1796 and August of the next year Jane wrote 'First Impressions'; it was her unique way of thinking about Tom Lefroy and of celebrating her delight at being in love – and at being loved. The novel that she later called 'my own darling Child' was to be a gift of love for Tom Lefroy.[29] Writing it was her natural way of filling the time as she waited for him to finish his law studies and return to Steventon to marry her.

While Jane was falling in love with Tom Lefroy, and Henry was hankering after the Regulars and courting Mary Pearson, James Austen was looking for a new wife. He appeared to have shaken off the melancholy that had plagued him after his wife's death, and by January 1796 he was attending balls. Jane wrote to Cassandra that James 'deserves encouragement for the very great improvement which has lately taken place in his dancing'.[30] In her next letter she reported that he was going to another ball 'for a Ball is nothing without *him*'.[31] James's eagerness – at least in Jane's account – seems a bit forced, a little too enthusiastic. He was exerting himself against his grief and trying to get on with his life, which above all meant finding a wife to be mother to his child.

At about the same time that Henry became engaged to Mary Pearson, James proposed to Mary Lloyd and was accepted. On 30 November 1796 Mrs Austen wrote to Mary to give her approval of the engagement,[32] and a month later Eliza wrote to Philadelphia Walter: 'Has Cassandra informed you of the wedding which is soon to take place in the family? James has chosen a second wife in the person of Miss Mary Floyd [sic] who is not either rich or handsome, but very sensible & good-humoured.'[33]

Eliza told Philadelphia that she had marriage prospects of her own.

> I am glad to find you have made up your mind to visiting the Rectory, but at the same time, and in spite of all your conjectures & belief, I do assert that Preliminaries are so far from settled that I do not believe the parties ever will come together, not however that they have quarrelled, but one of them cannot bring her mind to give up dear Liberty, & yet dearer flirtation. After a few months stay in the country she sometimes thinks it possible to undertake sober matrimony, but a few weeks stay in London convinces her how little the state suits her taste. Lord S___'s card has this moment been brought me which I think very ominous considering I was talking of matrimony, but it does not signify, I shall certainly escape both peer & parson.[34]

The 'parson' was Eliza's way of sarcastically referring to Henry. Not until the following May was she able to tell Philadelphia that she believed Henry had given up all thoughts of the church. As for the peer, it would be interesting to know if Eliza really had a Lord S___ in her life or if he were a fanciful bit of embroidery inspired by Lord Sparkle in *Which is the Man?*

Philadelphia was Eliza's confidante and must have been excited by the drama of the engaged Henry pursuing Eliza. But we have to be wary of Eliza's accounts of her romantic life. She later told Warren Hastings that she had withheld her acceptance from Henry for two years,[35] but her actions show that she, as much as Henry, was doing the pursuing. Not that Henry didn't collude with her – she reports his visiting her in London several times in 1796 and 1797.

As the affair of Henry and Eliza worked its way to a conclusion, Jane sat in Hampshire writing 'First Impressions' and thinking of Tom Lefroy.

She and Cassandra were both waiting for their lovers. There were, however, some significant differences. Cassandra's engagement was public and her waiting acknowledged. Jane's waiting was secret and not sanctioned by an engagement; it was an act of faith. She did not know how long she would have to wait, whereas Tom Fowle's return to England in April would bring Cassandra a husband.

The theme of waiting in Austen's later novels – Fanny for Edmund in *Mansfield Park*, Anne for Wentworth in *Persuasion*, even Jane Fairfax for Frank Churchill in *Emma* – had its origin here in Jane's own life, but her heroines abide in almost complete isolation without the consolation or encouragement of a sympathetic confidante. Cassandra made an immense difference to Jane's life, and Jane was fully aware of it.

The waiting of Austen's heroines is finally rewarded, but Cassandra was not so lucky. Instead of Tom Fowle's return, the news came in April that he had died of yellow fever in San Domingo in February. Before he had left England, Tom Fowle, well aware of the dangers of such a voyage, had made a will in which he left Cassandra £1000. Eliza wrote to Philadelphia Walter: 'Jane says that her sister behaves with a degree of resolution & propriety which no common mind could evince in so trying a situation.'[36] This is a rare but telling glimpse of Cassandra. She was a woman of extraordinary emotional control. Jane measured herself against her sister all her life, and she always found herself wanting.

She was still writing 'First Impressions' when the news of Tom Fowle's death reached England, but she did not put aside her work for very long. She persevered and finished the book in August, less than a year after she had begun it. But with Tom Fowle's death things had begun to go wrong, and other blows were to follow.

Hard upon the family's learning of Fowle's death, Henry finally got what he wanted – what he had been trying to get for more than a year. He purchased the adjutancy of the Oxfordshire regiment, and was raised to the rank of captain and made regimental paymaster. We can pretty much guess what Jane and her family thought of the business. But Henry was very persuasive and must have had his family's consent to take this step – the money to buy the commission had come from somewhere, probably Edward.

Eliza announced Henry's move in a crowing tone to Philadelphia:

Captain Austen has just spent a few days in town. I suppose you know that our cousin Henry is now Captain, Paymaster, & Adjutant. He is a very lucky young man & bids fair to possess a considerable share of riches & honours. I believe he has now given up all thoughts of the Church, & he is right for he certainly is not so fit for a parson as a soldier.[37]

Eliza was not a disinterested observer; she had a personal stake in Henry's choice of profession. In spite of all her insistence to Philadelphia that she didn't want to give up her freedom, Eliza was now determined to marry Henry. His engagement was an impediment she could do away with, so she acted.

By September she was no longer content to wait in Manchester Street for Henry's occasional visits. She took the offensive and went to him. All that autumn she was at Lowestoft and Henry at nearby Yarmouth. She knew what Philadelphia would rightly conclude but pretended to forestall her by claiming a doctor had recommended the place for the health of her son Hastings:

> Thus my dear friend you see that the contiguity of Suffolk & Norfolk was not my motive for visiting this place, & indeed had you known that Lowestoffe is no less than twenty-eight miles from Norwich, you would probably have dismissed all your *wicked* surmises for you must allow that a person who cannot absent himself from his corps for more than a few hours at a time, cannot very conveniently travel fifty-six miles to pay a visit.[38]

But in fact Henry was often – perhaps wholly – at Great Yarmouth, only a few miles from Lowestoft, and Eliza says she occasionally drives over to Yarmouth, 'with which I am delighted'.[39] She enjoyed a little game of telling the truth by pretending to deny it.

She returned to London in mid December, and Henry soon followed. They were married at St Marylebone parish church on New Year's Eve, but they did not tell the Austens until after the wedding. For once Henry was able to keep a secret. He had somehow managed to extricate himself from his engagement to Mary Pearson, and there was no open scandal as a result of the break. Whatever the family thought of Henry's choice they kept to themselves. Eliza's £10,000 made the match notably prudent. The money would have provided a great temptation to Henry with his worldly ambitions, and it relieved the family of any worry about his future financial security. Anyway, the drama that had been going on by fits and starts for more than ten years was now over. Henry and Eliza went to live at Ipswich, where he was stationed, and there they spent the first year of their married life.

Jane had finished 'First Impressions' in August and in November had begun recasting 'Elinor and Marianne' as *Sense and Sensibility*. In writing 'First Impressions' she had found her own narrative mode. Whether Willoughby was the name given to Marianne's faithless lover in the first version of the novel is impossible to say. Like Bennet and Bingley, it is a name connected to the Leigh family – the Duke of Chandos's second wife was Cassandra Willoughby – but the name Willoughby also appears in *Tom Jones*.[40] Jane Austen probably completed *Sense and Sensibility* in the late spring or early summer of 1798.

In early August came word that Jane Cooper, the Austens' beloved first cousin, had been killed in a carriage accident on the Isle of Wight. She was by then Lady Williams; her husband, Captain Sir Thomas Williams, had been knighted two years before her death. The Austens had been very close to both Jane and her husband, not only because of the family tie but because Sir Thomas had commanded the three ships Charles Austen had served on as a midshipman.

Soon after Jane Cooper's death, Mr and Mrs Austen and their daughters went to Kent to visit Edward and his family. Edward's adoptive father, Thomas Knight, had died in 1794, leaving everything to his wife for her lifetime and then to Edward. Mrs Knight had at first continued to live at Godmersham, but after a couple of years of widowhood she initiated procedures for making over the estates to Edward, reserving for herself an income of £2000 a year. When she told Edward she intended resigning her rights to him, he asked her not to give up the place that had for so long been her home,[41] but she had thought the matter over very carefully and had made up her mind.

Catherine Knight was a person of shrewd good sense. She argued that the activities on the estate, 'entirely lost on me at present',[42] would be interesting to Edward, a clever and energetic young man of thirty. It would give her pleasure to see him perform these duties and to observe his family's enjoyment of the house. She wanted Edward to rely on his own judgement, even to make his own mistakes. If she maintained actual ownership of the estates, he would not be completely free but always subject to the possibility of her interference. Recognising this as a danger, Mrs Knight chose to give everything to Edward outright, 'for your being kept in a state of dependence on my wish, or perhaps caprice, would not be less painful to you, than disagreeable to myself'.[43] Jane came to admire Mrs Knight and to value her friendship.

By the summer of 1798 Edward and his family were living at Godmersham Park, and the Steventon Austens were there on 10 October when Elizabeth had her fifth child and fourth son. Two weeks later Jane and her parents returned home, leaving Cassandra at Godmersham to help care for the children and run the house while Elizabeth recovered. This was Cassandra's role, not Jane's – Jane had many virtues and talents, but managing children, servants and a large house was not among them.

She wrote to Cassandra en route to Steventon on 24 October and again when they got home on 27 October. The next letter is dated 17 November; Cassandra destroyed the letters written in the interval. During that time Jane had learned that Tom Lefroy was again expected at Ashe.

Tom came to Ashe but he did not go to Steventon to see Jane. She received instead a message from Anne Lefroy saying she would come to see Jane on Wednesday, 14 November. She came, and the two friends sat alone together. Anne had foreseen the need for a distraction and so brought with her a letter she had received from a Samuel Blackall which she gave to Jane to read. Blackall, a young clergyman, had stayed at Ashe with the Lefroys the previous Christmas, and had been very attentive to Jane. In his letter, however, he said in effect that he would not be able to pursue her with a view to marriage. To show Jane the letter might seem almost cruel – she had lost not one suitor but two. But Mrs Lefroy knew that Jane was not in love with Blackall, and Jane's comments to Cassandra confirm her indifference:

> There seems no likelihood of [Blackall's] coming into Hampshire this Christmas, and it is therefore most probable that our indifference will soon be mutual, unless his regard, which appeared to spring from knowing nothing of me at first, is best supported by never seeing me.[44]

Blackall's letter served its purpose as a screen, a much needed diversion from the subject of Tom Lefroy.

Under the calm surface, the visit was tense. Neither Mrs Lefroy nor

Jane brought up Tom. Yet in ordinary circumstances what could have been more natural than for Mrs Lefroy to chat about her nephew's recent visit? Jane told Cassandra that she had been too proud to ask about him. And Mrs Lefroy was too considerate of Jane's feelings and had too much tact and delicacy to mention him. She knew that anything she said about Tom would cause Jane pain. Their silence was not an attempt to evade the truth: both women knew what Tom's failure to come to Steventon meant. The silence enabled Jane to maintain a facade of composure. Nevertheless, she did want to hear *something*.

Like a comic figure in a play, Mr Austen bumbled in – a kind, generous, good-hearted man. He broke the tension; he asked the question. He had heard Tom was at Ashe. He remembered the Lefroys' lively nephew and politely asked where he was and what he was doing now. Mrs Lefroy told him – in Jane's presence – that Tom had left Ashe to return to London and would then proceed back to Ireland to begin his law career. This could not have been much of a revelation to Jane, though it did confirm that Tom had finished his studies and was going home to Ireland. Jane knew that Mrs Lefroy was sympathetic; but everything was communicated in silence.

No one afterwards spoke of what Jane's feelings were, but within her own family Mrs Lefroy expressed her own dislike of Tom. After her children were grown up, they still remembered how their mother 'had disliked Tom Lefroy because he had behaved so ill to Jane Austen',[45] as Jane's niece Anna, who eventually married one of the Lefroy sons, reported. Anna's brother-in-law George, who had gone with Tom when he called on Jane after the Manydown ball, was sixteen by 1798 and had himself danced with Jane at balls. He would have remembered and understood his mother's opinion. Mrs Lefroy believed Tom had encouraged Jane and had then reneged. Perhaps she herself felt betrayed, especially if she had had a hand in arranging the meeting in Cork Street.

Mrs Lefroy would have been in correspondence with the family in Ireland, and so knew by 1798 that Tom had been back to Ireland in late 1797 and become engaged to the sister of a school friend. That she concealed this from Jane might appear dishonest, but Mrs Lefroy could discern the subtle difference between honesty and brutality. Perhaps she herself had insisted on Tom coming down to Hampshire again. To come and not to go to Steventon would put an end to Jane's expectations before she heard he had married someone else.

Jane should by now have been prepared for this outcome to her romance. During the two years following her visit to Cork Street Tom was in London. He could have managed, if he had wanted to, to pay another visit to his uncle's family. Jane must have made excuses for him to herself – his studies, his difficult uncle. But the fact remained that he did not come. Why he decided not to marry Jane remains hidden. It is easy to blame Benjamin Langlois, knowing as we do his views on marriage. But Tom's own father had risked Langlois's displeasure.

Tom's situation, however, was different from his father's. Anthony Lefroy had only one sister and one brother. Tom had ten surviving brothers and sisters, and as the eldest son (by some accounts the only one of much talent), he was expected to make the whole family's fortune. He had heavy responsibilities as a brother – especially to his sisters.

Tom may not have been quite as heartless and irresponsible as his aunt thought. The sad truth may be that three warm, romantic, impulsive people – Jane, Tom and Mrs Lefroy – got swept away by their feelings, and their enthusiasm and optimism were misplaced. In the hard realities of the social context Tom's marrying Jane would have shown a disregard for his obligations to his family, obligations that in those days had great weight and exerted more influence on an individual's choices than we are able to credit today.

Perhaps Tom thought over the whole situation and decided that to marry Jane would be a selfish act. He was wrong, though, to leave her with false expectations. Perhaps he believed his aunt would tell Jane about his engagement in Ireland; perhaps he thought his staying away from Hampshire was itself enough of a sign. His behaviour wasn't necessarily crass or callous, just muddled and evasive. He did not quite have the courage to face up to the scene. Jane herself could only speculate on what caused Tom to change his mind.

If Jane's own family knew what had happened, they kept quiet about it. Even James's second wife, Mary Lloyd, believed the romance had been a mere flirtation lasting only a couple of weeks. She did not know about the visit to Cork Street; and she thought Jane and Tom never met again after mid January 1796. At the time of Tom's second visit to Ashe, Mary was in the last few days of her first pregnancy. Confined at home, she might not have heard that he had come to Ashe; or, being preoccupied with the imminent birth, she perhaps hardly registered his coming and soon forgot he had been there. Mary is not a reliable source of information about the relationship. She later told her daughter that Jane and Tom had been infatuated but that Mrs Lefroy, knowing the romance could come to nothing because neither Jane nor Tom had money, had sent him speedily off to London before their attachment could develop into anything serious. From what we know of Mary Lloyd's view of marriage and money, it appears her story is speculation based her on own way of looking at the situation rather than on any real knowledge of what actually happened. *She* would have broken up a romance between two young people without money.

Tom Lefroy himself is the source we have to rely on. He died in 1869 at the age of ninety-three, and in the last years of his life one of his nephews asked him if he had been in love with Jane Austen. Tom said that he had been but that it was 'a boyish love'.[46] Whatever his qualification means, his admission confirms that Jane was not mistaken: Tom Lefroy had been in love with her. But of no less significance than Tom's answer is the fact that the question was asked at all. You might expect the nephew to have asked if his uncle had known the novelist Jane Austen; that would have been the natural question. But to ask if Tom had been in love with her shows that the question had lingered in family lore for more than seventy years. That in itself tells us a lot.

There is no reason to suppose that Tom and Jane were secretly engaged, but nearly twenty years later Jane was to warn one of her nieces of the danger of engaging herself 'in word or mind' if there was uncertainty as to when the marriage could take place.[47] In her own mind she had engaged herself to Tom Lefroy, and had believed their attachment had the same force in his mind.

Jane Austen had already created women in the situation she now found herself in – Jane Bennet when she thinks Bingley does not love her, and Marianne Dashwood after Willoughby rejects her. But the most vivid to her must have been Cassandra's conduct since Tom Fowle's death only a year and a half before. Jane had to try to endure her own disappointment with the same control and courage, the same quiet forbearance.

Mrs Lefroy came to Steventon on Wednesday 14 November, but Jane did not write to Cassandra until the following Saturday. She waited three days until she was able to write with composure and an implicit acceptance of what had happened. She did not even begin the letter with Mrs Lefroy's visit. This was not to hide what she was feeling or to pretend the event had less significance than it actually did. Cassandra knew what a blow it was. Jane's aim was to reassure her sister.

She began her letter with other subjects, clearing the way for what she really needed to write about. She gives a report on James's wife, who was about to have her first child – and in fact did so on the day Jane started the letter; and then on the state of Mrs Austen's health, for their mother had not been well for several months. Jane leads into her account of Mrs Lefroy's visit calmly and sensibly: 'So much for my patient [their mother] – now for myself.'[48] What she wrote about the visit was very much about herself:

> Mrs Lefroy did come last Wednesday, and the Harwoods came likewise, but very considerately paid their visit before Mrs Lefroy's arrival, with whom, in spite of interruptions both from my father and James, I was enough alone to hear all that was interesting, which you will easily credit when I tell you that of her nephew she said nothing at all, and of her friend very little. She did not once mention the name of the former to *me*, and I was too proud to make any enquiries; but on my father's afterwards asking where he was, I learnt that he was gone back to London in his way to Ireland, where he is called to the Bar and means to practise.[49]

This is how Jane told Cassandra what had happened. Oblique as it is, it was all Cassandra needed to know.

Jane never again mentioned Tom Lefroy in her letters, at least not in any Cassandra kept. And certainly with everyone except Cassandra she availed herself of the dignity of silence. She had loved Tom Lefroy and had waited for him but he had not come. There was no more to be said. It was as absolute as the death of Cassandra's fiancé. Jane probably thought of it in something like those terms. Many years later she told her niece Fanny that 'it is no creed of mine, as you must be well aware, that such sort of Disappointments kill anybody'.[50] She had earned the right to say that in the autumn of 1798.

Cassandra's loss was different from Jane's. She grieved not only for herself, for what had been taken from her, but for Tom Fowle's having lost his own life. And she did not have to suffer alone. Jane was with her, to talk to her, to distract her, to console her. Everyone had been concerned about Cassandra – her family, her friends, her neighbours were all aware of her loss. Jane, however, was virtually isolated – Cassandra was at Godmersham, and Jane and Mrs Lefroy had tacitly agreed not to acknowledge what had happened. No one else seems to have known about it.

The actual presence of Cassandra would have made a big difference to Jane, but it could not have turned her into Cassandra. The characters of the two sisters were very different. In the first biography of Jane Austen, her nephew James Edward Austen-Leigh says that in the family 'Cassandra had the merit of a temper always under command, but that Jane had the *happiness* of a temper that never required to be commanded'.[51] This was the family view, but it is one of those rhetorical statements about Jane Austen that does not bear close scrutiny. Jane's letters contradict this picture of her; even those Cassandra preserved show Jane sometimes being sharp, tetchy, irritated, even complaining. Austen-Leigh's comment denies Jane's real merit. She was a woman of feeling and imagination, full of conflicts and contradictions, no less vulnerable to pain and disappointment than anyone else. She had to struggle and endure. Her nephew's remark is a testament to how well she managed to conceal her efforts from her family and friends.

Cassandra knew the truth and did what she could to sustain her sister. Jane often mentions her sister's humour and once wrote to her: 'The letter which I have this moment received from you has diverted me beyond moderation. I could die of laughter at it, as they used to say at school. You are indeed the finest comic writer of the present age.'[52] Even taking into account a bit of sisterly hyperbole, there must have been some truth in the compliment.

In late 1798 and early 1799, Jane twice mentions how amusing Cassandra's letters are. 'You must read your letters over *five* times in future before you send them', Jane begins one letter, '& then perhaps you may find them as entertaining as I do. I laughed at several parts of the one which I am now answering.'[53] Cassandra worked hard to amuse Jane, to distract her, to take her out of herself. A couple of weeks later Jane again wrote of the pleasure she got from one of Cassandra's letters and singled out two particular bits for commendation: 'Your letter has pleased and amused me very much. Your essay on happy fortnights is highly ingenious, and the talobert skin made me laugh a good deal.'[54] Jane did not take her sister's efforts for granted, and she tried to reply in kind.

Jane's letters between mid November and March, when Cassandra returned, are not different from one another in subject, nor indeed different from most of the letters she wrote throughout her life. She always wrote about what she was doing, where she was going, what she saw and heard. She relates family news and news of friends and acquaintances. She comments on what she is reading, what she wears to balls; tells of plans for making dresses or putting new trimmings on bonnets. The subjects of the letters tell us almost nothing about Jane's frame of mind at any given time, but the tone of the letters is by no means as uniform as the subjects, and in the individual tone of each letter we find subtle indications of her mood.

The letters she wrote en route from Godmersham and announcing their arrival at Steventon are cheerful and playful, even making fun of herself a bit, as effortless as chatting with Cassandra face to face. When Cassandra was absent, all the housekeeping duties fell to Jane, who disliked domestic tasks and writes of her duties with self-mocking pomposity: 'I carry about the keys of the Wine & Closet; & twice since I began this letter, have had orders to give in the Kitchen.'[55] Her other duty was to nurse their mother, who was not well, and Jane reported with light self-irony: 'I am very grand indeed; I had the dignity of dropping out my mother's Laudanum last night.'[56] This kind of relaxed pleasure in writing disappears from the letters after the one reporting Mrs Lefroy's visit. In that letter Jane reassured Cassandra by making another joke about housekeeping:

> My mother desires me to tell you that I am a very good housekeeper, which I have no reluctance in doing, because I really think it my peculiar excellence, and for this reason – I always take care to provide such things as please my own appetite, which I consider as the chief merit in housekeeping.[57]

But this was the last time for a while that she enlivened the mundane subjects of nursing or housekeeping with spontaneous and seemingly effortless humour.

The letters over the next few months chart Jane's coming to terms with her disappointment in Tom Lefroy. In her daily life, as reflected in her letters, she at first fell back on a steady, willed engagement with what was going on at Steventon. This sustained her through the first month, and by mid December recitation of information begins to give way to cheerful reporting, which soon yields to a spirited attempt to make her subjects amusing, and the unselfconscious pleasure in communicating with Cassandra for its own sake returns.

Jane cultivated acceptance, not unhappiness. She let the activity of daily life draw her out of herself and into the flow and rhythm of her world. She was lucky because life at Steventon offered the machinery for keeping up her connection with ordinary life. She went through the motions, fulfilled her duties, however apparently trivial, inconsequential and unexciting. Tom Lefroy did not dwindle to insignificance. He found his natural place in her imagination, and he remained there for the rest of her life.

Almost the only outward sign that anything was amiss during these months was Jane's losing patience with her mother. In the first month or two after the return from Godmersham she attentively recorded the state of her mother's health. By December Jane considered her mother well enough to be left in the care of Mr Austen and the servants while she went to Manydown to visit her friends Catherine and Alethea Bigg for a few days. She needed a change of scene. When she returned home she reported their mother's condition to Cassandra with less solicitude than before: 'I returned from Manydown this morning, & found my Mother certainly in no respect worse than I left her. She does not like the cold Weather, but that we cannot help.'[58] With that the careful reports cease. As Mrs Austen improved, Jane became irritated because her mother continued to complain. Illness was one thing, complaint quite another.

After years of energy and bustle, Mrs Austen had lapsed into a querulous lassitude. This was the first sign of the change in her. She had once been as annoyed by complaining as Jane now was. Twenty-eight years before she had briskly dismissed the dissatisfactions of her sister-in-law Susannah Walter, but now she did not see herself quite so clearly. She believed her own complaints were real and justified, as no doubt Susannah had done. Jane thought her mother was being self-indulgent. She complained about things that could not be helped.

When Jane decided her mother enjoyed being ill, she lost sympathy and stopped believing she really was ailing. Jane was struggling against the impulse to be self-indulgently unhappy, and she was in no mood to be tolerant of anyone else's dissatisfactions. She particularly disliked people who enjoyed being sick and magnified every twinge into an illness. In late January 1799 she tartly commented to Cassandra:

> It began to occur to me before you mentioned it that I had been somewhat silent as to my mother's health for some time, but I thought you could have no difficulty in divining its exact state – you, who have guessed so much stranger things. She is tolerably well – better upon the whole than she was some weeks ago. She would tell you herself that she has a very dreadful cold in her head at present; but I have not much compassion for colds in the head without fever or sore throat.[59]

Her mother's ill health, real or fancied, had turned into an occasion for a 'parade of feeling'. She stopped reporting the maladies because she thought they were exaggerated, even imaginary.

Jane didn't find her mother a congenial companion, so little so in fact that she sometimes in her letters says she is alone when she means that only her mother is with her. Some element essential to easy intimacy and warmth was missing in their relationship.[60] They were a lot alike, which sometimes exacerbated Jane's annoyance. She took a sharp view of her mother's giving free rein to tendencies she had to work to check in herself.

With Cassandra at Godmersham, the family circle was reduced to Jane and her parents. The three elder sons were married and established. But Charles and Frank had their fortunes to make and were special objects of Jane and Cassandra's interest in late 1798. Frank had received his lieutenancy in 1792 and Charles his in 1797. Although separated from them by their duties at sea, Jane corresponded with both and followed their careers eagerly.

She took her brother Charles's complaints more seriously and in better humour than she did her mother's, perhaps because his were not about his health. Charles saw Cassandra at Godmersham in the autumn of 1798 and confided to her that his first assignment as a lieutenant was a disappointment. The vessel was small and he had little to do. Things were dull and he itched for action. Action was the way to get on in the navy. He wanted to be transferred to a frigate. His sisters became his go-betweens. Cassandra informed Jane of Charles's dissatisfactions, and she conveyed them to their father. Always ready to do what he could for his sons, Mr Austen sent an inquiry to Admiral Gambier, Frank's patron, asking that Charles be moved. Jane in turn suggested to Charles that he seek the advice of his former captain, Sir Thomas Williams, widower of their late cousin Jane Cooper.

In reporting to Cassandra her advice to Charles, Jane makes her only mention of having had a dream. 'I cannot approve of *your* scheme of writing to [Sir Thomas]', she wrote to Cassandra, '(which you communicated to me a few nights ago) to request him to come home & convey You to Steventon. To do you justice however, You had some doubts of the propriety of such a measure yourself.'[61] The dream has several possible interpretations. On the most literal level it shows Jane's wish for Cassandra to come home. More deeply, it may hint that Jane hoped Sir Thomas would fall in love with Cassandra or that Jane herself was attracted to Sir Thomas and in her dream-mind replaced herself with Cassandra. But the unconscious mind knows many tricks: Sir Thomas's given name might have made him a surrogate for Tom Lefroy and Cassandra a stand-in for Jane herself. The dream may be a sign of Jane's still yearning for Tom Lefroy to come and take her away, even after all conscious hope was gone.

Admiral Gambier answered Mr Austen's letter about Charles with an explanation of why young officers were kept for a time on a small vessel, but he assured him Charles would be moved to a frigate at the proper time. The admiral also had some exciting news: Frank was to be promoted to the rank of commander very soon. Jane saw that Frank's promotion was not likely to be much consolation to Charles: 'I have sent the same extract of the sweets of Gambier to Charles, who poor fellow! though he sinks into nothing but an humble attendant on the Hero of the peice, will I hope be contented with the prospect held out to him.'[62]

Four days after the receipt of Admiral Gambier's letter another arrived from the son of General Mathew, the father of James Austen's first wife and the uncle of the admiral's wife. Jane immediately relayed the news to Cassandra. 'Frank is made. He was yesterday raised to the Rank of Commander, & appointed to the Petterel Sloop, now at Gibraltar.'[63] Frank's promotion somewhat overshadowed the news that Charles was to be transferred to a frigate, the *Tamar*, but these two events in late December put Jane in brighter spirits than she had been in since October. The good fortune of her brothers was as important to her as her own, and to hear good of them always raised her spirits.

Frank's promotion brings out what Jane valued in the Steventon world. When her friend Catherine Bigg congratulated her on Frank's promotion, Jane was moved because, as she wrote to Cassandra, Catherine 'really felt the Joy she talked of'.[64] Their friend's words were not a mere form of politeness. She knew Frank, knew his worthy character, and knew how much his promotion meant to her friend Jane and the rest of the family. Catherine's joy included a whole circle of people.

About a week later, a different kind of feeling arose, but one that also depended on knowledge. Catherine's father fell seriously ill, and Jane wrote to Cassandra: 'Poor man! ... his life is so useful, his character so respectable and worthy, that I really believe there was a good deal of sincerity in the general concern expressed on his account.'[65] Jane hated sentimentality because she valued real feeling.

To Jane, knowledge of a person earned you the right to feel; knowledge enabled you to feel – and to feel justly. This is why she later wrote of the battle of Almeida: 'How horrible it is to have so many people killed! And what a blessing that one cares for none of them!'[66] She wasn't callous. She cared, as she said, that so many people were killed; but to say she felt for them what she would have felt for people she knew would have been dishonest, the second-hand thrill of the emotional pickpocket.

Early in the new year Charles came to Steventon on leave before taking up his new posting. Jane told Cassandra that Mrs Lefroy 'never saw anyone so much improved in her life, and thinks him handsomer than Henry'.[67] He also went to Kintbury to see the Fowle family and was said to have impressed everybody there. The opinion of Charles at Godmersham the previous autumn had not been so high. Like Jane, he was at his best with people he knew well. 'He appears to far more advantage here than he did at Godmersham', she wrote Cassandra, 'not surrounded by strangers and neither oppressed by a pain in his face or powder in his hair.' [68] But Charles was still something of a malcontent, however much improved.

Even though he had been transferred to a frigate, he did not want that particular frigate. When he left Steventon he hoped he would not get to Deal in time to join the *Tamar* before she sailed, leaving him free to look about for a better station. Charles was lucky this time. The *Tamar* was waiting to be refitted, and he contrived a posting to Captain Sir Thomas Williams's frigate, the *Endymion*, the vessel he had served on under Sir Thomas before he received his commission.

In the months following Mrs Lefroy's visit, we see Jane in her everyday roles as daughter, sister, friend and neighbour. The lover of Tom Lefroy seems to disappear into the background. She makes only one oblique reference to not being in the best spirits. In December she went to a ball and reported to Cassandra: 'There were twenty dances & I danced them all, & without any fatigue. I was glad to find myself capable of dancing so much & with so much satisfaction as I did.' [69] This was an objective indication of her spirits. She had energy, she danced, and she took pleasure in it. Nevertheless, in January she wrote to Cassandra: 'Pray mention the name of Maria Montresor's lover when you write next, my mother wants to know it, & I have not courage to look back into your letters to find it out.' [70] You would expect rereading Cassandra's letters to be a treat, not something requiring courage, but Jane was not ready to do anything that might conjure the pain of late November and early December or to risk reopening the wound she was trying to allow to heal. She kept her mind fixed on happier matters. She had started a new novel, and she got on with the work.

Cassandra was vaguer about the dates of composition of *Northanger Abbey* (or 'Susan', as Austen first called it) than she was about any of Jane's other novels. She simply notes it was 'written about 98 & 99' – the months of disappointment fall squarely in the middle of this time. [71] When Jane finished *Sense and Sensibility* in mid 1798 she began *Northanger Abbey*.

The conception of *Northanger Abbey* probably does not belong to the time of the end of her relationship with Tom Lefroy; it is more closely connected with the marriage of Henry and Eliza. The novel was meant to be a sign of her acceptance of the marriage and a gesture of reconciliation. The original name of the heroine, Susan, was deeply connected in Austen's mind with her cousin, and she named the agreeable and witty hero after her favourite brother. She fulfilled her own wish by making him a clergyman.

Austen purges the name Susan of the associations it had accumulated in her writing of 'Lesley Castle' and *Lady Susan*. Susan Morland (as the heroine would originally have been named) bears no resemblance to Eliza de Feuillide as we know her, but the famous episode of the mock-Gothic discovery of the laundry lists in the old chest can be directly connected to Eliza herself. On 7 November 1796, Eliza had written to Philadelphia Walter describing a visit to her doctor, where she was shown into a room:

> Here I waited nearly two hours which gave me an opportunity of reading various physical Books filled with shocking cases, and also inspecting two large presses (this part of the story you must keep secret) where I expected to find skeletons, but however met with nothing but crooked Scissors and other formidable Surgical instruments, and a few Embryos in Spirits. At length the doctor came in, and the grave face which he put on sufficiently alarmed me.[72]

It is not likely that Austen read this letter, but the echo of it in *Northanger Abbey* is too strong to be coincidental. Eliza corresponded with Jane and must have repeated the anecdote to more than one correspondent. Eliza's lively, self-mocking play of mind is one of the things Jane had always found most attractive about her; she used Eliza's anecdote as the basis for the incident in her novel – a tribute to her new sister-in-law.

The novel soon also became an expression of her acceptance of her disappointment in Tom Lefroy. She put aside whatever anger or bitterness she might have felt about Henry's marriage or Tom's rejection and wrote her novel in a spirit of generosity. She again connected her novel with Tom Lefroy through *Tom Jones*, in which Fielding mentions the name Allen.[73]

At the conclusion of the novel she comes closest to what she herself was experiencing in her own emotional life. James Morland's unhappiness at Isabella's breaking their engagement is only hinted at; the emphasis is on his certain recovery. Catherine's belief that she has lost Henry Tilney forever is treated more fully, and in a tender and philosophical way. She is young, she has a cheerful temperament; these two things will make it possible for her to get over Henry Tilney.

Austen conveys her sense of reconciliation so successfully that *Northanger Abbey* has a special distinction among her six novels. It is the only one that could have ended without the marriage of the hero and heroine and yet still have seemed to have a happy conclusion. Catherine Morland's happiness is inherent in her nature, in her relations with her loving family and in her attachment to the neighbourhood of Fullerton.

The last chapters of *Northanger Abbey* bring us back to Jane Austen's own life at the time that she was writing the novel. She sees Catherine's loss of Henry Tilney in the context of what her heroine has *not* lost. Jane herself still had her home, her family, her friends, and her happy engagement with her daily life. Moreover, she had her work. She had not allowed herself to be overwhelmed by her unhappiness. She did not complain about Cassandra's long absence, but just before her sister's return, she wrote, almost parenthetically, 'I shall be very glad to see you at home again'.[74]

7

Place

Cassandra returned from Godmersham in March, and in mid May Jane and Mrs Austen went to Bath for about six weeks with Edward, his wife, Elizabeth, and their two eldest children. Edward had been vaguely unwell and wanted to consult a doctor and take the waters.

Jane Austen disliked Bath. After being a novelist and a parson's daughter, it is one of the best known things about her. But nobody quite believes it. Bath is a beautiful city, full of architectural gems in a lovely landscape. In Jane Austen's time it was a fashionable spa – with parties, balls, concerts, plays and the constant toing and froing around the Pump Room where people met to gossip and take the waters. For us the attractiveness of the place is enhanced by what Austen imagined taking place there in *Northanger Abbey* and *Persuasion*. We see the town as the topographical image of the charm of her novels and think that Bath is just the right setting for Jane Austen. In a good mood she would have been amused by this misapprehension and enjoyed its irony.

Edward had taken a house at Queen Square for their stay, and Jane – the first sign of what was to be a lifelong habit – tried to make her holiday life as much like her home life as possible. She was later in *Emma* to refer to 'all those little matters on which the daily happiness of private life depends',[1] and in Bath she created a routine within the family and visited a few acquaintances. She doesn't seem to have thought it worth the trouble to make much effort with people she would never really get to know. Not even when the people were friends of Anne Lefroy, as the Mapleton daughters were. 'I do not see the Miss Mapletons very often, but just as often as I like', she wrote to Cassandra. 'We are always very glad to meet, & I do not wish to wear out our satisfaction.'[2]

Edward, being a rich and active man, inevitably ran into acquaintances from the large circle of people he knew. In Bath he encountered a Mr Evelyn, Jane wrote to Cassandra, '& was invited to a family dinner, which I beleive at first Elizabeth was rather sorry at his accepting, but yesterday Mrs Evelyn called on us & her manners were so pleasing that we liked the idea of going very much'.[3] Dining with the Evelyns, however, did not provide Jane with much material for a letter to Cassandra. All she mentions, in passing, is that 'the visit was very quiet & uneventful; pleasant enough. We met only another Mr Evelyn, his cousin, whose wife came to Tea'.[4] Hardly enthusiastic, and this is typical of Jane's accounts of social activities in Bath.

Accordingly, Bath only figures incidentally in these letters. Jane's real subject is her family and matters connected to Steventon. Each letter contains a report on Edward's treatment and the progress of his health. Jane was a little dubious from the beginning about the healing powers of Bath. She thought the best cure for any malady was to forget you were sick. On the day after their arrival she wrote that 'Edward seemed rather fagged last night, & not very brisk this morning, but I trust the bustle of sending for Tea, Coffee & Sugar &c., & going out to taste a cheese himself will do him good'.[5] Exertion, or getting on with it, was Jane's panacea and home was the best place to avail yourself of its efficacy.

Edward and Elizabeth were not of the watering-place world, as Eliza de Feuillide and her mother had been in their heyday, judging from Philadelphia Walter's accounts of what she called their 'dissipated life' in Tunbridge Wells.[6] Jane approved of Edward and Elizabeth's preference for domestic pleasures and routine, and after a couple of weeks in Bath she thought they looked forward to going home: 'He is more comfortable here than I thought he would be, & so is Elizabeth – though they will both I beleive be very glad to get away, the latter especially. Which one can't wonder at *somehow*.'[7] Most that really mattered to Edward and Elizabeth was at Godmersham – his duties, their younger children, and Elizabeth's relatives, the Bridges family, who lived nearby.

The only family the Austens had in Bath were James and Jane Leigh-Perrot, Mrs Austen's brother and sister-in-law. The Leigh-Perrots had spent part of the year at Bath for a long time and the Austens sometimes visited them there. James Leigh-Perrot's character is not very well defined. He is said to have had something of the wit and intelligence of his uncle Theophilus Leigh, Master of Balliol College. That would have stood him in good stead with Jane – she liked people with quick minds – but what endeared him to her even more was the interest he took in her younger brothers' naval careers. 'I had not been two minutes in the Dining room', she once wrote Cassandra after arriving at the Leigh-Perrots', 'before [our uncle] questioned me with all his accustomary eager interest about Frank & Charles, their veiws & intentions.'[8] This is practically the only thing Jane ever wrote that reflects Leigh-Perrot's character. But we know he adored his wife.

Jane Leigh-Perrot was proud, selfish, domineering and manipulative. No one loved her except her husband. The Leigh-Perrots were very rich and Mrs Leigh-Perrot was very stingy. She found it hard to part with cold cash, as Jane on one occasion wrote to Cassandra: 'My Aunt is in a great hurry to pay me for my Cap, but cannot find in her heart to give me good money.'[9] Her meanness, though, could sometimes be useful. She knew all the shops in Bath where you could get good bargains. During the stay Jane took advantage of her aunt's knowledge because Cassandra and friends had asked her to do shopping for them. These commissions are the chief subject of Jane's Bath letters.

Among other things, Cassandra wanted some artificial flowers to trim a hat. Jane looked about and wrote to inform her:

> Flowers are very much worn, & Fruit is still more the thing. A plumb or green gage would cost three shillings; Cherries & Grapes about five I beleive but this is at some of the dearest Shops; My Aunt has told me of a very cheap one near Walcot Church, to which I shall go in quest of something for You.[10]

A week or so later she reported:

> We have been to the cheap Shop, & very cheap we found it, but there are only flowers made there, no fruit & as I could get four or five very pretty sprigs of the former for the same money which would procure only one Orleans plumb, in short could get more for three or four Shillings than I could have means of bringing home, I cannot decide on the fruit till I hear from you again. Besides, I cannot help thinking that it is more natural to have flowers grow out of the head than fruit.[11]

As inconsequential as artificial fruit and flowers for bonnets might seem, they were important to Jane because her observations about what was fashionable were of interest at Steventon, and her tasks gave her something to do in Bath that was connected with her real life, her life at home.

She even found time to write to Henry's former fiancée, Mary Pearson, from Bath. Earlier in the year Henry had been posted to Ireland with his regiment, but Eliza had not gone with him, probably because of her ailing son. Before he left he seems to have asked Jane to do him a favour, and it was this business that led her to write to Mary Pearson. Jane told Cassandra:

> You may remember that I wrote to [Mary] above two months ago about the parcel under my care, & as I had heard nothing from her since, I thought myself obliged to write again two or three days ago, for after all that had passed I was determined that the Correspondence should never cease through my means. The exchange of packets is to take place through the medium of Mr Nutt, probably one of the Sons belonging to Woolwich Academy, who comes to Overton in the beginning of July.[12]

Jane seems to have taken the role of Henry's agent, returning the letters Mary had written to him during their engagement ('the parcel under my care') and receiving those he had written to Mary – hence the exchange of parcels she was trying to arrange. That this exchange did not take place before Henry's marriage to Eliza suggests that the ending of the engagement was a hurried and somewhat confused affair. Jane's correspondence with Mary Pearson did lapse. In 1807 when she was living in Southampton at the same time as Mary Pearson and her sisters, Jane referred to the Pearsons as 'the only Family in the place whom we cannot visit'.[13] Nevertheless, writing to Mary in the spring of 1799 was one of Jane's ways of maintaining a hold on ordinary life during the stay in Bath.

She began the holiday in good spirits, but though she kept up a brisk, lively tone in her letters this does not conceal that she would rather not be there. She could see the point of Bath to young and inexperienced people like Catherine Morland in *Northanger Abbey*, but for older, settled people to like Bath was not quite comprehensible to her. She was past the Catherine Morland stage of excitement with novelty or with watering-place pleasures. She was only twenty-three, but the three years she had waited for Tom Lefroy had changed her. A few weeks in Bath made her fidgety:

> I do not know what is the matter with me to day, but I cannot write quietly; I am always wandering away into some exclamation or other. Fortunately I

have nothing very particular to say. We walked to Weston one evening last week, & liked it very much. Liked *what* very much? Weston? – no – *walking* to Weston. I have not expressed myself properly, but I hope you will understand me.[14]

She felt a bit incoherent, a bit disjointed. This was the way Bath affected her. A week later she reported to Cassandra:

Edward has not been well these last two days; his appetite has failed him, & he has complained of sick & uncomfortable feelings, which with other Symptoms make us think of the Gout – perhaps a fit of it might cure him, but I cannot wish it to begin at Bath.[15]

If he came down with gout, it would mean staying in Bath longer. In the same letter she expressed her own wish quite clearly: 'The Play on Saturday is *I hope* to conclude our Gaieties here, for nothing but a lengthened stay will make it otherwise.'[16] She had had enough of 'gaieties' and was ready to go home.

Jane and her mother had been back at Steventon for only a month or so when the family heard that Mrs Leigh-Perrot's knowledge of cheap shops had led her into trouble. Early in August she had been into such a place at the corner of Bath Street and Stall Street and bought a piece of black lace, which she paid for and had wrapped. She left with the parcel and soon afterwards ran into her husband in the street. They strolled together for about half an hour before their way brought them back to Bath Street and past the shop. The owner saw them and came out and demanded to examine the parcel. It contained not only the lace Mrs Leigh-Perrot had bought but another piece of lace as well, possibly planted by the shop assistant who had wrapped the parcel.

Mrs Leigh-Perrot was arrested and charged. Bail was denied because theft of property worth more than a shilling was a capital offence. If found guilty, she could have been hanged, but would more likely have been transported to Australia for fourteen years. She was confined to the jail-keeper's house at Ilchester until her trial. At the trial, the shopkeeper and two assistants gave evidence that seemed to confirm Mrs Leigh-Perrot's guilt, but under cross-examination one of the assistants was shown to have perjured himself. The tide turned in Mrs Leigh-Perrot's favour. Seven witnesses for the defence testified that they had had goods other than what they had bought in the shop put in their parcels but had discovered the items and returned them before they could be accused of theft. This suggested Mrs Leigh-Perrot had been the victim of a scam that had been tried unsuccessfully on others. Finally, Mrs Leigh-Perrot made a statement in her own defence. It took the jury half an hour to reach a verdict of not guilty.

A few letters that she wrote to her cousin Mountague Cholmeley at the time tell us a lot about Mrs Leigh-Perrot's character. She was not totally selfish. She worried about the effect of the ordeal on her husband's health, and she refused Mrs Austen's offer to send Jane or Cassandra to stay with her until the trial because, as she wrote to her cousin, she did not want her nieces exposed to such a sordid place. This was her finest hour, but was not the whole of her character, as the letters to her cousin reveal.

Before, during and after her ordeal, Jane Leigh-Perrot always saw herself as pitiable and deprived – deprived of money, of health, and of her devoted old servant, Chambers, who was dead. From her confinement awaiting trial, she wrote that 'had my poor old quiet Chambers been living she would have been a real Comfort to me *here*'.[17] Chambers being dead must have been a favourite complaint, for in one of Jane's letters several years later she mentions her aunt's rehearsal of her dissatisfactions and notes: 'She does not forget to wish for Chambers, you may be sure.'[18] Mrs Leigh-Perrot's favourite theme was expense, and her favourite pretence that her husband was not rich.

Testifying on her own behalf at her trial, she described herself as being married to a man 'whose Supply of Money is so ample as to leave me rich even after every desire is gratified'.[19] That public admission must have cost her a lot, but much was at stake: being rich was her defence. 'What inducement', she asked the court, 'could I have to commit this offence?'[20] Once she had been acquitted, she stopped rejoicing in how rich she was and started complaining about the expense of the trial. Even before her acquittal, she wrote to her cousin Cholmeley fretting over how much the trial was costing: 'This ruinous Expense is what we shall long feel.'[21] Her use of the word 'ruinous' tips her hand. It was unfortunate – and unjust – that they had to pay so much to establish her innocence; but to call it ruinous was absurd. They did not even feel the pinch.

After her acquittal, she really warmed to the theme of the cost:

> The frightful expense I cannot estimate. I am told it will be nearer *two* than one thousand pounds and from the large demands already made only for conveying the witnesses (and the *two* days' expences for the *house* and *eating* at Taunton which alone amounted to £93 odd money), I can easily suppose it will be full that sum. What a comfort that we have no children! [22]

This ridiculous cant is as good as anything Jane put in the mouth of Mrs Norris in *Mansfield Park*.

Once she was free, Mrs Leigh-Perrot even begrudged paying for the transportation, lodging and food of the people who had come to testify to her character. Her dislike of providing room and board to guests seems to have been one of her particular foibles. Jane refers to it in a letter to Cassandra about the Leigh-Perrots' inviting Mrs Austen and *one* of the daughters to stay with them in Bath. Jane wanted both herself and Cassandra to go, 'though to be sure the keep of two will be more than of one, I will endeavour to make the difference less by disordering my Stomach with Bath bunns; & as to the *trouble* of accommodating us, whether there are one or two, it is much the same'.[23]

Jane seems to shift into another voice here – she may be mimicking her aunt. Austen's novels show that she could do many voices, and in *Emma* she gives the heroine the talent of mimicry. Cassandra would easily have picked up when Jane was mocking their aunt. Mimicry was Jane's way of getting a bit of her own back.

By the autumn of 1800 Jane was in her best form again for the first time since she had faced the fact that Tom Lefroy was not going to marry her. Her life was full: taking walks, dining out, attending balls, hearing news of matters serious and trivial, eager for details of romances, quick in her concern about Harris Bigg-Wither's illness, Earle Harwood's accidental gunshot wound, Mr Heathcote's broken ankle. Something happened every day. The news was brought to Steventon. Jane didn't have to look far for subjects for her letters. But it is the manner, the verve and style of her writing that is the true sign of her equanimity and makes you think she was on the brink of writing fiction again.

She is keenly interested in everything. She walked to their neighbours the Bramstons and ate sandwiches 'all over mustard' and got Mrs

Bramston to promise roots of heartsease (yellow and purple) for Cassandra's flower garden. [24] The nurseryman from Basingstoke came and put in thorns and beeches on one side of what Jane called the Elm Walk in the Steventon garden. A scattering of ornamental hardwoods was to be planted on the other side of the path, but before this could be done a severe wind during a storm blew down several big trees in the garden and in the fields that could be seen from the house. The nurseryman came again and suggested a little orchard of apples, pears and cherries.

She recounts to Cassandra a saga concerning new tables, beginning with James urging the cabinet-maker in Winchester to get the tables and chiffonier his father had ordered finished as soon as possible. That simple bit of information is wittily elaborated:

> James called by my father's desire on Mr Bayle to inquire into the cause of his being so horrid. Mr Bayle did not attempt to deny his being horrid, & made many apologies for it; he did not plead his having a drunken self, he talked only of a drunken foreman &c, &c, & gave hopes of the Table's being at Steventon on monday se'night next.[25]

The tables finally come, more or less on the day James was promised. The family decides where to put them and how they are to be used. Jane informs Cassandra:

> I had not expected that they would so perfectly suit the fancy of us all three, or that we should so well agree in the disposition of them; but nothing except their own surface can have been smoother. The two ends put together form our constant Table for everything, & the centre peice stands exceedingly well under the glass; holds a great deal most commodiously, without looking awkwardly. They are both covered with green baize & send their best Love.[26]

The old table was moved to Jane and Cassandra's room – which she calls 'the best bed-room'.[27]

This is only the beginning of all that is conveyed with enthusiasm to Cassandra, who was again at Godmersham: writing and receiving letters take their place in the happy progress of the days. Jane's words flow, everything is natural and unforced. It is hard for her not to be amusing, jokes seem to make themselves. She takes the most ordinary, insignificant bits of information and effortlessly enlivens them with wit and fresh turns of phrase. A nephew had left behind some chestnuts he

had intended to plant at Godmersham and a drawing he had planned
to take to his brother – 'the former will therefore be deposited in the
soil of Hampshire instead of Kent; the latter, I have already consigned
to another Element [the fire]'.[28] These facts couldn't in themselves
have interested Cassandra even if she were as fond of 'particulars' as
Jane; Jane's way of conveying the information was its justification. All
through November she celebrated her life at Steventon – the garden,
the furniture, the neighbours.

At the end of the month, she went to Ibthorpe to visit Martha Lloyd.
Her letter from there continues the vein of lively, spontaneous jokes.
She lapses into the voice of Mrs Stent, a muddled old lady who lived
with the Lloyds: 'I have been here ever since a quarter after three on
thursday last, by the Shrewsbury Clock, which I am fortunately enabled
absolutely to ascertain, because Mrs Stent once lived at Shrewsbury, or
at least at Tewksbury.'[29] The 'Endless Debaries', as Jane often called a
large family in the neighbourhood, lived at a nearby parsonage, and
three of the daughters called at Ibthorpe the morning after Jane's arrival,
'but I have not yet been able to return their civility; you know it is not
an uncommon circumstance in this parish to have the road from Ibthrop
to the Parsonage much dirtier & more impracticable for walking than
the road from the Parsonage to Ibthrop.'[30] Martha agreed to return to
Steventon with Jane, '& our plan is to [have] a nice black frost for
walking to Whitchurch, & there throw ourselves into a postchaise, one
upon the other, our heads hanging out at one door, & our feet at the
opposite'.[31] Jane saw nothing but fun in her immediate prospect.

But while she was enjoying herself at Ibthorpe and writing exuberant
letters to Cassandra, Mr and Mrs Austen were at home coming to a
decision that would destroy with one stroke Jane's equanimity and with
it her good spirits and playfulness.

Left alone at Steventon for a week or two, Mr and Mrs Austen talked
over the family's situation. The decision they reached is simple to state:
he would retire, and they and their daughters would go to live in Bath.
The retirement is easy to understand. Mr Austen was seventy. The choice
of Bath is harder to fathom. There were two good reasons for *not* going
to Bath. First, Jane – and probably Cassandra as well – disliked Bath.
Their parents could easily brush aside this objection – once they were

settled there and got used to the ways of the town, their daughters would like it well enough. The second objection was not so easy to dismiss and should have carried real weight. A fashionable watering-place like Bath would be more expensive than a country village.

The Austens were practical, sensible people, but launching their sons in the world had prevented them from being able to save money over the years. They had no margin for the extra cost of life in a watering-place. So the reasons for choosing Bath had to override the concern about expense. The wish for holiday pleasures of the kind offered by Bath was not the Austens' reason for going to live there. No one ever stated directly why they chose Bath for their retirement. And there are so many possible reasons for the decision that we cannot be sure what their real motive was. There was precedent – Mrs Austen's father had retired to Bath. But he had had an independent income. Like her father, Mrs Austen wasn't in good health. The waters might restore her, and perhaps her husband thought a change of scene, the bustle and activity of a watering-place, might give her new interests. Steventon had been dull for her since her sons had left home and Mr Austen had stopped taking pupils.

Jane and Cassandra were both still unmarried, and Bath was a magnet for eligible men. In the country the girls had little opportunity to meet prospective husbands, and it was by now clear that there was little chance of their being chosen by men in the Steventon neighbourhood. Bath would offer new possibilities. When Mr Austen died his wife would have to live on the income from her inheritance. Although it was sufficient for her, if she had to support her daughters as well she would be in straitened circumstances.

Not least of Bath's attractions was the presence of the Leigh-Perrots. James Leigh-Perrot was Mrs Austen's closest relative. It was natural for her to want to be near him. Of her sons, Frank and Charles had no settled home and were usually at sea. James, Edward and Henry were married and had lives of their own. Mrs Austen might one day go as a widow to live with one of her sons, or perhaps she hoped for a situation more like that of her own mother: one of her daughters would marry and she would go to live with her, not as a penniless dependant but with the dignity of an income from her £3350.

None of these motives seems to have persuaded Jane that Bath was the place to live. All she could see was that she would lose her home of twenty-five years and would have to live in a place she hated. To her Bath was a town with a population of rootless, shifting, idle, transient people. She knew what watering-place values were, and she knew what she would be according to those values. In Bath your identity was your situation in life, and she would be just another penniless spinster daughter of just another retired parson living on a reduced income. That her uncle and aunt Leigh-Perrot were in Bath made the prospect of living there even worse. Their presence would not elevate the Austens' status; it would define them as poor relatives. This was not a part Jane was keen to play.

When, at the end of her life, Jane Austen began to write a novel set in a watering-place, she gave a grim picture of what it is to be a poor relative. Charlotte Hayward observes the rich Lady Denham surrounded by her relatives who are hoping for a legacy:

> She is thoroughly mean ... I can see no good in her. Poor Miss Brereton [Lady Denham's poor relative]! And she makes every body mean about her. This poor Sir Edward & his sister [more poor relatives], how far Nature meant them to be respectable I cannot tell, but they are *obliged* to be mean in their servility to her. And I am mean too, in giving her my attention, with the appearance of coinciding with her. Thus it is, when rich people are sordid.[32]

Perhaps Jane feared that by going to live in Bath her parents would appear to be pursuing money from the Leigh-Perrots. Maybe they were, and perhaps that was what Jane found most intolerable about the place.

When Jane and Martha Lloyd arrived at Steventon from Ibthorpe that December day, Mrs Austen is said to have greeted them with a bald announcement of the decision. Maybe this was an instance of her being plain-spoken or even tactless. She might have been determined to brazen out what she knew her younger daughter would object to. Whatever the case, it had a strong effect on Jane: one account says she fainted when she heard her mother's words.[33] The blow was intensified because it was totally unexpected. That autumn the Austens had bought some new furniture, which they turned around and sold before they went to Bath; they had planted trees they would see come into leaf only once. Nothing had indicated a withdrawal from the place.

Mr Austen at first said they would have to live in the very plainest possible way in Bath, perhaps countering Jane's argument that the place would be too expensive for them. Jane alluded to this when she wrote to Cassandra in mid January. '[Our father's] veiws on the subject [of where they would live in Bath] are much advanced since I came home; he grows quite ambitious, & actually requires now a comfortable & a creditable looking house.'[34] This is not Jane's amused irony, delighting in human inconsistency; this is her edgy sarcasm. Her father had come round to thinking they would live in a house they would not be ashamed of. It was a point gained, but Jane did not seem much consoled by it.

Cassandra destroyed the letters Jane wrote in the first month after their parents announced the plan to move to Bath, but Jane's remark about their father slipped through Cassandra's net. It is usually assumed that Jane expressed her unhappiness too openly in these letters; but perhaps her unhappiness manifested itself in angry criticism of her parents. She had good reason to feel resentment. She and Cassandra had not been consulted, even though the decision concerned them as much as it did their parents. They should have had a say in the matter. Whatever objections Jane might have made were brushed aside; her parents had made up their minds.

Jane was lucky to have Martha Lloyd at Steventon to talk to about the whole business. After Cassandra, Martha was the person Jane was most intimate with. She respected Martha's judgement and trusted her discretion. She could speak freely to her. Martha's presence must have helped because Jane became querulous, tetchy, fidgety after her friend returned to Ibthorpe. All Jane had now were Cassandra's letters.

Not a single one of Cassandra's letters to Jane survives. We hear Cassandra's own voice only in a few letters written to Philadelphia Walter, and only two of these were written in Jane's lifetime. These two letters deepen the mystery, for they give no hint of the humour Jane said she appreciated so much in Cassandra's letters. Perhaps Cassandra did sometimes write the kind of condescending stuff to Jane that she wrote to their cousin Philadelphia, but she must have known that her sister did not need lectures on the acceptance of things as they are as the first duty of life. Jane had breathed that in with the air of Steventon, as her misquotation of Pope confirms: 'Whatever is, is best.'[35] Jane's remarks about Cassandra's letters suggest Cassandra knew that with Jane jokes were more effective than platitudes. Jane's problem was not a failure of rational understanding; she needed to be amused, distracted from her tendency to brood.

A month after the decision to move to Bath, Jane wrote to Cassandra: 'I suppose I need not tell you that [your letter] was very long, being written on a foolscap sheet, & very entertaining, being written by You.'[36] The letter she had just received from Cassandra inspired this splendid remark. We're back to the autumn of 1798 at the time of the Tom Lefroy disappointment. The pattern is repeated. The blow comes; the sisters are apart; Cassandra writes diverting letters to help Jane get through the crisis.

The letter Jane received on 6 January 1801 amused her, and she tried to reply in kind, responding to Cassandra's good intentions. The strategy had worked two years before. But now epistolary diversion was not enough. At best Jane pretended to be resigned to leaving Steventon:

> I get more & more reconciled to the idea of our removal. We have lived long enough in this Neighbourhood, the Basingstoke Balls are certainly on the decline, there is something interesting in the bustle of going away, & the prospect of spending future summers by the Sea or in Wales is very delightful. For a time we shall now possess many of the advantages which I have often thought of with Envy in the wives of Sailors or Soldiers.[37]

She claims she has found something positive in the situation; yet the prevailing tendency of what she says is self-persuasion and a hollow bravado. It might be true that she would not miss the Basingstoke balls, and equally that she would enjoy spending summers by the sea. But balls and holidays were not the basis of her well being, as she and Cassandra both knew.

She concluded this letter with an attempt at lightness: 'It must not be generally known however that I am not sacrificing a great deal in quitting the Country or I can expect to inspire no tenderness, no interest in those we leave behind.'[38] Jane was reduced to insincere playfulness. She was able to express something closer to the truth when she was not writing about herself. Ten days later she reported that Mr Austen had arranged for his bailiff, John Bond, to carry on under the new tenant of the farm, Mr Holder: 'The comfort of not changing his home is a very material one to [Bond]. And since such are his unnatural feelings his belonging to Mr Holder is the every thing needful.'[39] She understood such 'unnatural' feelings.

She could not be cheerful but she tried to be brisk; she kept Cassandra posted about the preparations for leaving Steventon. All the details of what was to happen to the servants, to the pictures, the furniture, the books, were sent off to Cassandra. Jane set them down, but to her every detail had a painful significance: Each meant the loss of home and departure for Bath. The very activities that might have taken her out of herself actually exacerbated her feelings of unhappiness.

James Austen and his wife and children were now to move to Steventon, and that Jane seemed to blame them for depriving her of her home gives a hint of the rage she felt. The character of James's wife, Mary Lloyd, made it easy for Jane to find fault with the way the change-over was handled. Mary was a bustler and arranger and an interferer in other people's business, and the take-over of Steventon provided her with plenty to bustle about. Sometimes Jane could laugh at Mary. When there seemed a possibility that Mrs Lefroy's son-in-law, Henry Rice, might take the curacy of Deane, Jane foresaw Mary's pleasure in trying to oversee the Rices' domestic arrangements: 'It will be an amusement to Mary to superintend [the Rices'] Household management, & abuse them for expense, especially as Mrs L[efroy] means to advise them to put their washing out;'[40] that is, have the washing done by a washer-woman at extra expense instead of having it done at home by their own servants.

This is the kind of interest Mary took in other people. Her love of interference and of money were both so strong that she could not resist the impulse to tell other people how to run their houses – motives and a habit Jane was to give to Mrs Norris in *Mansfield Park*. (After the novel was published, Jane recorded, no doubt with great amusement, that Mary particularly enjoyed Mrs Norris.) Mary would have been relentlessly on the look-out for her own material advantage. Losing her home was bad enough for Jane; to see someone she disliked, someone grasping and greedy, benefiting from her loss was hard to tolerate.

Even when she starts to pass something off as a joke, Jane's resentment comes through:

My father's old Ministers [his farm horses] are already deserting him to pay their court to his Son; the brown Mare, which as well as the black was to devolve on James at our removal, has not had patience to wait for that, & has settled herself even now at Deane. The death of Hugh Capet, which like that of Mr Skipsey, though undesired was not wholly unexpected, being purposely effected, has made the immediate possession of the Mare very convenient; & everything else I suppose will be seized by degrees in the same manner.[41]

Mary and James became the scapegoats, but Jane's parents were the real cause of her anger.

Through these letters is a stream of uneasiness sometimes giving way to irritation and annoyance with Cassandra herself. This is the most striking contrast to those written after the end of the Tom Lefroy affair. By mid January, when Jane should have been getting back on an even keel, she comments that she is writing to Cassandra too often. And she was fast running out of the will required to be alert and chatty. By the end of January she complains of having to write to Cassandra at all. 'Neither my affection for you nor for letter-writing can stand out against a Kentish visit. For a three months' absence I can be a very loving relation and a very excellent correspondent, but beyond that I degenerate into negligence and indifference.'[42] This is not really about letter-writing; it's about Cassandra's continuing absence. Jane thought the visit had been unreasonably prolonged. She felt herself deprived and neglected. She wanted more than amusing letters; she needed Cassandra's presence.

When Cassandra left Godmersham, she was to spend three weeks with Henry and Eliza in London. Henry had resigned his commission and entered a banking partnership with one of his fellow army officers. Eliza's £10,000 must have been his principal stake in this venture. Years before, Jane had foreseen that a marriage to Eliza would lead Henry eventually to London and the great world it signified. This would be the last time Cassandra would see poor Hastings de Feuillide, who died in the autumn at the age of fifteen and was buried beside his grandmother Hancock in Hampstead.

Cassandra's London visit was delayed in early January, and Jane wrote sharply: 'I think you judge very wisely in putting off your London visit & I am mistaken if it be not put off for some time.'[43] By the time Cassandra went to London in February, Jane gave vent to sarcastic anger that betrays a lapse into self-pity:

It is a great comfort to me to think that my cares have not been thrown away, and that you are respected in the world. Perhaps you may be prevailed on to return with [Edward] and Elizabeth into Kent, when they leave us in April, and I rather suspect that your great wish of keeping yourself disengaged has been with that view. Do as you like; I have overcome my desire of your going to Bath with my mother and me. There is nothing which energy will not bring one to.[44]

But she had no energy left. She was exhausted. Her words are full of reproach. Edward and then Henry had monopolised Cassandra when Jane needed her. With Martha back at Ibthorpe, Jane felt herself completely alone.

Needing respite, a change of scene, Jane went to Manydown at the end of January to see the Bigg sisters, exactly as she had done after the end of the Tom Lefroy affair when Cassandra was away. At Manydown she discovered that Catherine Bigg was planning to be in London at the same time as Cassandra and was thinking she and Cassandra might return to Hampshire together. Jane's worry was that Cassandra would again delay her return in order to fit in with Catherine's plan:

[Catherine] meditates your returning into Hampshire together, & if the Time should accord, it would not be undesirable. She talks of staying only a fortnight, & as that will bring your visit in Berkeley Street to three weeks, I suppose you would not wish to make it longer. Do not let this however retard your coming down, if you had intended a much earlier return.[45]

The last sentence is a plaintive plea, without bitterness or anger, just need. Two years before, the occupations of her everyday life had sustained Jane in her loss of Tom Lefroy. Now it seemed to her that her everyday life itself was to be taken away. The prospect before her was of course not a void, but it looked that way to her.

Cassandra finally came home in late February, but this was only temporary relief. The Leigh-Perrots had invited Mrs Austen to stay with them in Bath while she looked for a house to rent. When the invitation was made, Jane had written to Cassandra: 'Your going [to Bath] I consider as indispensably necessary, & I shall not like being left behind.'[46] Jane's real desire was to be with Cassandra and her real worry that she would have to go to Bath alone with their mother. What she foresaw is precisely what happened. When the family left Steventon,

Mr Austen went to Kent to visit relatives, and Mrs Austen and Jane and Cassandra went to Ibthorpe to pay a farewell visit to the Lloyds. Cassandra stayed on there while Jane and Mrs Austen proceeded to Bath.

May in Bath was the end of the social season – there was only one more ball before the town emptied for the summer. Jane could not make the effort required to enjoy the people she met. 'I cannot', she wrote to Cassandra, 'anyhow continue to find people agreable.' [47] Or to make herself agreeable. After her third party she grudgingly admitted that 'it was not quite so stupid as the two preceding parties here'.[48] Not much of a recommendation. She went on: 'I hate tiny parties – they force one into constant exertion.' [49] Jane was sick of exertion; she had had enough. This is a mood and frame of mind without precedent in her earlier letters. She felt homeless and hopeless. The past few months had made her feel that her life was ruled by the decisions of other people.

Cassandra and Mr Austen joined Jane and her mother in Bath in June, and the family departed for Devon where they spent the summer. In the autumn, when the Austens returned to Bath from their holiday, they settled at 4 Sydney Place. As far as Jane knew she was going to spend the rest of her life there. While her parents were alive, she had to live where they chose; when they died, she would have to live wherever her brothers decided to place her.

8

Ways of Escape

The first year at Sydney Place did not change Jane's opinion of Bath, and the next summer she and Cassandra stayed away from the town as long as they could. After another holiday in Devon with their parents, they went to Godmersham, and in late October moved on to James and Mary at Steventon. While they were at Steventon, their friends the Bigg-Withers invited them to stay and at the end of November they went to Manydown.

Both Lovelace Bigg-Wither and his son Harris had survived serious illnesses in the past few years, but William Heathcote, Elizabeth Bigg's husband, had died the previous spring at the age of thirty. Elizabeth and her year-old son had returned to live at Manydown. Her sisters Catherine and Alethea were still unmarried.

Manydown had a lot of associations for Jane. She and Tom Lefroy had danced and flirted at a ball there on his twentieth birthday; they had given Elizabeth Bigg and William Heathcote 'lessons in how to be particular'. But it was not romantic nostalgia that drew Jane to Manydown. After the end of her relationship with Tom, and again after her parents decided to move to Bath, Jane had needed a change, and Manydown was her refuge. She could always be sure of finding harmony and order, ease and good sense among her friends there.

The Bigg-Wither family were warm and welcoming, pleased to have the Austen sisters with them again. Jane and Cassandra were so much at ease and off their guard that neither noticed that the twenty-one-year-old Harris was being particularly attentive and that Jane was responding to him with comfortable familiarity. A picture of Harris shows he had boyish good looks, not unlike Tom Lefroy's. At the end of the first week of their visit, Harris proposed to Jane.

For all her rationality, Jane Austen was an impulsive woman. She had come to adore Eliza after only a few days; she had fallen in love with

Tom the first time they met and had made no attempt to conceal it. This time it was not an individual Jane responded to; it was to all that Harris signified. She impulsively accepted his offer. She said yes to making Manydown her home, yes to returning to the Steventon neighbourhood and to being the mistress of a fine house, to having financial security and social position; she said yes to being a member of a family she admired and respected, a family she knew held her and her own family in high regard. She said yes to everything except what Harris had asked: would she accept him as her husband?

Harris immediately told his father and sisters of Jane's acceptance, and the happy party celebrated for the rest of the evening. By the next morning, however, Jane had sorted out and weighed her motives. She knew she could not marry Harris. She was fond of him as the brother of her friends; she yearned for the security he offered; but she did not want to be married to him. She was probably ashamed of not having seen the truth at once, and even more at having to withdraw her promise. However awkward it would be, though, she knew she had to rectify her mistake. She spoke to Harris and made hasty, embarrassed explanations to his sisters. The Manydown carriage took Jane and Cassandra back to Steventon at once.

Steventon was no longer Jane's home. It was now the domain of the bustling, interfering Mary Lloyd, who in telling the story of this incident to her daughter many years later did not forget to mention James's inconvenience when his sisters insisted that he take them back to Bath on the spur of the moment. Mary had not even been expecting them back at Steventon that December morning. She demanded an explanation, but she said Jane refused to give one. Jane knew Mary's bluntness, had known Mary would have plenty to say that would pain her and even offend her. She was not going to hang around at Steventon until the wheedling Mary found out what had happened. Mary did later find out what had happened. And she thought Jane's refusal of such a man incomprehensible.[1] In worldly terms – which are perhaps the only ones Mary understood – a marriage to Harris had offered everything.

On that December morning when they returned from Manydown, Cassandra stood by Jane. James set out with them for Bath immediately. Fleeing Steventon for Bath was bitterly ironic. It looks like a rather awkward defeat. But Jane turned it into a liberation. The incident with

Harris Bigg-Wither clarified things for her. In her relationship with Tom Lefroy she had not wanted a husband, she had wanted *him*. Other people, women like her sister-in-law Mary, thought nothing mattered but having a husband. Jane would not force herself to marry, but she became determined to move forward in her work as a novelist. *That* she could do.

Back in Bath Jane began revising 'Susan' (later to be retitled *Northanger Abbey*), and that spring Henry's lawyer sold the novel to the publisher Crosby and Co. for £10. This was an affirmation of talent and a source of hope for independence. £10 was very little, but it was a beginning. She could earn money by writing. Seven years before, in the high glee of first meeting Tom Lefroy, she had said to Cassandra: 'I write only for Fame, and without any view to pecuniary Emolument.'[2] Now she had come to understand that money meant independence, and independence would bring escape from Bath.

The summer after 'Susan' was sold, Jane ran into her friend Anne Lefroy's brother Egerton Brydges in Ramsgate, where Frank was stationed. Jane had known Egerton best during the years he had rented Deane parsonage and had taken part in the Steventon theatricals of 1787. At that time the perceptive and precocious girl had listened to enough of his conversation to be able to comment when she read his novel *Arthur Fitz-Albini* in 1798: 'Never did any book carry more internal evidence of its author. Every sentiment is completely Egerton's.'[3] The autobiographical hero is unintentionally comic, a silly poseur, though he is meant to be an intense and intelligent man of parts. Brydges was not a man who would have taken much notice of an eleven-year-old girl, but he remembered quite vividly the meeting in Ramsgate, the last time he saw Jane Austen.

By the time he wrote an account of the meeting, Jane was dead and known to be the author of six novels. Her fame, however, does not seem to have coloured Brydges' recollection of her. His picture comes across as quite objective: 'I remember Jane Austen, the novelist ... she was fair and handsome, slight and elegant, with cheeks a little too full. The last time I think I saw her was at Ramsgate in 1803: Perhaps she was then about twenty-seven years old.'[4] This is simple and straightforward, but Brydges never knew when to stop, and so added in his pompous and self-important way: 'Even then I did not know she was addicted to literary composition.'[5] Jane would have been delighted with this foolishness; no doubt he considered himself 'addicted to literary composition' too.

To give Brydges his due, he almost unwittingly sheds some interesting light on Jane Austen in a new paragraph, directly after the sentence quoted above: 'I have not lived much with authors [but] I have seen enough to observe that authors seldom exhibit their minds in conversation, and that the best writers have often been the worst talkers.'[6] Recollecting their last meeting caused this idea to pop into Brydges's mind. He wrote a lot of nonsense in his rambling memoirs, but sometimes, as in this instance, something interesting and perceptive bubbles to the top. In recalling their last meeting, he realised Jane was not a good talker – at least not in his presence. The twenty-seven-year-old Jane is recognisable from the awkward child she herself described and Philadelphia Walter met. She was more composed now, but a bit quiet, not a brilliant conversationalist. This was Jane Austen as she appeared outside her own family and circle of intimate friends. This was the woman people met in Bath. She was also, though, the woman who had just sold her novel 'Susan' and was soon to begin writing a new novel, now known as *The Watsons*.

She began her new book with what had become established as her secret sign: the family of the title takes its name from a family in *Tom Jones*.[7] Jane's connection with Tom Lefroy in life might be over; but in her imagination he had an abiding place that she wanted to acknowledge in her work. Did Cassandra know? Somehow, you feel, this may have been the one secret Jane kept from her sister. It is all too easy to imagine that Cassandra would have found the gesture self-indulgent.

Jane Austen had not attempted a novel since completing 'Susan' in 1799, but with the sale to Crosby she was encouraged to start writing again. Crosby advertised 'Susan' as a forthcoming publication. In her desk she had two more novels to follow it: *Sense and Sensibility* and 'First Impressions'. Starting *The Watsons* was an act of faith; even though she had a backlog of two novels, being a writer means writing. In her own mind, and in the mind of Crosby and Co., Jane Austen had become a novelist. So she wrote.

The Watsons is a dark and unhappy novel. The father is a near-invalid

1. Jane Austen, watercolour sketch by Cassandra Austen. National Portrait Gallery.

2. The Rev. George Austen, Jane Austen's father.

3. Cassandra Austen, *née* Leigh, Jane Austen's mother. Silhouette, *c.* 1800.

4. Steventon Rectory, Hampshire, where Jane Austen lived between 1775 and 1801.

5. Edward Austen being presented by his father to Mrs Knight for adoption.

6. Godmersham House (Kent), inherited by Jane Austen's brother Edward.

7. Philadelphia Hancock, *née* Austen, the mother of Eliza de Feuillide.

8. Eliza de Feullide, Jane Austen's cousin.

9. James Austen, miniature of about 1790.

10. Henry Austen, miniature of about 1820.

11. James Leigh, later James
Leigh-Perrot, Jane Austen's uncle.

12. Jane Leigh-Perrot.

13. The Paragon, Bath (on the right). Jane Austen stayed with the Leigh-Perrots
at No. 1 in 1797.

14. Anne Lefroy, Tom Lefroy's aunt and Jane Austen's particular friend.

15. Tom Lefroy, Jane Austen's Irish friend.

16. Manydown House, Hampshire, the home of Jane Austen's friends the Biggs, where Jane and Tom danced.

17. Jane Austen, steel engraving (1869), from Cassandra Austen's sketch.

18. Cassandra Austen, undated silhouette.

19. Cork Street, the home of Benjamin Lefroy.

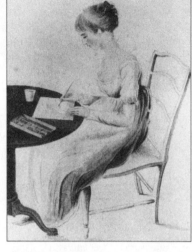

20. Anna Austen.

21. Fanny Austen.

22. Chawton Cottage, an early photograph.

who continues to try to fulfil his duties as a parson because he is too poor to retire. His elder son, Robert, is an attorney and has married a vulgar and pretentious woman with £6000; the younger son, Sam, is a surgeon just beginning his career. There are four unmarried daughters, ranging in age from nineteen to twenty-eight. When the father dies, which appears imminent, the daughters will be completely dependent on their brothers, neither of whom seems to be in a position to offer much support. Emma, the youngest, has been brought up and educated by a rich aunt and uncle, but has come home again, a stranger in her own family and with no better prospects than her sisters have.

The most poignant aspect of the work is Jane Austen's attempt to distance herself from her material by sending her heroine to just the sort of country village she herself was yearning to escape to. But the ruse did not work. The Watsons may live in a parsonage near a village, but in that place Emma Watson undergoes Jane Austen's experience of Bath: her loss of home, her sense of displacement and isolation, her unhappiness at having to live among strangers, people who are coarse, vulgar and unfeeling. As Austen worked on the novel, she must have begun to see aspects of the situation that were beyond her conscious intentions and, as it soon became apparent, beyond her control.

In the context of her story the theme of husband-hunting takes on a new colouring. Austen had treated the subject with plain ridicule in her first three novels, none more strongly than the picture in *Sense and Sensibility* of the Steele sisters, whose situation appears to be similar to that of the Watson sisters. Emma Watson does not laugh at her sisters for their crude open pursuits of husbands: she is shocked. One of her sisters dismisses Emma's attitude as over-refined. Austen herself seems ambivalent. She ridicules Emma's sisters, but beneath the ridicule lies a sense of the terrible necessity that drives the women.

She makes Emma's sisters crude and vulgar, selfish and unfeeling, indelicate and fretful. They are set up to be mocked, but their circumstances demand sympathy. Austen in full possession of her powers could have followed her imagination into the dark side of a theme she had intended to treat satirically. But her own personal preoccupations made it impossible for her to sustain the freedom and generosity of imagination necessary to do justice to the problem inherent in the Watson sisters' plight.

We can see Austen's defeat in the last paragraphs of the fragment. Up to that point she had maintained control in conveying Emma's unhappiness, communicated in her reticence; in her awkward feelings in trying to deal with other people, all virtual strangers; in her discomfort at her family's manners and values. When Austen came to the last paragraphs she was to write of *The Watsons*, she expressed directly what Emma Watson was feeling and thinking:

> Eager to be as little among [her family] as possible, Emma was delighted with the alternative of sitting above, with her father, & warmly entreated to be his constant Companion each Evening, & as Elizabeth loved company of any kind too well, not to prefer being below, at all risks, as she had rather talk of Croydon to Jane, with every interruption of Margaret's perverseness, than sit with only her father, who frequently could not endure Talking at all, the affair was so settled, as soon as she could be persuaded to beleive it no sacrifice on her Sister's part. To Emma, the exchange was most acceptable, & delightful. Her father, if ill, required little more than gentleness & silence; &, being a Man of Sense and Education, was if able to converse, a welcome companion.
>
> In *his* chamber, Emma was at peace from the dreadful mortifications of unequal Society, & family Discord, from the immediate endurance of Hard-hearted prosperity, low-minded Conceit, & wrong-headed folly, engrafted on an untoward Disposition. She still suffered from them in the Contemplation of their existence; in memory & in prospect, but for the moment, she ceased to be tortured by their effects. She was at leisure, she could read & think, though her situation was hardly such as to make reflection very soothing. The Evils arising from the loss of her Uncle, were neither trifling, nor likely to lessen; & when Thought had been freely indulged, in contrasting the past & the present, the employment of mind, the dissipation of unpleasant ideas which only reading could produce, made her thankfully turn to a book. The change in her home society, & stile of Life in consequence of the death of one friend and the imprudence of another had indeed been striking. From being the first object of Hope & Solicitude of an Uncle who had formed her mind with the care of a Parent, & of Tenderness to an Aunt whose amiable temper had delighted to give her every indulgence, from being the Life & Spirit of a House, where all had been comfort & Elegance, & the expected Heiress of an easy Independance, she was become of importance to no one, a burden on those, whose affection she could not expect, an addition in an House, already overstocked, surrounded by inferior minds with little chance

of domestic comfort, & as little hope of future support. It was well for her that she was naturally chearful; for the Change had been such as might have plunged weak spirits in Despondence.[8]

She struggled on for one more paragraph and then abruptly stopped writing the novel. She had given free rein to the expression of her own bitterness, and it signals her defeat in trying to write *The Watsons*. These paragraphs seem to have revealed to Austen the bleakness and bitterness that her own unhappiness was giving the work; and she did not want to write such a novel.

She did not have the equanimity necessary to write as she had to. An important aspect of Austen's genius was that she knew her tone, the tone that allowed her to express the truth. What she found herself writing in *The Watsons* might be truthful – she herself was feeling what Emma was feeling – and yet it was not her mode, her register. She gave up the novel, and her failure must have signified to her that at present she had neither the energy nor the composure of mind necessary for work. Too much was required just to maintain ordinary engagement with daily life; she had no margin for anything else.

The implications are devastating: without work there was no escape from Bath; but in Bath she could not work. Her only hope was that 'Susan' would be successful enough to bring about a change in her spirits or her circumstances that would enable her to start working again. In the autumn of 1804 the Austens gave up the lease on Sydney Place and moved to Green Park Buildings. They had now lived in Bath for three years.

A few months later, on 21 January 1805, George Austen died. He had been in a decline for several months, suffering from what Jane called a 'feverish complaint'.[9] He had an attack of fever, more violent than the previous ones, and died within forty-eight hours. Jane's letters to Frank informing him of their father's death are simple, unsentimental and deeply felt. She takes for granted that Frank knows what she is feeling. The letter is about their father, not about her own feelings at his death. She gives precise details of the event so that Frank can enter imaginatively into their father's death with exact specificity. She takes care to reassure him about their mother.

She gives credit to the Leigh-Perrots, who showed 'every imaginable kindness'.[10] When Henry wrote to Frank, he too mentioned the Leigh-Perrots: 'My Uncle & Aunt have both shewn much feeling and real affection during the whole of our severe trial. My Aunt *herself* could not help loving such a Being as the one whom we lament.'[11] Henry's remark is a backhanded way of saying it took an extraordinarily loveable person to touch their aunt's heart. Jane was not the only member of the family with a low opinion of the woman.

The most pressing concern was Mrs Austen's financial situation. According to Henry the banker, the income of his mother and Cassandra would now be £210 a year – about a third of what they had been living on since Mr Austen's retirement. Henry and James proposed to contribute £50 a year each and Edward £100. Frank was prepared to make a real sacrifice, and offered to give £100, but his mother would only accept £50.

All that is known of Charles's part in the scheme is hinted by a postscript to one of Henry's letters on the subject of the brothers' plan to help: 'Burn Charles's letter.'[12] Charles had no money to spare. He was trying to get himself into a sound enough position to marry and start his own family. There had always been a slight sense of his separateness from his brothers, and he probably felt, not unreasonably, that the whole support of their mother and sisters should come from the very rich Edward.

Even with the contributions from her sons, Mrs Austen could no longer afford to live at Green Park Buildings, and she and her daughters moved to lodgings in Gay Street. From there Jane wrote the only two surviving letters from her years in Bath that provide a glimpse of her life in the town. The sisters were rarely apart during these years, but in April 1805 Cassandra left Jane alone in Bath for a good reason, perhaps even at Jane's own insistence. Cassandra had not been well since their father's death and needed a change of scene and air. She went to Ibthorpe to stay with Martha Lloyd, and as it happened the visit coincided with Mrs Lloyd's final illness – she had been an invalid for a long time.

Jane's two letters are cheerful, even playful, so much so that she apologises to Cassandra for her tone. 'The Nonsense I have been writing in this & in my last letter, seems out of place at such a time; but I will not mind it, it will do you no harm, & nobody else will be attacked by it.'[13] She makes only one remark that gives a hint of what she felt about their life in Bath:

> This morning we have been to see Miss Chamberlayne look hot on horseback. Seven years & four months ago we went to the same Ridinghouse to see Miss Lefroy's performance! What a different set are we now moving in! But seven years I suppose are enough to change every pore of one's skin, & every feeling of one's mind.[14]

The difference between the Chamberlayne set and the Lefroys is left unspecified, but it does not sound as if Jane thought it a change for the better.

Whatever the difference, the Chamberlaynes were not socially inferior to the Lefroys. Miss Chamberlayne was a cousin, one of the Chamberlaynes of Maugersbury near Adlestrop Park. Soon after Jane had arrived to live in Bath she had become reacquainted with some of the family and had written to Cassandra that Mrs Chamberlayne 'remembers us in Gloucestershire when we were very charming young Women'.[15] Mrs Chamberlayne was recalling the visit Jane and Cassandra made to Adlestrop in 1794.

The Chamberlayne 'set' in Bath was a large one if we take into account all of its ramifications. The connections originated with Jane's maternal great-great grandfather James Brydges, Baron Chandos, and the Adlestrop Leighs, and include not only Chamberlaynes but Cookes, Stanhopes, Arnolds, Irvines, Twisletons, and even a Lady Furst, whose brother had married a Chamberlayne.[16] Bath doesn't at all sound like a place of strangers but of a large network of family, and there is no hint these people were ashamed of their Austen cousins. On the contrary, it appears they were willing, even eager, to get to know the Austens. It is Jane who sometimes expresses reticence about becoming more intimate with them. The hint of regret in Jane's comment about watching Miss Chamberlayne may have nothing to do with the girl or the 'set' she represented to Jane Austen, but to the memories the place evoked.

Only four months before, on Jane's twenty-ninth birthday, Mrs Lefroy had been thrown from a horse and killed, a loss Jane long felt. Anything that made her remember the Ashe Lefroys so soon after Mrs Lefroy's death would have been tinged with melancholy. A few years later she wrote the poem 'To the Memory of Mrs Lefroy', which begins with the coincidence of her friend dying on Jane's own birthday.

The only complaint Jane expresses about their Bath set is that she has too much social life. In addition to the Chamberlayne cousins and a couple of new Bath acquaintances, several other relatives and a very old friend were in the town in April. The person Jane was happiest to see was her father's old pupil Richard Buller, whom the Austens had visited in Devon and with whom Jane maintained a close friendship. Jane and Buller corresponded – unusual at that time for a man and woman who were not either engaged or brother and sister. He came to Bath with his wife because of his bad health. Jane pessimistically, but in the event rightly, told Cassandra that Buller's 'appearance is exactly that of a confirmed Decline'.[17] He died the next year at the age of only thirty.

The claustrophobic picture of Emma Watson's life in *The Watsons* may be what Jane feared or even sometimes felt in Bath, but her two letters convey nothing of that isolation and barrenness. If Jane lived in a desolation of spirit she learned to hide it from her acquaintance, and she shows in her letters to Cassandra that she was exerting herself to be active and busy. She makes a joke of the difficulties of keeping her social obligations from conflicting with one another: 'I shall endeavour as much as possible to keep my Intimacies in their proper place, & prevent their clashing.'[18] This is a marked contrast to her attitude when she and her mother had arrived in Bath four years before. She had been angry and querulous and determined to dislike everything. The people had been stupid, the parties demanding and tedious. Perhaps she still felt the same, but she expressed her feelings more lightly and noted what she found that gave satisfaction: 'There was a monstrous deal of stupid quizzing [teasing], & common-place nonsense talked, but scarcely any Wit; all that bordered on it, or on Sense came from my Cousin George [Cooke], whom altogether I like very well.'[19] She took what Bath offered and made what she could of it. But after the failure of *The Watsons*, she made no attempt to return to writing fiction.

Mrs Lloyd died on 16 April, and Cassandra remained at Ibthorpe with Martha for several more weeks. A few years earlier Jane had hoped that Martha and her mother would move to Bath, but nothing had come of that scheme. Now, Martha needed a home and decided to join her friends rather than going to live with relatives. With her sister Mary married to James Austen and Mrs Austen connected by the marriages of more than one Leigh to the Cravens, the women were almost relatives anyway. Martha's presence promised to be a great improvement to Jane's circumstances. Her living with them would make Jane less wholly dependent on Cassandra for companionship, and Martha seems to have had a good rapport with Mrs Austen. It was the first time in years that an event brought an enduring change for the better to Jane's life.

Setting out from Bath to Godmersham in June must have been more than the usual relief; when they returned Martha would be with them. The Austens travelled via Steventon to fetch Anna, James Austen's twelve-year-old daughter, who was going to Kent with them. Her step-mother, Mary Lloyd, was pregnant and had her second child, a daughter called Caroline, in mid June. Mrs Austen and Anna returned to Steven-ton at the end of July, and Jane and Cassandra stayed on at Godmersham until the middle of September.

Godmersham was a regular refuge from Bath, and Jane was attached to Edward's family circle. This included not only his wife, Elizabeth, and their children, but the Bridges family as well. Elizabeth had ten brothers and sisters so her connections were almost as numerous in Kent as the Leighs were in Gloucestershire. Jane liked being included in a wide network of family ties, as she once remarked to Cassandra: 'It is pleasant to be among people who know one's connections & care about them; & it amuses me to hear John Bridges [one of Elizabeth's brothers] talk of "Frank".' [20] She liked John's casual intimacy because it was a small but telling sign that the Austens were on easy, familiar terms with the Bridges clan, and were accepted as belonging to them.

The widowed Lady Bridges lived at Goodnestone Farm with her unmarried sons and daughters, while those who were married all lived close by. After Mrs Austen left Godmersham, Lady Bridges invited Jane and Cassandra to stay at Goodnestone by turns. Someone said they thought the Austen sisters would find Goodnestone dull, but Jane wrote Cassandra: 'I wished when I heard them say so, that they could have heard Mr E. Bridges's solicitude on the subject & have known all the amusements that were planned to prevent it.' [21] This was Edward Bridges, another of the Bridges sons, who lived with his mother. Jane was struck by Edward's kindness: 'It is impossible to do justice to the hospitality of his attentions towards me; he made a point of ordering toasted cheese for supper entirely on my account.' [22] Jane's fondness for toasted cheese was not what was uppermost in Edward's mind. The gesture was his awkward way of courting her. It looks as though he proposed to Jane and was refused. There is something almost comical about the whole scene, especially when seen in juxtaposition to the Manydown incident a few years before. Again Jane had found a haven and again a man had mistaken her attachment to the place and his family for an interest in himself.

Jane had blamed herself for what happened at Manydown, but she had no such feelings of self-reproach regarding Edward's proposal. She even made a sly joke about it to Cassandra a couple of years later when Cassandra wrote that Lady Bridges had invited her to Goodnestone Farm: 'I wish you may be able to accept Lady Bridges's invitation, though *I* could not her son Edward's.' [23] Jane wasn't ruffled by the incident, nor did her refusal offend Edward or his mother. The next time she saw them she was able to report that they were both friendly and good-humoured, their manners to her unaltered.

She implies that Lady Bridges knew what had happened. There is no hint that anyone else did except, of course, Cassandra. But if it were known, it must have caused some perplexity, even disapproval. By the time Jane turned Edward down, she was completely dependent on her brothers to support her. They were ostensibly giving money to their mother, but everyone knew Mrs Austen had an income of her own and that Cassandra had the £1000 Tom Fowle had left her. Only Jane was absolutely penniless. She had now had proposals from two upright, pleasant, respectable men, one of them very rich, the other a clergyman from a wealthy family. Her letters give no indication that anyone put pressure on her to marry or that she even felt unspoken demand. But she must have examined her own motives and questioned her *right* to have refused Harris and Edward.

When Jane did at last write a new novel, she would make the problem a central theme. In *Mansfield Park* we get some sense of what must have been going on in her mind at the time she received the proposals. The reader knows that Fanny Price has two strong reasons for refusing Henry Crawford: she is in love with someone else, and she thinks Crawford is unprincipled. But no one else is aware of the reasons, and most of them find Fanny's refusal of Crawford incomprehensible. Fanny doesn't reveal her motives. She only tells her uncle, 'I – I cannot like him, Sir, well enough to marry him'.[24] And she later almost angrily insists on a woman's right not to like a man even though he happens to like her:

> 'I *should* have thought ... that every woman must have felt the possibility of a man's not being approved, not being loved by some one of her sex, at least, let him be ever so generally agreeable. Let him have all the perfections in the world, I think it ought not to be set down as certain, that a man must be acceptable to every woman he may happen to like himself.'[25]

Jane Austen had her reasons for not marrying Harris or Edward. What they were she never revealed. She followed her principle, and her principle was that the decision belonged to her alone.

Jane and Cassandra did not return to Bath at the end of their 1805 Godmersham visit. They went to the seaside village of Worthing where Mrs Austen and Martha Lloyd joined them, and the women settled in lodgings there until the end of the year, when they returned to Bath and gave up the lodgings in Gay Street. They took rooms in Trim Street until they could find something better. Good lodgings were difficult to come by. Mrs Austen expressed her exasperation in the heading of a letter to Mary Lloyd in April: '*Trim Street Still.*'[26]

9

Money

Frank now became the hero of the piece. We don't hear his private voice during Jane Austen's lifetime; we know him, appropriately, through his actions. We got a hint of his character when he generously offered to contribute £100 a year to his mother and sisters – double what James and Henry gave, and the same as the rich Edward. Imprudent perhaps, but where his mother and sisters were concerned prudence was not the virtue called for. In the spring of 1806 he showed imagination as well as generosity. The women needed to get out of Bath, because it was too expensive, and because Jane was unhappy there.

Frank had a plan. He had decided he was securely established in his career and could now afford to marry. He had met Mary Gibson in Ramsgate in 1803 when he was twenty-nine and she was nineteen. He had not rushed into marriage, but once he had made up his mind, and Mary had accepted him, he proposed that his mother and sisters and Martha Lloyd share a house with him and his bride in Southampton. It would be financially advantageous for all of them. Even taking into consideration that in those days people were used to living in extended families, for a man to bring his bride to live in a small house with four other women took a lot of courage – on everyone's part. Perhaps the potential difficulties actually appealed to Mrs Austen's brave and brisk side.

Frank's gesture brings up questions we might before have taken for granted. Was he the first of the sons to think of sharing a home with his mother and sisters? When their father died, didn't it occur to James or Henry to make such an offer? Above all, didn't Edward with his three estates think of trying to find a cottage for them in the country? Perhaps they all offered and were refused, though Mrs Austen's motive for insisting on staying in Bath remains hidden. When Frank came up with his plan, though, she let herself be persuaded to leave.

Mrs Austen and Jane and Cassandra left Bath on 2 July 1806 'with what happy feelings of Escape!',[1] as Jane later remembered. On the same day Mrs Austen's cousin the Hon. Mary Leigh died in London. She was a very distant relative, one of the Leighs of Stoneleigh Abbey, while Mrs Austen came from the line of Adlestrop Leighs. The Stoneleigh family had been created barons in the seventeenth century, but the line had ended in 1786 with Mary Leigh's brother, who died insane, leaving the family fortune and estate to his sister for her lifetime. Her brother's will is somewhat ambiguous about the disposal of the property after Mary's death, but she left a will laying out her own intentions. The estate was to go in order of seniority to the surviving male of the Adlestrop Leighs: first, the Rev Thomas Leigh, then James Leigh-Perrot, and finally, since both men were childless, to Thomas's nephew, James Leigh of Adlestrop Park and his heirs.

When Mary died in London her lawyer wrote to the three heirs summoning them to London for the reading of the will. Mrs Austen's brother Leigh-Perrot arrived on the night of 3 July and wrote to his wife the next morning and again the following day. The letters tell us a lot about Leigh-Perrot's relationship with his wife.

Although they had been married for more than forty years, he wrote with something like a young lover's insistence on his devotion: 'You may be sure my thoughts and wishes are at Scarlets, and I will be there as soon as I can.'[2] He ended this letter: 'If I was able to say how much I love you and how much I long to be with you perhaps you would not believe me.'[3]

The next day he wrote again: 'My Dearest Jenny, once more I am obliged to write to you instead of coming to you.'[4] He explained why he had to stay in London – the prospect of money from the Stoneleigh estate. Thomas Leigh wanted the property to pass directly from himself to his nephew James Leigh, which meant persuading James Leigh-Perrot to renounce his own claim to it. Thomas and James Leigh were prepared to pay Leigh-Perrot to do this.

Seeing how profitable this might be to himself and his wife, he decided to stay on in London to discuss the matter and wrote to his wife to explain: 'I therefore agreed not to quit Town today, though I feel very uneasy at this delay; for indeed I am very very anxious to be again with you.'[5] Uneasy and agitated, he couldn't bear being separated from his wife. He ends his letter: 'How glad shall I be to tell you how dearly I love and value you, instead of employing my Pen for that Purpose!' [6] His concern seems excessive for someone who has only been away a day or two. After more than forty years of marriage, he was still so besotted with his wife that to be separated from her caused him acute anxiety.

Mrs Austen and her daughters were in Clifton near Bristol at this time, but later in July they went to Adlestrop to visit Thomas Leigh and his sister Elizabeth at the rectory – his wife, the family historian, had died ten years before. They were not at Adlestrop very long, but long enough for Jane to become intrigued with the idea of landscape improvements: Humphry Repton had recently completed redesigning the park there. It was probably from the Leighs that Jane learned that Repton charged five guineas a day, a detail she was to mention in *Mansfield Park*.

At the beginning of August, Thomas Leigh had a letter from Mary Leigh's lawyer asking him to come to Stoneleigh to deal with business relating to his role as executor of the estate. A party including the Austens set out for Warwickshire and arrived at Stoneleigh on 4 August. Mrs Austen had never been there before and wrote to Mary Lloyd in some detail about the house and grounds. She hadn't realised how large or how pleasant the place was and was struck by its not being heavy and gloomy:

> The house is larger than I could have supposed. We can *now* find our way about it … I expected to find every thing about the place very fine and all that, but I had no idea of its being so beautiful. I had figured to myself long Avenues dark Rookeries and dismal Yew Trees, but here are no such melancholy things.[7]

She mentions the estate as now being owned by Thomas Leigh and makes no reference at all to her brother Leigh-Perrot's present or future interest in it. By the end of the year, however, the Austens had formed their own expectations concerning the Stoneleigh money.

With the move to Southampton, everyone seems to have considered that things were back to normal. Perhaps Jane herself, in the exhilaration of having escaped from Bath, had believed it would be a peaceful scene without vexations. Mrs Austen, Cassandra, Jane and Martha joined Mary

Gibson and Frank early in October, and they took lodgings while they looked for a house to rent. They had hardly had time to settle in when Edward's wife had her ninth child in mid November, and for the first time in five years Cassandra left Jane behind and went off to Kent to help. Soon Martha too was off on a round of Christmas visits that would go on until the end of February, and Jane was left without the consolation of an intimate companion or the calming influence of a capable, sensible woman.

With Mrs Austen always teetering on the brink of illness and Mary Gibson five months pregnant and subject to 'fainting fits', Jane found herself having to be the active, sensible, capable woman in the household. She found it a strain. Behind her light remarks is a reminder to Cassandra that housekeeping was not Jane's forte. James and his family came for a visit and Jane declared: 'When you receive this, our guests will be all gone or going; and I shall be left to the comfortable disposal of my time, to ease of mind from the torments of rice puddings and apple dumplings, and probably to regret that I did not take more pains to please them all.'8 The cook was on holiday and so Jane had to supervise the scene in the kitchen more closely than usual. The irksome tasks were not rewarded; Jane did not enjoy Mary Lloyd's company.

Mary talked too much about money, indirectly boasting about James's income, and she took no pleasure in the books they read aloud in the evening. Jane's irritations with Mary built up to something like anger at the effect her sister-in-law had on James:

> I am sorry & angry that [James's] Visits should not give one more pleasure; the company of so good & so clever a Man ought to be gratifying in itself; but his Chat seems all forced, his Opinions on many points too much copied from his Wife's, & his time here is spent I think in walking about the House & banging the Doors, or ringing the Bell for a glass of Water.9

Jane felt a real loss at seeing the brother whose lively conversation and inventive stories and essays in the *Loiterer* had once given her so much pleasure now subside into dullness, parroting his inferior wife's ideas and opinions.

Once the Steventon family left, Jane was involved in preparations for the move to the house in Castle Square they had taken from the end of March, and she wanted Cassandra at home to share in the plans. But just as in the old days, once Cassandra got to Godmersham, her return kept being postponed. Jane grumbled about the delays and pretended that Frank and his wife wanted Cassandra in Southampton:

> Frank & Mary cannot at all approve of your not being at home in time to help them in their finishing purchases, & desire me to say that, if you are not, they shall be as spiteful as possible & chuse everything in the stile most likely to vex you, Knives that will not cut, glasses that will not hold, a sofa without a seat, & a Bookcase without shelves.[10]

Behind the teasing is Jane's own annoyance at Cassandra's lingering in Kent.

Social life offered some distractions but not many that were to Jane's taste. Her general comment was: 'Our acquaintance increase too fast.'[11] One of the best things about Southampton, however, was that there the Austens had a new social identity: they belonged to the naval society of the town, Frank's friends among his fellow officers and their families, people like Captain John Foote whose company did please Jane, as she wrote to Cassandra:

> He dined with us on Friday, and I fear will not soon venture again, for the strength of our dinner was a boiled leg of mutton, underdone even for James; and Captain Foote has a particular dislike to underdone mutton; but he was so good-humoured and pleasant that I did not much mind his being starved. He gives us all the most cordial invitation to his house in the country.[12]

It is an easy, cosy domestic scene, everyone natural, no one bothered by a mishap like an underdone leg of mutton.

To show her appreciation and regard for Captain Foote, Jane one day offered to take care of his ten-year-old daughter Kitty after his wife had just had a baby. Jane took to the little girl and was led to recollect, by contrast, what she herself had been like as a child. She was writing to Cassandra when Kitty arrived, and Jane described the scene as she wrote: 'She is now talking away at my side & examining the Treasures of my Writing-desk drawer; very happy I beleive; not at all shy of course.'[13] Reflecting on Kitty's manners, she wonders:

> What is become of all the Shyness in the World? Moral as well as Natural Diseases disappear in the progress of time, & new ones take their place.

Shyness & the Sweating Sickness have given way to Confidence & Paralytic complaints.[14]

Jane makes clear which of these 'moral' diseases she considers worse. After Kitty had gone home, she added in her letter to Cassandra:

Our little visitor has just left us, & left us highly pleased with her; she is a nice, natural, openhearted, affectionate girl, with all the ready civility which one sees in the best Children of the present day; so unlike anything that I was myself at her age, that I am often all astonishment & shame.[15]

In truth Jane retained some of the awkwardness and reserve she had had as a child. With new people she could be stiff and anxious; she needed someone like Captain Foote to put her at her ease. Not everyone had that talent, especially people Jane feared were weighing her up socially.

Southampton was a fashionable watering-place like Bath, and sometimes the Austens were brought into contact with people Jane did not want to know – and feared *they* didn't want to know her. At best she was indifferent, as when Admiral Bertie, who had encountered Frank one day, brought his daughter to call on them: 'There was nothing to like or dislike in either', she informed Cassandra.[16] But Jane was defensive when the Lances, people whose relatives were friends of Martha Lloyd, introduced themselves:

I suppose they must be acting by the orders of Mr Lance of Netherton in this civility, as there seems no other reason for their coming near us. They will not come often, I dare say. They live in a handsome style and are rich, and she seemed to like to be rich, and we gave her to understand that we were far from being so; she will soon feel therefore that we are not worth her acquaintance.[17]

Such were Jane's speculations; how much basis they had in reality we don't know. Even the possibility that someone was being condescending made Jane bristle. Up came her self-protective mechanism.

It sounds as if Jane Austen at thirty-two retained more than a touch of Jane at eleven when she had thought she wouldn't like her cousin Eliza for the same reasons – she was too rich and too grand. From Mrs Lance's perspective, Jane probably seemed too cold, even haughty – in spite of the profession of being far from rich – to make her want to cultivate the acquaintance. Jane was just the kind of person she herself didn't like to meet. This made living in new places among strangers particularly hard for her. Whether it was Bath or Southampton, any town was overwhelming. She needed a village where everyone knew where they belonged in the social hierarchy, where she knew her place and everyone knew what that place was. In reality of course, no such place existed, as she was to imply in her picture of Highbury in *Emma*, a village with a society as fluid and ambiguous as that of any watering-place.

The unexpected element in the background to life in Southampton was the Stoneleigh inheritance. It turned out to be confusing (at least to the Austens) and quite drawn out. But the Austens began to think some of the money might come their way. Sometimes Jane's remarks make it sound as if her mother might get money directly as a part of the actual settlement, but they usually suggest Mrs Austen expected a gift from her brother Leigh-Perrot as a result of his windfall. Six months after Mary Leigh's death, the Austens thought Leigh-Perrot had reached an agreement with Thomas Leigh and his nephew. Jane mentions the 'termination of the family treaty' in January 1807. [18]

The whole family was talking about the money, and Mrs Austen was waiting in tense expectation to see what her brother would do for her. She could not ask outright and was careful not to give hints about the matter. This made her correspondence with her sister-in-law difficult. Jane told Cassandra that for their mother writing to their aunt 'always hangs a little upon her mind'.[19] And she assumed that when Cassandra, who was in Kent, visited Edward's benefactor Mrs Knight in Canterbury they would discuss the settlement: 'You will have a great deal of un-reserved discourse with Mrs K., I dare say, upon this subject [the Stoneleigh business], as well as upon many other of our family matters. Abuse everybody but me.'[20] Jane ventures nothing except this wry comment about the situation.

At this point we have only the Austens' sense of what they thought would be the outcome of the matter with regard to Mrs Austen. Their hopes do seem to have been more than just groundless fantasy. The Leigh-Perrots were already rich, and Mrs Austen, James Leigh-Perrot's only living sister, was so poor that her sons had to give her £250 a year to support her two unmarried daughters. A couple of thousand pounds would have relieved her sons of their burden and made the daughters secure for life. Leigh-Perrot had so much money that such a gift would not have involved sacrifice. He was already over seventy and his wife over sixty, and they were childless. If James Austen was to inherit his uncle's fortune, why not go ahead and give Mrs Austen enough to live on now?

Believing the settlement had been reached, the Austens waited for some sign from the Leigh-Perrots, some announcement of their intentions. The letter that should have carried the news arrived, and Jane reported to Cassandra that their aunt made no reference to the subject.

> My Mother has heard this morning from Paragon [where the Leigh-Perrots lived in Bath]. My Aunt talks much of the violent colds prevailing in Bath, from which my Uncle has suffered ever since their return, & she has herself a cough much worse than any she ever had before, subject as she has always been to bad ones. She writes in good humour & chearful spirits however. The negociation between them & Adlestrop [Thomas Leigh] so happily over indeed, what can have power to vex her materially? [21]

Mrs Leigh-Perrot pointedly avoided mentioning the money, and all the Austens could do was make excuses for her evasiveness. Perhaps the Leigh-Perrots were still making up their mind how much to give Mrs Austen; perhaps they were waiting until they actually had the money in hand.

In fact the negotiations were still going on. A part of a game like this was delay, and delay was a good gamble in this case. Both Thomas Leigh and James Leigh-Perrot were over seventy; if one of them were suddenly to die the matter would be resolved; the survivor would get everything without having to pay or renounce anything.

In February 1807 Mrs Leigh-Perrot, far from encouraging the Austens to hope, seems to have been signalling them to expect nothing. Yet in the next year or so something was hinted or said to make the Austens more than optimistic; Jane herself was almost excited. When she went to Godmersham in June 1808, legacies, inheritance, gifts, even the Stoneleigh 'business' itself, recur again and again in her letters. No subject had turned up again and again so insistently since she had met Tom Lefroy at the beginning of 1796. She never wrote details or speculated about the financial arrangements, but her allusions would have spoken volumes to Cassandra. To us they indicate how persistently the affair loomed in Jane's mind. The possibility of independence seemed very real and very near.

She wrote to Cassandra that their sister-in-law Elizabeth's sister Louisa had inherited some money – 'legacies are very wholesome diet'.[22] That hint of what was preoccupying her became more explicit when Elizabeth talked of Jane and Cassandra coming to Godmersham at Christmas. 'A Legacy might make it very feasible; a Legacy is our sovereign good.'[23] She reported that 'Mr Thomas Leigh is again in Town – or was very lately. Henry met with him last sunday in St James's Church. He owned being come up unexpectedly on Business, which we of course think can be only *one* business'.[24]

While at Godmersham Jane visited Edward's benefactor, Mrs Knight, and reported to Cassandra that they had 'had time to say a little of Everything'.[25] One of the subjects they found time to discuss was the Stoneleigh money. 'Mrs Knight is kindly anxious for our Good, & thinks Mr L. P. *must* be desirous for his *Family's* sake to have everything settled. Indeed, I do not know where we are to get our Legacy – but we will keep a sharp look-out.'[26] Jane writes with a hardly repressed thrill of expectation; she believed some of the Stoneleigh money would somehow make its way to her mother.

Mrs Austen's old friend Mrs Birch, like Mrs Knight, was also certain Leigh-Perrot would give money to his sister and declared she would 'not be at all satisfied unless a very *handsome* present is made us immediately, from one Quarter' – the quarter obviously being uncle Leigh-Perrot.[27] Probably Jane and Cassandra shored up their hopes by reminding each other that these were not just based on a groundless fantasy and wishful thinking; disinterested people like Mrs Knight and Mrs Birch believed Leigh-Perrot would now have to respond to his sister's need.

Jane had travelled to Godmersham with James and Mary and their two children, James Edward and Caroline. The boy was ten, the girl only three. 'We were rather crowded yesterday', Jane wrote to Cassandra when they arrived, 'though it does not become me to say so, as I and my boa were of the party, and it is not to be supposed but that a child of three years of age was fidgety.'[28] This is not Jane's irritated voice but her amused one. She was in a good mood.

But at the beginning of the visit she found it odd to be there without Cassandra. Then she caught a cold and felt languid and lonely. Nevertheless she was alert enough to take note of the contrast between the lively and confident Godmersham children and their shy little cousin Caroline. This observation lodged in her imagination, later re-emerging to excellent effect in *Mansfield Park*.

Jane stayed on for a while after James and his family left, and she planned to return to Southampton in July. In late June Henry wrote suggesting that she stay on until September when he would come and take her home. Edward and Elizabeth kindly pressed her to accept Henry's offer and extend her visit. Jane did not want to refuse their invitation because it might seem ungrateful, but she felt she had to. She had heard that Catherine and Alethea Bigg were planning be in Southampton in July – it would be their first visit to Jane since their brother Harris's proposal. She felt that she had to explain to Edward and Elizabeth why it was important for her to be in Southampton to see Catherine and Alethea.

Jane confided that Harris had proposed to her; she told them of her acceptance and then withdrawal. They understood why she had to see Harris's sisters and also why the story of the proposal should remain secret. Jane was so intensely private that it cannot have been easy to reveal the circumstances of her refusal of Harris, even to her brother and sister-in-law. If she had cared less about them, she would have let them think what they pleased about her insisting on going home in July, even that she was tired of them and their many children. But she wanted to be frank and open. She plucked up her courage and told them. 'I have felt myself obliged to give Edward & Elizabeth one private reason for my wishing to be at home in July', she wrote to Cassandra. 'They feel the strength of it, & say no more; & one can rely on their secrecy. After this, I hope we shall not be disappointed of our Friends' visit; my honour, as well as my affection will be concerned in it.' [29]

Jane returned to Southampton in July, and near the end of September Cassandra went to Godmersham, where Elizabeth was expecting her eleventh child. Cassandra arrived too late for the birth but wrote to Jane that Elizabeth and the baby were doing well.

Frank and Mary were in lodgings on the Isle of Wight where Frank was now stationed, and Martha was also away but expected back on 10 October. Jane thought Martha would be delayed: 'I shall not much regard it on my own account [if Martha's return is delayed], for I am now got into such a way of being alone that I do not wish even for her.'³⁰ Being with her mother was being alone. Jane sounds as if she is trying to forestall disappointment. To her surprise, Martha returned three days early and was at the house in Castle Square when the news came on 12 October that Elizabeth Austen had died two days before. She was thirty-five years old and had had eleven children in less than seventeen years.

The Austens had been very lucky, considering how common untimely deaths were in the early nineteenth century. Until Elizabeth died, the immediate family circle had only been touched by the early deaths of James's first wife, Anne, in 1795, and Cassandra's fiancé, Tom Fowle, in 1797. Mr Austen had died peacefully at the age of seventy-four.

All the children of George and Cassandra Austen were in good health, and Charles and Frank, though actively engaged in the Napoleonic Wars and often at sea, had come through their perils safely. Not one of the fifteen grandchildren had died in infancy, as was so common then, nor, before Elizabeth, had any of the wives died in childbirth. Yet child bearing was as treacherous as soldiering or sailoring – at about the time Mary Lloyd's first child was born, two women in the Steventon neighbourhood had died giving birth.

In the death of Elizabeth Austen we see the fullness of Jane's life. Her imagination carried her out of herself, not only into those fictional worlds and characters she created, but into the real world and into the feelings and thoughts and situations of many other people, making her life richer and more varied than might casually appear. She was not limited by the emotions and experiences that were directly her own. In observing Jane's habits of mind and imagination at this time we see how she practised imaginative engagement as a moral activity – an exercise in turning outward from herself.

Jane directed her thoughts to Godmersham, especially to Edward. 'All that you say of Edward is truly comfortable', she wrote to Cassandra; 'I began to fear that when the bustle of the first week was over, his spirits might for a time be more depressed; and perhaps one must still expect something of the kind.'³¹ She believed he would be supported in his grief by his religion and that his natural disposition to be active and cheerful would carry him through.

Jane thought of the particular suffering her brother would endure when he saw Elizabeth's mother, Fanny Lady Bridges. Her imagination moved outward to every detail of the days at Godmersham.

> I see your mournful party in my mind's eye under every varying circumstance of the day; & in the Evening especially, figure to myself its' sad gloom – the efforts to talk; the frequent summons to melancholy orders & cares; & poor Edward restless in Misery going from one room to the other, & perhaps not seldom upstairs to see all that remains of his Elizabeth.[32]

She connected herself to the mourning at Godmersham by keeping the family there in her thoughts and pondering deeply Cassandra's part and the strength her sister required. Her letters at this time contain more instances than usual of such phrases as 'my dearest Cassandra' and 'my dearest Sister'.

Jane was engaged with equal intensity in thoughts of the children, especially Fanny, the eldest. Fanny was now fifteen, and on her fell the heaviest burden. Before Elizabeth's death Cassandra had written in praise of Fanny, and Jane had replied: 'I found her in the summer just what you describe, almost another Sister, & could not have supposed that a neice would ever have been so much to me.'[33] She rejoiced that Cassandra was there to comfort Fanny, who Jane saw would now have to take her mother's place.

Even at such a distance from Godmersham, Jane had practical tasks to perform. Cassandra asked her to write letters to some members of the family to inform them of Elizabeth's death. Another task was to send mourning clothes to Cassandra, and she reported what her own were to be: '*I* am to be in Bombazeen & Crape, according to what we are told is universal *here*; & which agrees with Martha's previous observation.'[34]

Jane once had written that as they were entering Bath they 'met a Gentleman in a Buggy, who on a minute examination turned out to be Dr Hall – & Dr Hall in such very deep mourning that either his Mother, his Wife, or himself must be dead'.[35] She noted a similar tendency in the 'Endless Debaries': 'The Debaries persist in being afflicted at the death of their Uncle, of whom they now say they saw a great deal.'[36] About two weeks later, she was more specific: 'Miss Debary, Susan & Sally all in black, but without any Statues, made their appearance.'[37] What she means by 'without any Statues' is opaque, but the implication of their being all in black is enough for us to get the drift. Jane considered such excessive or unusual show in mourning clothes to be a particularly distasteful parade of self-advertising and self-dramatising feeling.

When Jane saw Edward's two eldest sons a week later, she discussed their clothes with them. 'I find that black pantaloons are considered by them as necessary', she reported to Cassandra, 'and of course one would not have them made uncomfortable by the want of what is usual on such occasions.'[38] Her sensibility is apparent in her concern for her nephews' feelings. Her attention to form was not for its own sake but reveals a deeper principle with her: conform to what is customary in a particular place so as to be unobtrusive, so as not to draw attention to yourself.

Coming home to Southampton early in October, Martha had seen both boys, Edward and George, in Winchester, where they were at school, and had reported her admiration of Edward's manners. She had noticed a bit of their uncle Henry in George – which was certain to endear him to Jane. Young Edward was a favourite of Cassandra, with whom he corresponded.

When the news of their mother's death reached Winchester, Edward and George went to Steventon to stay with their uncle James and his family. Then they came to Southampton for a few days before returning to school. Jane and her mother were impressed by the feeling the boys showed, and Jane wrote to Cassandra that 'Miss Lloyd, who is a more impartial judge than I can be, is exceedingly pleased with them'.[39] Jane talked to the boys about the gravity of their loss, but she also sensibly did what she could to provide them with distractions to prevent them from dwelling too much on their grief.

The younger boy, George, was thirteen and described by Jane as 'almost a new acquaintance to me, and I find him in a different way as engaging as Edward'.[40] Ten years before at the age of three, George had first captivated his aunt Jane. After Jane's visit to Godmersham in the early autumn of 1798, Cassandra had written to her that George remembered her and had asked Cassandra to tell her he had learned a new song. Jane, who like her father was insistently unsentimental even when deeply attached to children, wrote back:

> My dear itty Dordy's [George's name for himself in those days] remembrance of me is very pleasing to me; foolishly pleasing, because I know it will be over so soon. My attachment to him will be more durable; I shall think with tenderness & delight on his beautiful & smiling Countenance & interesting Manners, till a few years have turned him into an ungovernable, ungracious fellow.[41]

But George hadn't yet become the boy Jane predicted, and she was delighted with him and Edward.

They played games indefatigably and took long walks. On Sunday young Edward was deeply affected by the parson's sermon, but Jane had realistic expectations of the boys. 'In the evening we had the Psalms and Lessons, and a sermon at home, to which they were very attentive; but you will not expect to hear that they did not return to conundrums the moment it was over.' [42] With their natural liveliness and spontaneous sense of fun, the boys themselves did a lot to dispel the gloom from the Southampton household. Jane arranged a water party on the river. Both boys rowed, and 'their questions and remarks, as well as their enjoyment, were very amusing; George's inquiries were endless, and his eagerness in everything reminds me often of his Uncle Henry'.[43] George worked the same charm on his aunt that he had when he was a little child.

Something of the flow of ordinary life was already beginning to reassert itself when the nephews came to Castle Square. Jane did not forget or ignore what had occurred in October, and she particularly noted what a sad day 27 December – the wedding anniversary of Edward and Elizabeth – must have been at Godmersham. But midway through her letter describing the boys' visit, she turned to subjects wholly unconnected to Elizabeth's death and its aftermath. To Cassandra's writing she would not be returning to Southampton as early as she had intended, Jane replied with resignation: 'As to your lengthened stay, it is no more than I expected, and what must be, but you cannot suppose I like it.' [44]

Even before Elizabeth's death, a plan was afoot that would change Jane Austen's life, and she understood the possibilities the change offered.

In the summer Mrs Austen had already decided they should leave Southampton. Frank and his wife were now settled on the Isle of Wight, and the Austen women and Martha would move to a place in the country rather than take a smaller house in Southampton. They were considering both Kent and Hampshire. Alton had been chosen as the best place in Hampshire because Henry's bank had a branch there and he frequently went there on business; Edward's estate at Chawton, only a mile from Alton, brought him to the town from time to time; and it was close enough to Steventon for convenience but far enough away to keep Mary Lloyd from being a nuisance.

Edward did just the sort of thing the Austens favoured in the face of grief: he looked outward from his sorrow to the concerns of the living. By 24 October, two weeks after his wife's death, he had offered Chawton Cottage on his Chawton estate to his mother and she had accepted. The plans for Chawton began with eager exchanges of information about the house. The cottage had six bedrooms, and garrets for storage. Other questions were asked and answered. In spite of all the information they gleaned, they longed for more and depended on Cassandra's report, for she was actually to see the house on her return journey to Southampton. 'We are very desirous of receiving *your* account of the House', Jane wrote to Cassandra, 'for your observations will have a motive which can leave nothing to conjecture & suffer nothing from want of Memory. For one's own dear Self, one ascertains & remembers everything.' [45]

The subdued and consoling tone of Jane's letters to Cassandra after Elizabeth's death gives way now to cheerfulness and more than cheerfulness. Her letters crackle with excitement at the prospect of living in the country again, of having brothers and nieces and nephews coming to visit; of having a *place* again. At some time she must have recalled her earlier stay in Southampton with Mrs Cawley, from which she was delivered by the outbreak of typhus. This time she was leaving Southampton for a home that would become no less dear to her than Steventon itself had been.

With the prospect of Chawton in view Jane could be philosophical, even when their hopes for some of the Stoneleigh money came to nothing. But it must have been a bitter disappointment. In November she reported to Cassandra that the business was indeed concluded. Their uncle finally signed the document renouncing his interest in the inheritance. He accepted £24,000 and an annuity of £2000 for himself or his widow for life. Mrs Austen had heard from her sister-in-law: 'My Aunt says as little as may be on the subject by way of information, & nothing at all by way of satisfaction.'[46] Mrs Leigh-Perrot was evasive as usual and emphasised her own poor pitiful self.

> She reflects on Mr T. Leigh's dilatoriness [in paying the money], & looks about with great diligence & success for Inconvenience & Evil – among which she ingeniously places the danger of her new Housemaids catching cold on the outside of the Coach, when she goes down to Bath – for a carriage makes her sick.[47]

Aunt Leigh-Perrot's letter, with its self-pitying referral of everything to herself, was precisely what Jane had come to expect from her. Not so Mrs Austen:

> In spite of all my Mother's long & intimate knowledge of the Writer, she was not up to the expectation of such a Letter as this; the discontentedness of it shocked & surprised her but *I* see nothing in it out of Nature – though a sad nature.[48]

The real point of the letter, implicit in what was *not* said, was that the Leigh-Perrots did not have any intention of giving Mrs Austen money from the Stoneleigh settlement.

Soon after the unsatisfactory letter to Mrs Austen, Mrs Leigh-Perrot wrote to James Austen to announce that she and his uncle intended to give him £100 a year. The wily Leigh-Perrots completely dissociated this gift from their having just come into a large amount of money; they claimed it was to show their approval of James's having turned down the rectorship of Hampstead Marshall because he had a moral objection to clergymen not living in the parish they served.

The future history of this £100 throws more light on Mrs Leigh-Perrot's character. A year after her husband died, she stopped paying the money to James. 'My Aunt has withdrawn the Annuity of £100 a year which she and my Uncle had allowed me for these eight or nine years past', James wrote to his son. 'The ostensible reasons are her own *poverty* & my having £200 a year to support T. Leigh,[49] of which I certainly clear more than half, but who is very unlikely to live long. The real reasons I leave you to guess.'[50] James's son, James Edward, replied: 'I am very sorry and certainly surprised at this last motion of

Mrs L. Perrot, but I have long thought too meanly of her, to be much astonished at any fresh instance of want of feeling or of hypocrisy.' [51] Mrs Leigh-Perrot had a whimsical streak as well. Less than a month after James died in December 1819, she wrote to his mother offering *her* the £100 a year – and on Mrs Austen's death, once again channelled the money back to James's widow, Mary Lloyd, rather than continuing to give it to Cassandra. Mrs Leigh-Perrot enjoyed making everyone grateful to her – by turns. She got a lot of mileage out of £100 a year. Such was the character she bore in the Austen family – and it appears she gave frequent evidence of it. James Edward, however, learned to hide his opinion of her and became her principal heir. Her final will was made less than two months before she died – she kept everyone guessing until the very end.

James acknowledged her uncle and aunt's generosity to her brother, but she understood the significance of their giving James £100 a year. 'My Expectations for my Mother do not rise with this Event', she wrote to Cassandra. 'We will allow a little more time however, before we fly out.' [52] But this was just bluster. She must have seen that to hope for money from the Leigh-Perrots was useless, but she still couldn't bring herself to say directly, even to Cassandra, that there was nothing to be done but to forget the whole matter. She later reported dryly: 'The Letter from Paragon, before mentioned, was much like those which had preceded it, as to the felicity of its Writer.' [53] So ended the Stoneleigh business that had for two years seemed so certain to make the Austen women independent.

James Leigh-Perrot did outlive Thomas Leigh, and consequently would have inherited the Stoneleigh property for the last years of his life had he not agreed to the settlement. When Thomas Leigh died, in 1813, Jane wrote to Frank about his death and about his sister, Elizabeth, who had lived with him. She continues: 'There is another female sufferer on the occasion to be pitied. Poor Mrs L. P., who would now have been Mistress of Stonleigh had there been none of that vile compromise, which in good truth has never been allowed to be of much use to them. It will be a hard trial.' [54] The remark has often been mistaken to state Jane's opinion of the settlement, but it is yet another instance of her lapsing into her aunt's own voice, saying what she imagines she would say about the situation. It is Mrs Leigh-Perrot who would say it was a 'vile compromise'. Jane's final comment is heavily ironic; Frank would have understood exactly what she was saying.

Without the prospect of Chawton, the disappointment at getting none of the Stoneleigh money might have weighed heavily on Jane and made her both angry and depressed. But with Chawton before her, nothing really had the power to disturb her. She was thirty-three years old, and she was about to obtain the thing she had most longed for since she left Steventon – a home in the depths of the country.

The most explicit indication of the good effect of the prospect of Chawton on Jane is her account of a ball in Southampton early in December 1808. 'It was the same room in which we danced fifteen years ago! I thought it all over & inspite of the shame of being so much older, felt with thankfulness that I was quite as happy now as then.' [55] Our first impulse might be to think it somehow unlike Jane Austen to be ashamed of something as absolute as the certainty of passing time and growing older. Perhaps it was her sense of having accomplished so little in the past decade. More worth notice, however, is her claim that she is as happy now as she had been fifteen years before when she danced at Southampton, full of optimism about what she believed the future held for her. Now, without Chawton in view she could not have made this claim and expected to be believed. Chawton changed her perception of her life. In a sense it made fulfilment possible by generating in her a renewed spirit and energy.

The first manifestation of the new Jane Austen – new at least to us because, whatever we may imagine to have been going on in her mind, this is the first overt sign of it – appears in early April 1809 before she left Southampton. She wrote to Crosby and Co. herself rather than having Henry or his lawyer make discreet inquiries for her. There is nothing discreet about *her* letter. It is direct, forthright and businesslike:

Gentlemen
   In the spring of 1803 a MS Novel in two volumes Entitled Susan was sold to you by a Gentleman of the name of Seymour, & the purchase money £10 received at the same time. Six years have since passed, & this work of which I avow myself the Authoress, has never to the best of my knowledge, appeared in print, though an early publication was stipulated for at the time of Sale. I can only account for such an extraordinary circumstance by supposing the

MS by some carelessness to have been lost; & if that was the case, am willing
to supply You with another Copy if you are disposed to avail yourselves of
it, & will engage for no farther delay when it comes into your hands. It will
not be in my power from particular circumstances to command this Copy
before the Month of August, but then, if you accept my proposal, you may
depend on receiving it. Be so good as to send me a Line in answer, as soon
as possible, as my stay in this place will not exceed a few days. Should no
notice be taken of this Address, I shall feel myself at liberty to secure the
publication of my work, by applying elsewhere. I am Gentlemen &c &c

                                                                      MAD.
Direct to Mrs Ashton Dennis
Post office, Southampton   April 5 1809 [56]

The witty acronymic battle cry of 'I am Gentlemen MAD' comes from
a Jane Austen we already know, but this is the first time we have heard
her business voice. The letter is a clear, bold, direct challenge, and she
gave Crosby a ready-made excuse for not having published the novel
and a way to resume publication without having to make tedious
explanations. But it is not a letter from a 'lady'. It is from an author
who was fed up with a stalled career and determined to get things
moving.

The letter is a good corrective to Henry Austen's insistence on his
sister's ladylike disregard for the vulgarity of money – a euphemistic
way of attributing to her what Henry thought was a correct feminine
propriety, with its attendant implications of milky modesty. He wrote
after her death: 'She became an authoress entirely from taste and
inclination. Neither the hopes of fame nor profit mixed with her early
motives.' [57] Henry's loophole is the word 'early', but the statement is
still misleading and inane. Henry refused to admit what his sister was
– a determined individual driven by the desire for autonomy and
independence, just as if she were a man.

Of course she began writing from taste and inclination, and in the
early days fame and profit were probably insignificant as incentives. But
at some point Jane Austen stopped calling what she did 'writing' and
started referring to it as 'work'. She had at first accepted, as did most
ordinary women of her time and class, that her talents and accomplishments were ornamental, that she would get married, have children, and
be taken care of by an industrious husband. Perhaps she did not stop

to imagine deeply where her writing would fit into this conventional picture of a woman's life. It took her rejection of Harris Bigg-Wither in late 1802 to bring home to her the real point and the real value of her talent: it could be turned into money.

Austen's letter to Crosby has nothing to do with 'taste and inclination', nothing even to do with fame. It was prompted by a desire for profit – not the £10 she had been paid for the manuscript but the profit that might follow. She saw the publication of 'Susan' not as a single event but as the launching of her career. The publication of the novel would give her career a footing in the world, and with luck would gain her work an audience. Then would come another novel, perhaps making more money, and then yet another novel. Austen had a strategy: her letter to Crosby shows that she was looking at the way she could develop her career as certainly as any ambitious man might. Her sailor brothers were always on the look out for promotions, for prizes, for good ships and fruitful commands; Henry had got himself appointed paymaster of his regiment, had sold his commission and had set up as a banker. Jane was ready to be just as cunning, just as much on the look-out for her advantage, and she was just as intent as her brothers on becoming a success.

Before she left Southampton, she received a reply from Crosby saying they were under no obligation to publish 'Susan' but would sue anyone else who did. They offered to sell the manuscript back for the £10 they had paid for it. Jane's spirits were too high and her determination too great for her to be daunted by the setback. She left 'Susan' where it was, but by the time she had settled at Chawton in July she had formed a new plan for realising her ambitions.

10

Work

Jane spent the first eighteen months at Chawton preparing *Sense and Sensibility* and 'First Impressions' for publication. Just what she did or even the order in which she did it is unknown. We assume she began with *Sense and Sensibility* because it is the first novel she published, and because it seems to have required less work than 'First Impressions' – Cassandra doesn't mention any revision of *Sense and Sensibility* at Chawton. The work must have been a minor job of recopying and polishing the manuscript. 'First Impressions', however, underwent more radical changes – 'alterations & contractions' Cassandra called the process; Jane later said she had 'lopt and cropt' the manuscript. She changed the title to *Pride and Prejudice*.

Jane Austen's only consistent habit of revision seems to have been her need to make her work contemporary – up to date. She intended to give pictures of the world her readers inhabited more or less at the moment of reading. When in 1816 she finally prepared 'Susan' for publication, she prefixed an author's note to the novel giving a partial history of its composition and subsequent fate. To her keen eye, the thirteen years between 1803 (when she said the novel was completed) and 1816 dated some aspects of the work and made it 'comparatively obsolete'.[1]

Even when she reread the pieces in *Volume the Third* in 1809, she made slight changes to bring them up to date. The last couple of pages of 'Evelyn' seem to have been written in another hand and so the date given of 19 August 1809 may not be a revision but the actual date of composition. But in 'Catharine' Jane put in a reference to *Coelebs in Search of a Wife*, which was published in early 1809. Jane Austen did not want readers to think of her books as belonging to the past; even thirteen years was too distant for her taste. The revisions of both *Sense and Sensibility* and *Pride and Prejudice* must have followed this principle. She expunged details, even opinions, that anchored the books in the final years of the eighteenth century, when they were written.

At some point during the year and a half that all this work was going on, Jane consulted Henry about her next move. She had three options: she could try to sell the manuscripts outright as she had 'Susan'; she could look for a publisher who would bring them out on a profit-sharing plan; or she could get them published at her own expense. Henry maintained that 'It was with extreme difficulty that her friends, whose partiality she suspected whilst she honoured their judgement, could prevail on her to publish her first work'.[2] Whatever truth may be the basis for this statement, it was patently not true in the spring of 1809. Her letter to Crosby is not that of someone who thinks her friends have flattered her into a false estimation of the value of her work. She knew her stuff was good. Her concern was to get as much money for it as she could. Her biggest problem was not a lack of talent or boldness but of money. Jane Austen had no money to risk on a self-publishing venture. The 'extreme difficulty' Henry recalled in getting his sister to publish was probably her being hesitant to let somebody risk their money backing her.

Perhaps Jane thought she ought to sell *Sense and Sensibility* or *Pride and Prejudice* outright, taking what money she could get and leaving the risk to a publisher. She knew, though, that the problem with such a scheme was that she would have no guarantee the publisher would actually bring out the book. Publication itself had become more important in the long view than immediate recompense. She was thinking beyond the sale of a manuscript or the publishing of a single novel. She had three books now ready to be published – more than a start for creating the momentum of a career. She was not dabbling in novel writing; she was ready to get things moving, to see something substantial and profitable building up that would keep her at work and in money for the rest of her life.

The Austens had some information about self-publishing. In 1799 Mrs Austen's first cousin Cassandra Cooke, the daughter of Theophilus Leigh, Master of Balliol, had paid for the publication of her novel, *Battleridge*. She had complained about the publisher and said she would never use him again. We don't know what her specific complaints were or if she made any money from her book, but we can be pretty sure Jane Austen knew the details. The Austens themselves already had connections with another publisher – Thomas Egerton, who was probably a remote cousin on the Leigh side of the family. Egerton had published the *Loiterer* for James Austen back in 1789 and 1790, so it was natural for Henry to consult him about details of publication at the author's expense. It may be that Henry first tried to sell the book outright to Egerton, but Egerton was a hardened businessman and took no risks himself.

Hesitant as Jane must have been, Henry convinced her the publication of her novel was a good gamble. He said 'she actually made a reserve from her very moderate income to meet the expected loss'.[3] This income is mythical; Jane Austen had no income. Whatever money she got came as an allowance from her mother or an occasional gift – £5 now and then from Edward or his benefactor Mrs Knight. (£5 was about £250 in today's money.) Jane had no money to put aside to cover the loss if her novel did not sell.

Henry is smoothing over the fact of his sister's financial dependence in 1810. He may even have been prompted by a certain modesty about his own part in her career. He must have put up the money for the publication of *Sense and Sensibility* himself. Jane's quandary was that she knew all too well how unreasonably optimistic and enthusiastic Henry was. Of course he would have insisted that the success of the novel was a certainty.

Henry could afford to put up the money because he had married Eliza de Feuillide. This was a consequence Jane had not foreseen when she was trying to prevent Henry's marrying Eliza and urging him to become a clergyman. She had written stories about the dangers of marrying a woman like Eliza; she had promoted his engagement to Mary Pearson; she had tried to laugh him out of his military ambitions; she had again and again hinted that not least among the ill consequences of his relationship with Eliza and the pursuit of his ambitions would be his ending up in London. Everything Jane had feared and deplored had come true. Yet if Henry had made other choices, Jane's career as a novelist would have been very different. It might never even have got off the ground.

Henry had failed to be the kind of hero Jane thought he could be;

but he was a great success as an instrument of fate. Perhaps he was destined to marry for money and go and live in London so as to be in the position to serve the mechanical function of facilitating his sister's literary career. That is certainly the way it turned out. Perceptive Jane must have sometimes pondered with some amusement and not a little awe this particular manoeuvre on the part of Providence.

Jane agreed to what Henry arranged: Egerton was to bring out *Sense and Sensibility* at the author's expense. The choice looks odd in one respect. You would think that taking all things into account, particularly the need to make money but yet wanting to take the least risk possible, Jane would have published *Pride and Prejudice* first. Few readers would disagree that it is the masterpiece among her early novels. Moreover, it is not just the best, it is the most entertaining – the book most certain to sell. It has all the earmarks of a popular success, and Jane Austen knew it, as her later remarks about the novel indicate. Yet she held it back.

This suggests a lot more confidence than Henry would have us believe his sister felt. If she had had any serious doubts about the power of *Sense and Sensibility* to pay its own way, she would not have ventured to publish it first. Jane did not want to begin her career with her best work. She knew *Pride and Prejudice* was a special novel, a unique production: she could never repeat that particular performance. Her plan was to hold it back a little and to use it to increase her reputation once she had a base.

The decision to publish *Sense and Sensibility* must have been made in late 1810 or early 1811. With her first novel in the hands of the publisher, and *Pride and Prejudice* in her desk ready to follow, the time had come to get on with something new. This was the real test: in 1803 she had been able to make 'Susan' ready for publication and to sell it to Crosby, but her attempt to write a new novel had failed. According to Cassandra, Jane began *Mansfield Park* 'about February 1811'. The novel had had the longest gestation of any of her books. She had been thinking about it in one form or another for at least a decade. It is her most autobiographical novel.

Even though *Mansfield Park* in a way belongs to the period of Jane Austen's life before she met Tom Lefroy, she yet again acknowledges some deep connection between him and her art. It was more than fifteen years since she had met and fallen in love with him, and ten years since she had written anything new, but she again gave her sign that she had not forgotten him: Tom Bertram's friends the Andersons take their name from a family in *Tom Jones*.[4]

Mansfield Park brings together a lot of the apparently unconnected and disparate stories, incidents, places and people in Austen's experience and history, and they are all fused together by her imagination: the story of her great-grandfather Theophilus Leigh's three sisters; Repton's improvement of Adlestrop Park; the theatricals at Steventon at Christmas 1787, including even Philadelphia Walter's refusal to act; the slave plantation in Jamaica of her Freeman cousins, and the dangers of the hot climate and the long ocean voyage to that part of the world. At the centre of the novel is Jane's complicated and troubling relationship with Eliza.

She had first tried to tell the story of Henry and Eliza in *The Watsons*, but had had to give up before she had even come to the heart of the story. The unfinished work shares with *Mansfield Park* not only the same themes but the same situations. The summary of the planned plot of *The Watsons* states that 'much of the interest in the tale was to arise from Lady Osborne's love for Mr Howard and his counter affection for the heroine, Emma Watson, whom he was finally to marry'.[5] This is the rudimentary outline common to the two works. Lady Osborne became Mary Crawford; Mr Howard became Edmund Bertram. In *The Watsons* Austen had made Lady Osborne more than ten years older than Mr Howard, but in *Mansfield Park* she discarded the age difference and focused on the influence of Mary Crawford and her objection to Edmund's profession.

The heroine underwent an even more radical change from Emma Watson to Fanny Price. Austen was no longer inclined to linger for the length of the novel over the heroine's displacement – Fanny's first weeks at Mansfield and her later return home to Portsmouth were enough to encompass Austen's feelings about her loss of Steventon. The change in the heroine's situation from *The Watsons* had its origin in Jane's 1808 visit to Kent when she noticed the contrast between her brother James's little daughter, Caroline, and the child's lively, confident Godmersham cousins. Not that Caroline (who was only three in 1808) is in any sense Fanny Price nor the Godmersham children the Bertrams. But the contrast, with all its possibilities, struck Austen's imagination and developed quite independently of the reality.

She remarked to Cassandra at the time that Caroline wasn't 'so headstrong or humoursome' as her cousins, but that this didn't make her 'more engaging'.[6] Although Caroline was less selfish and demanding than the Godmersham children, Jane didn't find her more attractive. This points to that worrisome, yet deeply satisfying, ambiguity in *Mansfield Park*. We think we *ought* to like Fanny Price more than we do the fine, handsome Bertram girls and the warm, lively Mary Crawford. That it is difficult to do so, in our feelings if not in our reason, is precisely what Austen was determined to show. Our values tell us one thing, our hearts another. *Mansfield Park* is Austen's most profound attempt to capture this inevitable confusion of feelings in human life – and her strategy was to make readers themselves confused in their own feelings about the characters in the novel.

A couple of months into *Mansfield Park*, Jane had to go to London to take a part in the process of publishing *Sense and Sensibility*. Egerton's part was strictly business – arranging for the printer, the paper supplier, the binding, the distribution of the book. Jane had no editor and no proof-reader. Proof sheets from the printer were sent to the house in Sloane Street where Henry and Eliza were now living. Sloane Street became Jane's office – she made the corrections and sent the proofs back. The printer was slow, so she had a lot of time on her hands.

She had the usual commissions to perform for her friends in the country, and she paid calls on old and new acquaintances, and frequently dined out. Henry and Eliza had a busy social life, and Jane went with them to a lot of parties. She remarked to Cassandra: 'I find all these little parties very pleasant.'[7] This is quite a change from her mood in Bath ten years before when she complained that she hated small parties because they required too much exertion.

She sometimes went to museums and galleries, but she was not much interested in the visual arts. After going to exhibitions at the Liverpool Museum and the British Gallery, she commented: 'I had some amusement at each, though my preference for Men & Women, always inclines me to attend more to the company than to the sight.'[8] When she looked at pictures, what interested her most was finding a likeness of one of her characters.

She had so many London pleasures to write to Cassandra about that she hardly mentions Godmersham, where Cassandra was visiting. She realised this was very unusual:

> I am a wretch, to be so occupied with all these Things, as to seem to have no Thoughts to give to people & circumstances which really supply a far more lasting interest – the Society in which You are – but I do think of you all I assure you, & want to know all about everybody, & especially about your visit to the W[hite] Friars [Mrs Knight's house in Canterbury]; *mais le moyen* not to be occupied by one's own concerns? [9]

This was a liberation – to have concerns she could take pleasure in. Mrs Knight was one of the few people who knew Jane was publishing a novel. 'Mrs K. regrets in the most flattering manner that she must wait *till* May [to read the novel], but I have scarcely a hope of its being out in June', she wrote to Cassandra. 'I am very much gratified by Mrs K.s interest in it; & whatever may be the event of it as to my credit with her, sincerely wish her curiosity could be satisfied sooner than is now probable. I think she will like my Elinor, but cannot build on any thing else.' [10]

Cassandra was surprised Jane hadn't mentioned *Sense and Sensibility* at all in her previous letter. Had she forgotten about the novel? 'No indeed', Jane replied, 'I am never too busy to think of S & S. I can no more forget it, than a mother can forget her sucking child; & I am much obliged to you for your enquires.' [11] More than just the outward bustle of publication was preoccupying her; about her reading she remarked: '[I] am always half afraid of finding a clever novel *too clever* & of finding my own story & my own people all forestalled.' [12] She had begun to think of herself as an author, a published one. On a more prosaic level, she reported details of the progress of publication – or lack of progress owing to delays by the printers, whom Henry hounded to get on with the work. He was not very effective in his attempts to hurry them; the process dragged on.

Henry and Eliza gave Jane a lot of practical support in bringing *Sense and Sensibility* to the light of day. At the end of April when Jane left London she did so knowing that the book was in good hands. Henry would take care of the work when he was at home. When he was away on business, as he often was, Eliza would be there to receive the proofs – maybe Eliza herself did some proof-reading.

After a short visit to Catherine Bigg, who had finally married and now lived in Streatham, Jane returned to Chawton in May and carried on writing *Mansfield Park*. From the time she moved to Chawton, Jane had taken a businesslike approach to her work. Writing came first. She was a working author, and everyone must have been made to understand this fact. She was not at liberty to go off paying long visits, and she probably didn't want to. After her 1809 visit she did not go to Godmersham again until she had finished *Mansfield Park* in June 1813. The only time she left Chawton was to go to London on business and to make relatively short annual visits to Steventon, probably at the insistence of her mother or the bossy Mary Lloyd.

In August 1811, with *Sense and Sensibility* still not yet out, Eliza paid a rare visit to her mother-in-law and sisters-in-law at Chawton. Cassandra wrote to Philadelphia Walter that she thought she had never seen Eliza 'in such good health before'.[13] The correspondence and evidently the old intimacy between Philadelphia and Eliza had by this time petered out. Fifty-year-old Philadelphia had written to Cassandra to announce her marriage. Like her mother before her, she took the opportunity to complain about her new home. Cassandra did not mention in her congratulatory reply that Jane had a novel in the press. Nor did she taunt the whinging Philadelphia with how happy she and Jane were at Chawton. Unlike Philadelphia, they had no complaints about their new home. Chawton was, in the hyperbolic phrase of their neighbour Mrs Harry Digweed, 'beyond anything & everything'.[14] Jane knew before she went to live there what she needed. It fulfilled her requirements – and held some surprises, not least Mrs Digweed herself.

Jane had known Jane Digweed in the Steventon years when she was still Jane Terry of Dummer. The Terrys sometimes seem more ubiquitous in Jane's letters than the 'Endless Debaries'. Jane Terry married Harry Digweed, whose father had been the tenant of Steventon Manor. After their father's death Harry and his brother William became co-tenants. William lived at Steventon, and Harry at Alton, near Chawton, where he had another farm. This arrangement was convenient for the Austens at Chawton Cottage and Steventon parsonage because the Digweed brothers were constantly going back and forth between the two villages and could handily carry letters and parcels for them.

When Jane heard Mrs Digweed was looking forward to their living at Chawton, she was dubious. 'Mrs H. Digweed looks forward with great satisfaction to our being her neighbours', she wrote to Cassandra; 'I would have her enjoy the idea to the utmost, as I suspect there will not [be] much in the reality.' [15] But she was wrong. The years had not turned Jane Digweed into a Martha Lloyd, an Anne Lefroy or a Catherine Knight, the sensible, intelligent kind of woman Jane preferred as a friend, but she came to take pleasure in Mrs Digweed and felt an amused tenderness for her. She laughed at her but the laughter was affectionate, not sharp or dismissive, as Jane's laughter sometimes was in her younger days.

Mrs Digweed was rather stupid in an unobtrusive, scatter-brained way that Jane now enjoyed more than she had in her youth. 'Dear Mrs Digweed! I cannot bear that she should not be foolishly happy after a Ball', [16] she wrote to Cassandra. And once, when she was staying in town, she told Martha Lloyd that she longed 'to hear Mrs Digweed's good-humoured communications. The language of London is flat; it wants her phrase', [17] the most famous being 'beyond anything and everything', which Jane quoted frequently, a shared joke with several correspondents. When one of Jane's nieces began writing a novel and said she intended modelling a character, a young man, on Mrs Digweed, Jane thought this was a splendid idea. 'I can readily imagine Mrs H. D. may be very like a profligate Young Lord. I dare say the likeness will be "beyond every thing".' [18]

Although Jane could not establish real intimacy with the Digweeds, they had a good humour she had learned to value. She wrote in expectation of a dull dinner, 'I do not think Mr & Mrs D. will add much to our wit'. [19] But afterwards she included in her account of the pleasures, 'Mr & Mrs Digweed taking kindly to our Charades, & other Games'. [20] They contributed to the harmonious little society of Chawton.

The village of Chawton did not offer much more than Highbury in *Emma* – a poor spinster, a bachelor parson and his sister, a few respectably genteel people to exchange news with, dine with, drink tea with, and even talk of books with, though Mrs Digweed tended to borrow books but never got around to reading them. Such were the pleasures of the place. The only extraordinary thing about Chawton was that Jane Austen lived there.

Even at Chawton Jane did not find everyone delightful. She had not taken to Mrs Webb and her two daughters (though the only fault she mentions is that they couldn't say their 'r's') and only felt a moment of regret when they left Chawton: 'When I saw the Waggons at the door, & thought of all the trouble they must have in moving, I began to reproach myself for not having liked them better, but since the Waggons have disappeared, my Conscience has been closed again, & I am excessively glad they are gone.'[21]

The real centre of Jane's social life was not her neighbours, important as they were to her general contentment, but her brothers and their families. Henry was often at Alton on banking business. When he didn't come down himself, he sent presents by his partners and clerks. Edward's Hampshire estates brought him there more and more, and after about 1812 Chawton House became his family's second home. Steventon was just far enough away to keep the bustling Mary Lloyd from being too much underfoot, but close enough to give ample opportunity for the two families to meet without the strain of extended visits. Although Frank was often at sea between 1809 and 1814, after 1815 he and his family lived first at Chawton House and then in Alton. Only Charles remained beyond the Chawton sphere, even after he came home in 1811 from a four-year tour in Bermuda, bringing his wife, Fanny Palmer, whom he had married there, and their two small daughters.

Jane was still not much of a housekeeper and took little pleasure in household matters. But the knowledge that the domestic was not her whole life was a part of the expansive freedom of Chawton. Released from the strain of those years between Steventon and Chawton, her mind was free to be engaged in a pleasantly desultory way with the household. 'Good apple pies are a considerable part of our domestic happiness' is not a totally ironical remark.[22] But writing had become her real occupation.

When Jane was in London in April she had hoped to see her first novel out in early summer, but *Sense and Sensibility* 'By a Lady' wasn't published until the end of October 1811, about six weeks before her thirty-sixth birthday. The months between April and November must have been increasingly anxious ones for her. A lot was riding on *Sense and Sensibility*; it may not be an exaggeration to say that *everything* was. Chawton probably proved its worth in a new way during these months. The quiet, equable life in the village must have helped keep Jane on an even keel.

Once the book was finally published, Jane's first concern became how well it was selling. Sales would prove one way or the other whether she had a career or not. The only publicity for the novel was the advertisements that announced its existence. These appeared first on the last two days of October and sporadically through the month of November. Probably more important to its success were recommendations by word of mouth.

Before the end of November the Countess of Bessborough was asking a correspondent if he had read the novel and reporting that her friends at Althorp (Earl Spencer's house) 'were full of it'.[23] The Duke of York read it and praised it to his niece Princess Charlotte, the only child of the Prince Regent. By late January Charlotte was writing enthusiastically, if a bit egotistically (she identified with Marianne), about the novel. Approbation in the circles of rich and leisured people certainly helped sales, but the first public approval came in the *Critical Review* of February 1812, followed in May by a notice in the *British Critic*. Jane was not indifferent to praise, but the most important verdict on the work came not in the form of words but money. What really counted was how many people paid fifteen shillings for *Sense and Sensibility*. A year after its publication, the edition had still not sold out, but the cost of publication had probably been recouped. The novel had not, though, made enough profit for Austen to use its success as leverage in negotiating the publication of *Pride and Prejudice*, which she was now eager to get into print.

By the autumn of 1812 Jane was ready to go forward with her second novel. But Eliza was ill and the family knew she was dying. Cassandra's finding her in such good health the year before when she visited Chawton had been Eliza's last bloom.

Jane had learned something about publishing from her experience with *Sense and Sensibility*. Bringing out a book entailed a lot more than just paying the bills. With Eliza dying, she could not ask Henry to take on the burden of seeing *Pride and Prejudice* through to publication, nor could she expect to be accommodated at Sloane Street in such circumstances as now prevailed there. She was faced with a choice. She could either postpone the publication of her novel, or she could sell the manuscript outright and leave it to the publisher to deal with the onerous and time-consuming details. This was not a dilemma she could ask Henry to advise her about. She had to make the decision herself. Now that her career was under way, Jane was too impatient to wait.

She sent *Pride and Prejudice* to Egerton, offering to sell the manuscript to him for £150. Egerton countered with an offer of £110 and Jane accepted. She wrote to Martha Lloyd about the sale of the manuscript and commented: 'Its' being sold will I hope be a great saving of Trouble to Henry, & therefore must be welcome to me.' [24] She alluded to the progress of Eliza's illness in the same letter.

Thomas Egerton brought out the novel quickly. *He* knew how to hurry up the printers when his own profit was concerned, and *Pride and Prejudice* was published only a couple of months after Jane sold it. She received the first copy on 29 January 1813. 'I want to tell you', she wrote to Cassandra who was visiting at Steventon, 'that I have got my own darling Child from London; on Wednesday I received one Copy, sent down by Falknor.' [25] The rest of the letter is devoted to matters relating to her darling child. She did not, however, begin the letter with this subject: as in her letter of November 1798 about Mrs Lefroy's visit, she got other matters out of the way first – a little epistolary habit of Jane's when she had very good or very bad news concerning herself.

Jane and her mother invited a neighbour, Miss Benn, to dine with them, and in the evening they read *Pride and Prejudice* aloud and Jane reported to Cassandra:

> She was amused, poor soul! *that* she could not help you know, with two such people to lead the way; but she really does seem to admire Elizabeth. I must confess that *I* think her as delightful a creature as ever appeared in print, & how I shall be able to tolerate those who do not like *her* at least, I do not know.[26]

After the second evening of reading, Jane was less pleased with the overall effect of the tone of the novel:

The work is rather too light & bright & sparkling; it wants shade; it wants to be stretched out here & there with a long Chapter – of sense if it could be had, if not of solemn specious nonsense – about something unconnected with the story; an Essay on Writing, a critique on Walter Scott, or the history of Buonaparte, or anything that would form a contrast & bring the reader with increased delight to the playfulness & Epigrammatism of the general stile; I doubt your quite agreeing with me here. I know your starched Notions.[27]

In spite of these reservations, Jane knew that the wit and celerity of the novel were the very qualities that would make it popular.

She expected the novel to be a success, and she was right. Six months after its publication, *Pride and Prejudice* was much talked of. The first edition sold out quickly, and Egerton brought out a second edition in the autumn. The popularity of the novel gave a boost to *Sense and Sensibility*, and the first edition of that novel finally sold out. Jane reported to Frank in July that all copies of her first novel had been sold and that she had made £140. *Pride and Prejudice* went through two more printings, from which Jane did not profit a penny. The popularity of her second novel, though, would help sell *Mansfield Park*. She told Frank that she had completed her new novel, 'which I hope on the credit of P. & P. will sell well, though not half so entertaining'.[28] Perhaps this is a hint as to why she had gone ahead and sold the copyright of *Pride and Prejudice*: she thought the publication of the book would increase her popularity and that the profit she lost on it would be made up by sales of her subsequent novels. Perhaps she was right.

The success of *Pride and Prejudice* did not bring *her* wealth, but it did bring some degree of fame. Henry told Jane a Miss Burdett wanted to meet her – clearly to meet Jane Austen the novelist. 'I should like to see Miss Burdett very well', Jane wrote to Cassandra, 'but that I am rather frightened by hearing that she wishes to be introduced to *me*. If I *am* a wild Beast, I cannot help it. It is not my own fault.'[29] A wild beast. The residue of Jane's shyness made her wish for anonymity, and yet her very nature had led her to do this shocking thing – to write novels.

Those in her family and among her acquaintance who knew her secret were prepared to keep it – all but the lively and talkative Henry. In the summer of 1813 he went to Scotland, and upon hearing Lady Robert

Kerr praise *Pride and Prejudice*, he could not resist the temptation to reveal the author's identity. 'He told her with as much satisfaction as if it were my wish', Jane wrote to Cassandra.[30] On his journey back from Scotland, he stopped at Daylesford, Warren Hastings's estate in Oxfordshire, and told the great man that Jane was the author of the much talked of *Pride and Prejudice*. Back in London, he sent Hastings a copy of the novel. Jane saw that Henry's tendency to tell signalled the end of her secret. 'A Thing once set going in that way – one knows how it spreads!' she wrote to Frank, 'and he, dear Creature, has set it going so much more than once.'[31]

Jane adored Henry, not only because he was such a delightful companion, but because she was so grateful to him. He had had his lawyer sell 'Susan'; he had arranged for Egerton to publish *Sense and Sensibility*; he had probably put up the money for the cost of publication; and he had dealt with the printers when the novel was in the press. Yet he knew he was wrong to violate Jane's wish. He told her Lady Robert liked *Pride and Prejudice*, but to their niece Fanny he confessed he had revealed the identity of the author to her. Henry, so utterly different in temperament from Jane, could not really imagine her need to remain anonymous.

Others, however, possessed a deeper understanding of her character. Or perhaps they just took her at her word. Cassandra had written to Jane that James and Mary were very careful not to say anything that would give away her identity when they received *Pride and Prejudice*, and Jane replied: 'The caution observed at Steventon with regard to the possession of the Book is an agreable surprise to me, & I heartily wish it may be the means of saving you from everything unpleasant.'[32] James and Mary were so discreet that even their own children had no inkling their aunt was a novelist until she chose to tell them.

When writing about Henry revealing her secret, Jane thanked Frank and his wife for respecting her wishes. 'I know [Henry's telling] is all done from affection & partiality – but at the same time, let me here again express to you & Mary [Frank's wife] my sense of the *superior* kindness which you have shewn on the occasion, in doing what I wished.'[33] Frank gave her permission to use the names of some of his ships in *Mansfield Park*, but warned her the association might give a hint as to her identity. Jane replied:

I was previously aware of what I should be laying myself open to, but the truth is that the Secret has spread so far as to be scarcely the Shadow of a secret now & that I beleive whenever the third appears, I shall not even attempt to tell Lies about it. I shall rather try to make all the Money than all the Mystery I can of it.[34]

As the books became more and more popular, and were read and talked of, and her identity as the author known, she accepted with humour and self-irony what was to be: 'I do not despair of having my picture in the Exhibition at last – all white & red, with my Head on one Side; or perhaps I may marry young Mr D'arblay.'[35]

Still working on *Mansfield Park*, Jane went to Sloane Street again a few days before Eliza died on 25 April 1813. This was unusual. Sick-rooms and death-watches were not Jane's sphere: it was capable Cassandra who sometimes took this role, going to Godmersham for the births of the children and attending Elizabeth afterwards; or staying at Ibthorpe with Martha when Mrs Lloyd was sick and dying. It must have been Jane's past affection for Eliza, not her practical abilities, that dictated she sit by Eliza's death-bed.

She had loved Eliza – probably still in some way did – but she did not like her and grieved because she could not. She had lost the Eliza she had adored as a child as certainly as she had lost Tom Lefroy. But Eliza had remained in her life as well as her imagination. Jane's going to Sloane Street when Eliza was dying was a sign of many things – love, gratitude, obligation, reconciliation, even respect, perhaps forgiveness. The experience must have been intense. Jane was accompanied by her twenty-five year relationship with Eliza, by the ghosts of Louisa Lesley, Lady Lesley, the various Susans, and now Mary Crawford and Lady Bertram, whom, as Eliza was dying, Jane was in the process of bringing into being.

We know little of what became of Eliza after her marriage to Henry. Jane seldom mentions her in her letters. A passage in one of Eliza's own letters to Philadelphia Walter in 1796 may, though, give a hint:

I once more thank you for your puggish intentions in my favour, and wish that you may be able to realise them, though to say truth I am already possessed of one of these bewitching animals. I shall joyfully receive as many more Pugs as you can procure for me. You would laugh to see me consulting my doctor about my dog.[36]

Eliza's love of pugs was unforgettably given to Lady Bertram in *Mansfield Park*; perhaps the older Eliza of whom we hear so little also spent her time nicely dressed sitting on a sofa doing some long piece of needlework of little use and no beauty. The picture has a certain ring of truth. Austen perceived in Eliza that the fate of a Mary Crawford – or of an Eliza de Feuillide – might be nothing so dramatic as a descent into 'a vortex of Dissipation' but a gradual decline into vacuous dullness. [37]

Jane did not speak of her own feelings when Eliza died and was buried beside her mother and son, Hastings, but a few months later she wrote to Frank of Henry's loss:

> Upon the whole his Spirits are very much recovered. If I may so express myself, his Mind is not a Mind for affliction. He is too Busy, too active, too sanguine. Sincerely as he was attached to poor Eliza moreover, & excellently as he behaved to her, he was always so used to be away from her at times, that her Loss is not felt as that of many a beloved Wife might be, especially when all the circumstances of her long & dreadful Illness are taken into the account. He very long knew that she must die, & it was indeed a release at last. [38]

About a month after Eliza's death, Jane went to London again to help Henry prepare to move to Henrietta Street. He planned to give up his house and live in rooms above his bank.

She was near the end of *Mansfield Park* and must have remembered the outing to Sotherton in Henry Crawford's barouche when she remarked on her pleasure in going about London alone in Henry Austen's carriage. 'I liked my solitary elegance very much, & was ready to laugh all the time, at my being where I was. I could not but feel that I had naturally small right to be parading about London in a Barouche.' [39] This was another consequence, trivial but not insignificant, of Henry's marriage to Eliza. Jane had now become Eliza's surrogate, out in the barouche being driven about London.

Writing *Mansfield Park* seems to have been harder for Jane Austen than the other novels. She had taken only about a year each to write 'First Impressions', *Sense and Sensibility* and 'Susan', but she laboured for more than two years on *Mansfield Park*. Cassandra says the novel was not finished until June 1813. How much of the time of composition was taken up with the difficulties posed by the novel itself and how much by Jane's having to combine her writing of the novel with other demands of her literary career is impossible to say.

There is no evidence that she took time out from her work on the novel to revise *Pride and Prejudice*. Even though the chronology of the latter coincides with the calendar of 1811–12, it also follows that of 1805–6. (*Mansfield Park* follows the calendar of 1808–9.) Besides, the meticulous and scrupulous Cassandra was there when Jane was writing, and even though she qualifies her dates with 'about' she was not talking about her sister's planning the novel but giving the dates of actual composition.

Jane Austen finished *Mansfield Park* in June but it took her several months to make a fair copy of the manuscript. In early March 1814 she gave it to Henry to read. If Jane felt any trepidation at how he would respond to finding his Eliza – either as shadow or substance – in the pages of the book, or to seeing elements of himself in Edmund Bertram and Henry Crawford, she gives no hint of it.

Henry had himself written about Eliza in two of his *Loiterer* stories and Jane had meant him to see Eliza in 'Lesley Castle' and *Lady Susan*. His marriage had apparently turned out much better than the one projected for Reginald and Susan in *Lady Susan*. And Jane had taken that into account in *Mansfield Park*. She did not let Mary and Edmund marry, but she acknowledged that a good marriage between them would have been possible. Perhaps that was enough to satisfy Henry's need for truth.

Henry Crawford is partly Austen's way of dealing with Eliza's 'masculine' nonchalance about sex. Jane was no puritan, and she is subtly tolerant of sexual weakness: what she is not tolerant of is vanity masquerading as passion. That is why Maria Bertram is ultimately a more sympathetic figure in *Mansfield Park* than Henry Crawford. When Mary Crawford asks Henry what Maria will say about his falling in love with Fanny Price, he replies:

> 'Mrs Rushworth will be very angry. It will be a bitter pill to her; that is, like other bitter pills, it will have two moments ill-flavour, and then be swallowed

and forgotten; for I am not such a coxcomb as to suppose her feeling more lasting than other women's, though *I* was the object of them.' [40]

His belief that women have no lasting feelings is his undoing, and Maria's giving up everything for him shows how strong a woman's feelings can be.

Austen had given her brother Henry's professional dilemma to Edmund Bertram, but far more intriguing is what Henry made of his namesake, Henry Crawford. The core of Henry Austen that makes its way into Henry Crawford has nothing to do with sex. Jane Austen explores her brother's protean nature, his trying on different parts, but being unable to recognise and commit himself to his true self. She had seen him as a prospective parson, an adherent of traditional country values, the part he played in his *Loiterer* stories; as an infatuated young man engaged in a potentially adulterous flirtation; as an enthusiastic but unsteady young army officer; as a confused and fickle fiancé; probably as a somewhat disillusioned husband; certainly as a rich and successful banker and man of the world. Perhaps Henry saw what she was getting at in Henry Crawford, or perhaps he saw nothing more than what Jane reported to Cassandra – that he thought Henry Crawford a pleasing, agreeable man.

One of the triumphs of *Mansfield Park* is Austen's drawing so much on real people without being unjust to them, without imposing her own subjective perceptions on them. She was at last able to convey in the creation of Mary Crawford her ambiguous feelings about Eliza de Feuillide and the unsettling experience of knowing her. She does not try to justify her adverse opinion of Eliza as she had in *Lady Susan*, or to manipulate the reader into disliking Mary. She leaves us to form our own judgements. Mary Crawford is not guilty of any morally reprehensible *act*; but she is an indefinably unsettling presence, far more so than her brother is.

Some critics have tried to confer on Mary the status of being the real heroine of *Mansfield Park*, but common sense tells us this is not the case. She has the potential for being the heroine and that is what her admirers are really getting at. As an anti-heroine Mary has an almost unique status in English literature. We know Becky Sharp, to take the most obvious example, is 'bad' but we like her anyway. Mary Crawford is interesting because we are never quite certain she really *is* bad. She is quick, lively and agreeable, and we feel she could be something even finer, more substantial. We believe she *is* something better, and consequently deserves a better fate than she has in the novel.

Novelists tend to settle matters in such a way that the sense of justice outweighs the sense of disappointment, but in *Mansfield Park* Jane Austen achieves something quite different. Nothing is fixed and definite, and paradoxically the *appearance* of everything being so heightens our sense that it is not. Austen creates such a strong, distinct possibility in *Mansfield Park* that things did not have to turn out as they do that we are left in confusion. What *might* have happened is as real as what *did* happen. This disturbs us, makes us angry. We have been arguing vehemently with Jane Austen about the ending of *Mansfield Park* for two hundred years, exactly as she intended. *She* was unsettled and angry about Eliza de Feuillide, and in *Mansfield Park* she recreates her own experience for her readers.

The ending of *Mansfield Park* is not supposed to be inevitable; its inevitability is an illusion, a sleight of hand. Put another way, there is not simply one inevitability. This is more like life than a novel, and few novels make us so consciously aware of it as *Mansfield Park*. It is a haunted and haunting novel because the ghosts of unrealised possibilities are as substantial as the realised.

It is said that Cassandra attempted to persuade Jane to change the ending of the novel, to allow Henry to marry Fanny and Edmund to marry Mary, but Jane refused. What makes this interesting is not how the possible change would affect our reading of the novel, but what Jane's refusal shows about her relationship with Cassandra. She always thought of Cassandra as her superior, but in the world of art Jane Austen was free. She knew what she wanted to do in her novel, and she knew what she had achieved. It is to Cassandra's credit that, in spite of her sister's refusal to change the ending, Cassandra always maintained that *Mansfield Park* was her favourite of the novels.

Had Jane Austen capitulated and made the change, she would have destroyed the theme that only emerges with the ending of the book: loss and disappointment. Only in its completeness is *Mansfield Park* about the loss we feel when people we care about turn out to be less than we think they might have been, the loss we feel when we ourselves fail to be what we might have been. To achieve this, Austen had to make us care about Mary Crawford, feel that she deserves better than what she gets. Otherwise she would be no different from the Steele sisters or Lydia Bennet, left inconsequentially and unobtrusively on the margin of the central happiness that concludes the novel. The profound sense of loss and consequent disappointment that *Mansfield Park* evokes is what we continue to find so disquieting.

Henry Austen liked the book from the first, and particularly praised Jane's drawing of the characters. He thought he foresaw the ending, but as he progressed he said he 'defied anybody to say whether H.C. would be reformed, or would forget Fanny in a fortnight'.[41] Jane Austen had tried for a new kind of tension, a real uncertainty as to whom her heroine would marry. 'Henry has finished Mansfield Park, & his approbation has not lessened', she told Cassandra. 'He found the last half of the last volume *extremely interesting.*'[42] With Henry's reading of it, *Mansfield Park* was, in a deeply personal way for Jane, at last finished. The novel was published two months later in early May 1814 and sold well.

'One does not care for girls till they are grown up',[43] Jane once wrote to her niece Anna, James's daughter from his first marriage. In the spring of 1813, when Eliza died and Jane was moving towards the end of *Mansfield Park*, Anna and her cousin Fanny, Edward's eldest girl, were both twenty and Jane was starting to find them interesting. They captured her imagination; in a way they filled the void left by the death of Eliza and the completion of *Mansfield Park*.

Anna had just become engaged – for the second time. At twenty she already had a rather chequered history. She had long been, from time to time, a difficult girl. When she was fifteen she was rebellious and attention-seeking: once she shocked everyone by cutting off her hair. As punishment, her father and stepmother refused to take her with them on the Godmersham visit in the summer of 1808 but instead sent her to stay with her grandmother and aunt Cassandra in Southampton.

When Cassandra at the time wrote to Godmersham complimenting Anna, Jane conveyed it to James but he did not seem to find it gratifying. 'I have tried to give James pleasure', she wrote to Cassandra, 'by telling him of his Daughter's Taste, but if he felt, he did not express it. *I* rejoice in it very sincerely.'[44] James seemed indifferent to Anna, but her step-mother, Mary Lloyd, was actively critical, tending to find fault with the girl even before she had done something wrong – 'it must be for the pleasure of fancying it', Jane remarked to Cassandra.[45]

Three years later, eighteen-year-old Anna became engaged to Michael Terry, rector of Dummer and brother of Mrs Harry Digweed. He was the same age as Jane. James and Mary did not approve of the match. This time they sent Anna to Godmersham to visit her cousin Fanny, and on her return she flightily broke off the engagement. This disturbed her parents even more than her having accepted him in the first place. So they sent her to Chawton.

At the time of Anna's exile to Chawton, Jane was in London working on the proofs of *Sense and Sensibility* and Cassandra was at Godmersham, but Mrs Austen and Martha Lloyd wrote to Jane 'with great satisfaction of Anna's behaviour'.[46] Jane was in a good mood with *Sense and Sensibility* imminent, and took a light and optimistic view of Anna's unformed and changeable character: 'She is quite an Anna with variations, but she cannot have reached her last, for that is always the most flourishing & shewey – she is at about her third or fourth which are generally simple & pretty.'[47] She sketched this little picture from her imagination; when she got back to Chawton and was confronted with the real Anna, she took a sterner view of her niece's character.

Anna had a restless, aimless social life at Chawton, visiting friends in nearby villages, always going somewhere. Once she missed a flying visit from her uncle Henry and his banking partner because she was at a fair on Selborne Common. Mrs Austen was sorry Anna had not been at home to see Henry but Jane found this 'a distress which I could not share'.[48] She continued: '[Anna] does not return from Faringdon till this evening, & I doubt not, has had plenty of the miscellaneous, unsettled sort of happiness which seems to suit her best.'[49] Anna's dependence on a succession of transient pleasures was in Jane's eyes evidence of a troubling disposition. Her opinion of Anna was to change several more times in the course of the next few years. Such was the background of the girl who in 1813 became engaged to Ben Lefroy.

The Austens were not very pleased with this engagement, though they had no objection to Ben himself. He was the youngest son of Jane's friend Anne Lefroy. His father had died two years after his mother, and

Ben's eldest brother had become rector of Ashe, where the family continued to live. He was twenty-two, had been at Merton College, Oxford, and was to be a clergyman. Jane gave him credit for being 'sensible, certainly very religious, well connected & with some Independance',[50] as she wrote to Frank, but she was worried about the difference between Anna's love of company and Ben's dislike of it, a difference heightened by (and perhaps even arising from) 'some queerness of Temper on his side & much unsteadiness on hers'.[51] She was not optimistic about Anna's prospects for happiness in any marriage. 'We are anxious to have it go on well', she concluded to Frank, 'there being quite as much in his favour as the Chances are likely to give her in any Matrimonial connection.'[52]

Mrs Austen, too, was disturbed by the match. Jane and Cassandra tried to keep her from knowing too many details of what was going on. They had learned to deal with their mother's nervous disorders, which gave rise to physical complaints, by avoiding disturbing topics. The patience and indulgence with which Emma Woodhouse treats her tiresome father may give a hint as to how Jane and Cassandra coped with Mrs Austen. Mary Lloyd, however, lacked the good sense of her sister Martha and of Jane and Cassandra. Mary was still Mary, though in the later years Jane seldom remarks on her demerits – perhaps the creation of Mrs Norris got the worst of Mary out of her system. But during Anna's engagement, Mary couldn't keep her mouth shut, and Jane lashed out to Cassandra:

> How can Mrs J. Austen be so provokingly ill-judging? I should have expected better from her professed if not her real regard for my Mother. Now my Mother will be unwell again. Every fault in Ben's blood does harm to hers, & every dinner-invitation he refuses will give her an Indigestion.[53]

Mary's uncontrolled outspokenness caused her to say things without considering the effect on other people. In that way she was rather like her mother-in-law.

The uneasiness of the family about the match seemed to them justified when Ben was offered a 'highly eligible' curacy but declined it because he was not yet ready to be ordained.[54] The Austens were still the prudent, practical people they had always been, and to them this refusal was not only imprudent and impractical in a man who was about to marry but showed an unsteady character. Jane didn't mince words. 'He must be maddish',[55] she wrote to Cassandra. James pressed Ben on the point, but he would not be moved. He wanted to marry Anna, but he would give her up rather than compromise his principles on the serious matter of when he should be ordained and take up his profession.

Ben could afford – up to a point – to exercise such scruples because he had inherited some money, though not enough to afford the full expense of a wife and family. The engagement, however, was not broken off. 'They are going on again, at present as before – but it cannot last', Jane told Cassandra.[56] To encourage Anna and Ben to think more seriously about their intentions, the usual remedy was applied: Anna was sent to stay with her grandmother and aunts. She made the visit unwillingly, even though it was agreed Ben could visit her at Chawton. There the matter rested for a while.

When Anna and Ben became engaged, Edward and his family were at Chawton House, where they now stayed for a few months every year. This change in the domestic pattern of the family coincided with the death of Mrs Knight in 1812 at the age of fifty-nine. Edward had been very attached to his adoptive mother and never spent long periods of time away from her in her last years. When she died, Edward and his children took the name of Knight. Jane declared to Martha Lloyd: 'I must learn to make a better K.'[57]

Jane finished *Mansfield Park* in the summer of 1813 during the Knights' visit and so was at her leisure for a few months before she began her next novel. When the family returned to Godmersham in the autumn, Jane went home with them for a long visit. Four years had passed since she had last been to Kent, and Godmersham was a very different place from what it had been on her previous visit, just before she went to live at Chawton. In 1809 Edward's wife had been dead for only a few months and his eldest child, Fanny, had been just sixteen. Godmersham in those days was still very much a place of children, from Fanny down to the baby of a few months old. Now the youngest, who was five, was away from home. The other boys were at school, one at Eltham and two at Winchester. Edward and George, the two eldest, were at home for most of their aunt's visit, but were going up to Oxford in late October. It was George's first term; Edward had been there since 1811.

In addition to twenty-year-old Fanny, the four other girls, ranging in age from seven to twelve, were at home. Yet it was not the female-dominated household this might lead you to assume. Edward and George were the princes of the place – if through nothing else but their own sheer energy. They were lively sportsmen, and Jane's observations of them show her in a new role, that of censorious aunt. After young Edward had been to Scotland with his uncle Henry, Jane discovered he had not been much struck by the beauties of nature, as she reported to Frank:

> His Enthusiasm is for the Sports of the field only. He is a very promising & pleasing young Man however upon the whole, behaves with great propriety to his Father & great kindness to his Brothers & Sisters & we must forgive his thinking more of Growse & Partridges than Lakes & Mountains.[58]

But after a few weeks at Godmersham she was less inclined to be so indulgent.

She wrote to Cassandra referring to her preceding letter in which she had been critical of George and Edward:

> As I wrote of my nephews with a little bitterness in my last, I think it particularly incumbent on me to do them justice now, & I have great pleasure in saying that they were both at the Sacrament yesterday. After having much praised or much blamed anybody, one is generally sensible of something just the reverse soon afterwards. Now, these two Boys who are out with the Foxhounds will come home & disgust me again by some habit of Luxury or some proof of sporting Mania – unless I keep it off by this prediction. They amuse themselves very comfortably in the Evening by netting; they are each about a rabbit net, & sit as deedily to it, side by side, as any two Uncle Franks could do.[59]

The last comment contains as much compliment to the boys as they themselves might have felt they deserved. Frank was well known and admired for his quiet domesticity and skilful handiwork of all kinds.

The activities of her nephews did not affect Jane's enjoyment at Godmersham, but did add to the general chaos – as it appeared to her – of the first three weeks of her visit. Since the move to Chawton, she had become accustomed to the quiet, regular, orderly life of the cottage. There was activity and interest there, but nothing so relentlessly demanding as at Godmersham.

Jane's natural companion at Godmersham was her niece Fanny, who had had to assume the place of mistress of the house and mother to her ten younger brothers and sisters when she was still only fifteen. She was now twenty and fully involved in the social obligations that her position entailed. These duties Jane found it wearing to share. Hardly a day went by without people calling or without Jane and Fanny going off in the carriage to pay morning visits or to dine. 'In this House there is a constant succession of small events, somebody is always going or coming', she half-complained in a letter to Frank.[60] She tried to settle into a routine, to regular employment, but that was hard to maintain with people always turning up unexpectedly and invitations always in the offing. 'Fanny & I are to go on with [reading a history book called] Modern Europe together, but hitherto have advanced only twenty-five Pages, something or other has always happened to delay or curtail the reading hour',[61] she told Cassandra. Early on Jane had said, 'We live in the Library except at Meals & have a fire every Evening'.[62] But that peaceful scene seems to have been pretty rare.

She did not complain, though she was happier when she did not have to go paying calls with Fanny. Nor did she object to the way of life itself. But for her it was too unsettled, had too many distractions. She saw, though, it must be that way at Godmersham, the Knights being a rich and prominent family in the county.

Jane was to be joined at Godmersham in mid October by Charles and his wife, Fanny Palmer, who were bringing their eldest child, Cassy, now almost five, and the baby, another girl. They were to leave the middle daughter in London in the care of Fanny Palmer's sister. The family was living on board Charles's ship, the *Namur*, at Sheerness – his hope of getting command of a frigate had been disappointed. As the time of their visit approached, Jane became a little uneasy. She had seen them several times since their return from Bermuda and had found Charles over-attached to his wife and children. He was too much affected by 'a cross Child or some such care pressing on him',[63] as she told Cassandra.

His little daughter Cassy had already shown a disposition that did not please the Austen women. '[She] *ought* to be a very nice Child – Nature has done enough for her – but Method has been wanting',[64] Jane wrote to Frank, adding, 'She will really be a very pleasing Child, if they will only exert themselves a little'.[65] When the two older girls had spent a

month at Chawton in June, the aunts had gone to work. By the time
Cassy went back to her parents, everyone thought her improved and
the girls 'had so endeared themselves that we were quite sorry to have
them go'.[66] You hope that Frank had enough confidence and enough
good humour not to worry about what his sisters thought of his own
methods of child-rearing. Anna's fiancé Ben Lefroy did not dub Cassandra and Jane 'the formidables' without good reason.

In spite of Cassy's improvement at Chawton, Jane thought she might
displease her at Godmersham 'by some immediate disagreableness'.[67]
But Cassy surprised her by being very affectionate. In the evenings
Charles and his wife and Jane sat quietly talking with Edward and Fanny
Knight, while the children were in bed and the assorted young men –
for young Edward and George often collected friends of their own at
Godmersham – played billiards.

As Jane had feared before his arrival, Charles did seem to find it
difficult to overcome a hovering concern for his wife and children, and
once at least Jane stepped in and made him get ready to go out shooting.
Sports of the field, as she called hunting and shooting, might sometimes
be a proper activity.

When Charles and his family left on 22 October, and young Edward
and George went to Oxford a few days later, things at last began to
settle down a little, and Jane was more at leisure to observe life in the
neighbourhood. One evening at Chilham Castle she saw for the second
time during her visit a Mrs Britton, 'a large, ungenteel Woman, with
self-satisfied & would-be elegant manners',[68] as Jane with delight had
described her to Cassandra. After the second meeting she declared, Mrs
Britton 'amuses me very much with her affected refinement & elegance'.[69] Jane was equally taken with Miss Milles, who also gave her
something entertaining to write Cassandra:

> Miss Milles was queer as usual & provided us with plenty to laugh at. She
> undertook in *three words* to give us the history of Mrs Scudamore's recon-
> ciliation, & then talked on about it for half an hour, using such odd
> expressions & so foolishly minute that I could hardly keep my countenance.[70]

Mrs Britton and Miss Milles gave her more than momentary amusement
and something to write to Cassandra. Jane was at this time preparing
to begin *Emma*.

In the peacefulness of the last two weeks at Godmersham she had some time to herself. 'At this present time I have five Tables, Eight & twenty Chairs & two fires all to myself', she announced to Cassandra on 3 November.[71] And three days later she was 'very snug, in my own room, lovely morning, excellent fire, fancy me'.[72] But she was ready to go home. And she was ready to work. She had already mused to Cassandra: 'I wonder whether the Ink bottle has been filled.'[73]

11

The World

Back at Chawton Austen began *Emma* on 21 January 1814, the ninth anniversary of her father's death. It is her longest novel but took about half as long to write as *Mansfield Park*, and little more time than *Persuasion*, which is much shorter.

She wrote steadily through the spring and summer, though she made two visits to Henry in London, the second to his new house at 23 Hans Place. While Henry was at the bank every day, she worked on the novel in the downstairs room, which opened into the garden. 'I go & refresh myself every now & then', she wrote to Cassandra, 'and then come back to Solitary Coolness.'[1] This is as close as we ever come to a picture from her own pen of Austen at work. A room of her own opening onto a garden; quietness and peace; no interruptions except when she needed to take a break.

She was not the only member of the family writing a novel that summer. A new Anna emerged in May or June – a variation that surprised even Jane. She was still engaged to Ben Lefroy, despite the obstacle of his refusing to take the offered curacy. After returning to Steventon from her banishment at Chawton, she settled down to pass the time fruitfully by writing a novel, just as Jane herself had done nearly twenty years before when she was waiting for Tom Lefroy. Writing a novel was not an undertaking for the aimless and the unfixed. It required application and perseverance. Jane was happy to see at last a real sign of steadiness and purpose in Anna.

Anna sent her effort to her aunt Jane. The consideration and encouragement Jane gave to her in this endeavour should be set beside the criticism of Anna's character that Jane sometimes expressed. Her sympathy was greater than might always appear. The close attention she gave to Anna's work shows the kindness her nieces and nephews later insisted was the dominant part of her character. She was liberal in her

praise of Anna's writing, but suggested improvements. She was careful
not to discourage her but, once Anna got further along, she suggested
that some scenes might ultimately be discarded. She amended some bits
stylistically, following the principle that the sense should be expressed
in as few words as possible, and cautioned Anna about using 'novel
slang',[2] phrases Jane said Adam must have found 'in the first novel he
opened'.[3] Gently and unemphatically she directed Anna away from life
as presented in novels to life in the world, to nature as the pattern to
be followed in the creation of character and situation. 'Henry Mellish
I am afraid will be too much in the common Novel style – a handsome,
amiable, unexceptionable Young Man (such as do not much abound in
real Life).'[4] But another character is commended: 'I like the beginning
of D. Forester very much – a great deal better than if he had been very
Good or very Bad.'[5]

The attention to nature Jane urged in the creation of character had
its parallel in her insistence on adhering to accepted social forms. She
sets down the general law in this warning to Anna: 'And we think you
had better not leave England. Let the Portmans go to Ireland, but as you
know nothing of the Manners there, you had better not go with them.
You will be in danger of giving false representation.'[6] In particular, she
corrected such lapses as Lady Helena's being introduced to Cecelia,
rather than Cecelia's being introduced to Lady Helena, and a country
surgeon's being introduced at all to a Lord P. and his brother.

On another level, the time required to travel from one place to another
had to be given accurately and topics of conversation be plausible: 'Lyme
is towards forty miles distance from Dawlish & would not be talked of
there. I have put Starcross instead.'[7] These changes derived from the
same law that led Jane to object to a character's going out on the day
he had broken his arm. Anna's father had done just that, but Jane
considered it an aberration, too unusual in real life to be used in a
novel. It would '*appear* unnatural in a book'.[8]

These are not merely instances of gratuitous niggling over superficial
reality. Austen herself worked through strict attention to the surface in
order to get at deeper truths. She found this principle in life as well as
in art – though life could be tantalisingly ambiguous, as she once wrote
to Fanny Knight: 'I do not know what to do about Jemima Branfill.
What does her dancing away with so much spirit, mean? – that she does

not care for him, or only wishes to *appear* not to care for him? Who can understand a young Lady?' 9

Implicit in Austen's attention to the surface is her concern with the relationship between reader and author: an artist loses authority when the surface reality is violated. She presents this idea in *Persuasion* through Admiral Croft's bluff, sensible remarks about the picture in a shop window:

> 'Here I am, you see, staring at a picture ... But what a thing here is, by way of a boat. Do look at it. Did you ever see the like? What queer fellows your fine painters must be to think that any body would venture their lives in such a shapeless old cockleshell as that. And yet, there are two gentlemen stuck up in it mightily at their ease, and looking about them at the rocks and mountains, as if they were not to be upset the next moment, which they certainly must be. I wonder where that boat was built! ... I would not venture over a horsepond in it.' 10

The Admiral knows more about the laws of ships and the sea than the artist. He perceives something in the picture the artist had not intended: the ship is about to capsize!

Jane reveals herself as a reader as well as a writer in her comments on Anna's book. By extension she indicates how she expected her own books to be read. She 'read' characters in novels by the same light that she 'read' people in life; assuming the world of the book to be continuous with the real world – a view she shared with her mother. A character in Anna's novel, Mrs Forster, didn't return a call as soon as she should have. This would have indicated a fault in the character that Jane and her mother assumed Anna had not intended. Jane pointed out other instances of characters doing things that might cause readers to mistake Anna's intention.

Writing led Anna to do something else that Jane took as a very good sign. When she wrote to Frank about Anna's engagement to Ben, she had remarked on a certain lack of openness in their niece. 'It came upon us without much preparation; at the same time, there was *that* about her which kept us in a constant preparation for something.' 11 Anna didn't at first tell Ben she was writing a novel – her lack of openness – but when she did, Jane approved. 'You have been perfectly right in telling Ben of your work, & I am very glad to hear how much he likes it', she wrote to Anna. '*His* encouragement & approbation must be quite "beyond everything".' 12

The secretive and mischievous sides of Anna found their way into *Emma*, but Fanny Knight contributed something to the novel too. Anna confided in Jane about her novel-writing but not about her romances. Fanny, however, was open with Jane about being in love. While Jane was writing *Emma*, Fanny was in the full throes of her first serious romance and her aunt was her confidante. Whether what Jane says in her letters to Fanny at this time about love and perfection came from her thinking about Fanny's situation or are echoes of what Austen had written in *Emma*, it is impossible to say.

Although Jane always praised Fanny, for a few years after her mother's death the girl's character seemed unnaturally staid and serious for her age. She had been forced into a partially pretended maturity too early in life. But during Jane's visit to Godmersham she had discovered that Fanny was beginning to have romances, which gave the girl spirits appropriate to her age. Jane was charmed and later wrote to her:

> You are inimitable, irresistible. You are the delight of my Life. I cannot express to you what I have felt in reading your history of yourself, how full of Pity & Concern & Admiration & Amusement I have been. You are the Paragon of all that is Silly & Sensible, common-place & eccentric, Sad & Lively, Provoking & Interesting. Who can keep pace with the fluctuations of your Fancy, the Capprizios of your Taste, the Contradictions of your Feelings? You are so odd! & all the time, so perfectly natural – so peculiar in yourself, & yet so like everybody else! 13

We seldom find quite such flights of fancy or expressions of affection in Jane's letters. Fanny inspired her. You can see why Jane was Fanny's confidante as her first romance was coming into bloom.

She had met Fanny's suitor, John Plumptre, but was less impressed with him than Fanny was. 'A handsome young Man certainly, with quiet, gentlemanlike manners', she wrote to Cassandra, 'I set him down as sensible rather than Brilliant. There is nobody Brilliant nowadays.' 14 Another aspect of Jane as a 'formidable'. The following spring Plumptre was on the scene when Jane and Fanny were in London, where he was studying law. They had seen him in the park one day, and he had called

at Henry's house. Henry invited the young man to join the family party
at the theatre that night and to dine with them the next day.

That was just the kind of thing that made Jane adore Henry. He took
an interest in their niece's romance, and entered into it with the same
enthusiastic spirit as Jane. In the autumn he sent Jane an account of
the ball after the Canterbury races, reporting that Fanny had had good
partners, but John Plumptre, whom Henry had thought in love with
their niece in the spring, had danced the second dance with her and
then no more. Henry did not think this promising; it was not *his* way.

Fanny confided to Jane that she was in love with John, but by
November 1814 she had decided her feelings had changed. She wrote
secretly to Jane and tried to find a reason for the change. Had she lost
interest now that she knew John was in love and wanted to marry her?
Or was it his Evangelical tendencies and his lack of wit and spirit that
had finally put her off? She compared him unfavourably to her brothers,
but Jane countered with the same comparison. 'You have no doubt of
his having superior Abilities – he has proved it at the University – he
is I dare say such a scholar as your agreable, idle Brothers would ill bear
a comparison with.' [15] But the reply to Fanny's letter was not actually
so balanced and rational as this sentence might suggest.

Jane's letter is her most mercurial, quite unlike any other letter of
hers we have. She herself was aware of how disorganised and full of
changes her response was. 'I am feeling differently every moment', she
wrote to Fanny, '& shall not be able to suggest a single thing that can
assist your Mind. I could lament in one sentence & laugh in the next.' [16]
She wrote down her thoughts as they arose or as Fanny's letter elicited
them. She wanted to reassure her niece that feelings do sometimes
change or are mistaken in the first place, and that Fanny's letter had
convinced her the girl had only fancied herself to be in love because
Plumptre was the first man to love her. 'That was the charm', she wrote,
'& most powerful it is.' [17]

But then her mind turned to John Plumptre himself, whom she quite
liked, as she had written to Cassandra the year before: 'He gives me the
idea of a very amiable young Man, only too diffident to be so agreable
as he might be.' [18] His diffidence was one of Fanny's complaints. True, he
was somewhat reserved, but he was good-looking and quietly personable;
he was the eldest son of a rich man, and his family and friends, all known

to Fanny, were good people. Above all, Jane pointed out the strength of his character, 'his uncommonly amiable mind, strict principles, just notions, good habits'.[19] Jane suddenly urged Fanny to think again before giving up such a man. 'Oh! my dear Fanny, the more I write about him, the warmer my feelings become, the more strongly I feel the sterling worth of such a young Man & the desirableness of your growing in love with him again. I recommend this most thoroughly.'[20]

She argued that Fanny should not wait for perfection, 'where Grace & Spirit are united to Worth, where the Manners are equal to the Heart & Understanding'.[21] Fanny's *love* would perfect him through its influence. This idea had been somewhat amended by her next letter two weeks later. If Fanny were in love the good qualities would seem to outweigh the bad. 'It is very true that you never may attach another Man, his equal altogether', Jane told her, 'but if that other Man has the power of attaching you *more*, he will be in your eyes the most perfect.'[22] This idea is exactly echoed in *Emma* in the relationship of Emma and Mr Knightley.

The postscript to Jane's first letter to Fanny has an even more explicit connection to *Emma*. 'Your trying to excite your own feelings by a visit to his room amused me excessively. The dirty Shaving Rag was exquisite! Such a circumstance ought to be in print. Much too good to be lost.'[23] And so she took the detail, transformed the shaving rag into a bit of court plaster and the stub of a pencil, and made them Harriet Smith's mementoes of her love for Mr Elton.

Fanny replied that Jane had convinced her she was not in love, but this letter elicited an immediate warning from Jane – Fanny had given too much weight to her aunt's opinion. 'You frighten me out of my wits by your reference. Your affection gives me the highest pleasure, but indeed you must not let anything depend on my opinion. Your own feelings & none but your own, should determine such an important point.'[24] These were her last words on the question of whether or not Fanny was really in love. But Fanny's second letter had given a new piece of information that in Jane's eyes changed the whole situation. She recognised the situation from her own life.

John Plumptre had revealed that he was not quite independent. He had begun his study of law at Lincoln's Inn in 1813 and did not know when he would finish and be called to the bar; he did not know when he would be able to marry. This called up Tom Lefroy's situation in 1796 and the ghost of her own indefinite arrangement with him. The deep impression her experience had made on her enabled Jane to give a decisive opinion to Fanny: 'I am at present more impressed with the possible Evil that may arise to *You* from engaging yourself to him – in word or mind – than with anything else.' [25]

With the degree of Fanny's affection and the worth of John Plumptre's character, Jane believed their love and suitability to each other would increase within marriage itself. But she thought an indefinite engagement would be a mistake. 'I should dread the continuance of this sort of tacit engagement, with such uncertainty as there is, of *when* it may be completed. Years may pass, before he is Independent. You like him well enough to marry, but not well enough to wait.' [26] Fanny refused John Plumptre. She was a tender-hearted girl and was worried about the pain the rejection would cause him, but Jane had a strong opinion on this point too, perhaps again derived from her own experience: 'I have no doubt of his suffering a good deal for a time, a great deal, when he feels that he must give you up; but it is no creed of mine, as you must be well aware, that such sort of Disappointments kill anybody.' [27]

Early in November 1814, at about the same time Fanny was trying to come to a decision about John Plumptre, Anna and Ben carried their point and were married at Steventon, even though he had held to his determination not to be ordained yet. Anna's parents and brother and sister were the only Austens who attended the wedding, but this was probably not owing to any reservations about the marriage itself. Less than two months earlier, following the birth of her fourth daughter, Charles's wife, Fanny Palmer, had died at the age of twenty-four. The baby lived only a couple of weeks.

After their wedding, Anna and Ben lived first at Hendon with one of Ben's brothers. To Fanny Knight, Jane praised Anna's bridal letters, saying they were 'very sensible & satisfactory, with no *parade* of happiness, which I liked them the better for. I have often known young married Women write in a way I did not like, in that respect.' [28] Years before, Jane had admired the same quality in a letter from her friend Richard Buller at the time of *his* marriage. [29]

Edward Knight and Jane soon paid the obligatory 'wedding visit' to Hendon. Afterwards Jane wrote to thank Anna and said they had talked of her after they left 'for about a mile & a half with great satisfaction'.[30] But she hadn't approved of all she had seen and heard. She did not like Anna's self-indulgence – she was to have a piano when she would need that twenty-four guineas 'in the shape of Sheets & Towels six months hence', Jane wrote to Fanny Knight.[31] But more irritating to Jane had been the purple pelisse Anna had been wearing. 'I thought we had known all Paraphernalia of that sort', she went on to Fanny. 'I do not mean to blame her, it looked very well & I dare say she wanted it. I suspect nothing worse than its' being got in secret, & not owned to anybody. She is capable of that you know.'[32] So the chief criticism returned to Anna's old fault of being secretive. Insignificant as the purchase of a frivolous article of clothing might be, Anna's concealing it was to Jane a flaw in her niece's character.

Anna seems to have had an inherent distrust of other people, owing perhaps to having grown up with an officious stepmother and unsympathetic father. We can hardly be surprised that she developed a certain furtiveness of character. Not being open gave Anna a kind of advantage: her way of springing things on her parents without any previous hint increased the impact of her ploys to get attention and gave her a little revenge for their apparent lack of interest in her. Jane herself was not without a certain tendency to be secretive, though of course she had Cassandra to share her secrets, and this might have made her less aware of how much she kept to herself. Anna had no Cassandra.

Anna sitting there in her secretly-bought purple pelisse and talking of buying a piano instead of sheets and towels was still the old Anna. And Jane was still the formidable, critical, judging, rational aunt. But with marriage Anna had embarked on the last of her 'variations' that Jane was to know.

Anna continued to work on her novel, and she apologised for asking her aunt to take up her own valuable time reading what she had written – Anna must have known Jane was working on *Emma*. Jane insisted it was not a burden: 'I have been very far from finding your Book an Evil I assure you; I read it immediately & with great pleasure. I think you are going on very well.'[33] She then comments specifically on what she had just read, and commends Anna for being able to make so much progress: 'Indeed, I *do* think you get on very fast. I wish other people of my acquaintance could compose as rapidly.' [34]

But an impediment to Anna's writing arose. A couple of months after she married, Anna became pregnant, which weakened her so much and made her so sick that she was forced to stop writing. Jane now saw something new in marriage, something besides sheets and towels, pianos and purple pelisses.

Anna wrote telling Jane she had had to give up work on her novel, and Jane tried to be encouraging. Only a scrap survives of the letter she wrote in response to Anna but it tells us enough – 'from the first, being *born* older, is a very good thing. I wish you perseverance & success with all my heart'.[35] She pretends Anna's pregnancy marks only an interruption in her work, not a cessation, that the delay in completing the novel will be a good thing for the quality of the work, will make the novel better. But the phrase 'with all my heart' is not idle, empty words – Jane *felt* the significance of what was happening. Once Anna had a child her life would be very different. It is the last we hear of Anna's writing in Jane Austen's lifetime.

Jane's perspective on marriage began to undergo a radical change. The deepest spring of her imagination was not those brief but astute observations (such as she made of the women around Godmersham during her 1813 visit) but observation over long years, seeing not just what people were but what they became, how the world acted upon them and they upon the world.

During the years in Bath and Southampton Jane was preoccupied with herself and her own problems, made all the worse because she could not *act* to solve them. She had had to wait, in a sense passively. It made her in a way selfish. She once wrote to a niece that she was 'all for Self' – a joke but also a rueful admission. [36] She had had to be selfish to survive. Chawton gave her the energy and equanimity to take a look at the world outside herself. She saw first what she had always seen – young women poised on the brink of marriage. Anna and Fanny with their charm and liveliness and intelligence revitalised that central vision as expressed in *Emma*, which Austen finished on 29 March 1815, at about the same time Anna's pregnancy forced her to give up her own work.

The impact of Anna's pregnancy with all its implications was brought home to Jane, quite literally, when in the summer Anna and Ben moved from Hendon to Wyards, a farmhouse within walking distance of Chawton. That spring Frank and his wife and their five children had come to live at Chawton House, almost within sight of Chawton Cottage. Mary was pregnant with her sixth child. Jane's eyes were now opened to something she had before only vaguely registered. The problem wasn't just that Anna had had to give up her work, though that circumstance might have first fixed Jane's attention. The problem lay deeper and had wider significance as she saw in Mary Gibson's sixth pregnancy. Marriage did not just prevent a woman from writing a novel; it could turn a woman into a 'Poor Animal',[37] the other side of the coin from 'a wild Beast'.

The subject of pregnancy is easy to evade when thinking about Jane Austen's life and even more when thinking about her novels.[38] Pregnancy is what comes after the ending. Austen herself had perhaps not given it a lot of thought. Her own life had not taken her in that direction; she had had different concerns. When Elizabeth Austen died at the age of thirty-five of complications following childbirth, Jane's imaginative focus had been on the living – Edward's loss of a beloved wife, the eleven children left without a mother, Fanny's having to take her mother's place. Elizabeth was dead; concern had to be for the living. Even as recently as the death of Charles's wife, Fanny Palmer, just before Anna's marriage, Jane's thoughts were probably similar – poor depressed and grieving Charles, poor motherless little girls. Fanny had not been very strong.

An account of how many children the Austen women had in a small number of years is quite staggering, but we tend to shrug it off: that is the way things were in those days. Elizabeth had eleven children in less than seventeen years – not a subject for nonchalance to *her*. From the birth of her first child a year after she married, she did not have a single full year between the birth of one child and becoming pregnant with the next until her last two; there was a lapse of about a year and three months before she became pregnant with her tenth child, and about a year before she was expecting her last. Fanny Palmer's story is similar but a lot shorter. Her first was only five months old when she became pregnant with the second; nine months after the second was born she was pregnant with the third; and ten months after the third she was expecting her last child, though the last was possibly a premature birth since the baby died soon after its mother.

Mary Gibson had had a difficult time during her first pregnancy and the birth of the child. This might account for her not becoming pregnant again until her first child was about two years and three months old. After that, though, she usually became pregnant when each preceding child was under a year old – nine or ten months – though two were conceived five or six months after she had given birth.

Mrs Austen seems to have understood something about her own body. She had her children in sets. James was born little more than nine months after his parents married. When he was nine months old, George was conceived. By the time George was four months old, Mrs Austen was pregnant with Edward. Then she gave her body a rest and did not become pregnant again – this time with Henry – until Edward was nearly three years old. Ten months after Henry was born, she was expecting Cassandra, and seven months after Cassandra, Frank. When Frank was eleven months old, she was pregnant with Jane. Then another hiatus. She became pregnant with Charles when Jane was about two years and nine months old. Mrs Austen had eight children, and over a span of more than fifteen years. The periods between sets of children seem too closely calculated to have been wholly accidental.

The women knew a child's life does not begin with its birth. But even to Jane the pregnancies of her sisters-in-law were for a long time little more than abstractions. Some of them she saw when they were pregnant, but Mary Gibson's first pregnancy was the only one she had observed every day; they were living in the same house in Southampton. Whatever she suffered, Mary had been young and strong. The first birth is often the most difficult. A commonplace piece of information. Now Jane saw in Mary Gibson where marriage had led; and she watched in Anna where it *would* lead.

At the beginning of October 1815 Mary Gibson and Anna were in the last month of their pregnancies. Jane wrote a short letter to arrange a time for calling on Anna before leaving for London on business related to the publication of *Emma*. She did not allude to Anna's pregnancy and her tone is light and casual, but the complimentary closing of the letter is unusual. Ordinarily Jane wrote 'Yours affectionately' or 'Your affectionate aunt', followed by her signature. But she ended this letter, 'Yours very affectionately My dear Anna J. Austen'.[39]

Two months before on 8 August, Austen had begun a new novel, *Persuasion.* She did not make her heroine as young as Anna and Fanny. Anne Elliot is twenty-seven; she has not given up her youth to what Austen later called 'the business of Mothering'.[40] This choice was Austen's first tentative step into new territory.

On 4 October Jane went to London with Henry, planning to stay for a week or two. She expected to be back at Chawton in time for the births of both Anna's baby and Mary Gibson's. Since neither woman had been in good health during her pregnancy, the approaching births were a cause of anxiety for everyone.

The purpose of going to London was to negotiate the publication of *Emma* by John Murray. Murray had read the book and liked it. He offered her £450 but wanted, for that sum, the copyrights of *Mansfield Park* and *Sense and Sensibility* as well. Jane did not accept this offer but liked Murray's letter to her. 'He is a Rogue of course, but a civil one', she wrote to Cassandra. 'He sends more praise however than I expected. It is an amusing Letter.'[41] She had already been in London for almost two weeks and hoped that in another week she would be able to return home.

But she knew her plan was very uncertain. Henry had been unwell, and on the day she wrote to Cassandra, Tuesday 17 October, he grew worse – 'something bilious, but cheifly Inflammatory'.[42] By Sunday he had gone into such a rapid decline that Jane wrote to Chawton and to Steventon, asking James and Cassandra to come to London; and to Godmersham summoning Edward. Frank couldn't leave his wife since her baby was due in the next couple of weeks, but Anna's baby, a daughter, had been born the Friday before, 20 October, and both were doing well.

Edward, James and Cassandra joined Jane and for a couple of days Henry's condition deteriorated. On Wednesday he was so much worse that Jane felt obliged to write a 'preparatory Letter' to the Leigh-Perrots, a letter to warn them of the possibility of Henry dying. But then he rallied and soon took a turn for the better. After a few more days he was declared out of danger. Jane stayed on in London to nurse Henry during his convalescence, and the others returned home. Mary Gibson was safely delivered of her sixth child, a son, on 8 November, but this was not the end of the family's worries that autumn.

Henry's banking business was on the brink of ruin. Banks had appeared to flourish during the years of war with France, but Napoleon's defeat at Waterloo in the summer of 1815 was followed by a sudden economic depression. This might have brought Henry's problems to a head, but Henry himself was ultimately responsible for his own financial catastrophe. He had used his power as a banker to cultivate the kind of acquaintances he wanted in the great world. It appears he was an easy touch for feckless and undependable aristocrats, making them large personal loans. The habit finally caught up with him, and of course none of these friends did anything to bail him out.[43]

In the last week of November Henry wrote to Edward about the state of his business affairs, in which Edward himself and, to a lesser extent, other members of the family were deeply implicated. Open and frank as ever, Henry read his letter out to Jane, who remained with him in London, and she reported to Cassandra with a calmness that conceals what must have now been considerable alarm:

> He read me what he wrote to Edward; part of it must have amused him I am sure; one part alas! cannot be very amusing to anybody. I wonder that with such Business to worry him, he can be getting better, but he certainly does gain strength.[44]

Four days later the Alton bank collapsed.

Although the Henrietta Street bank remained trading, albeit shakily, Henry found it prudent to leave London to avoid his creditors. He went to Hanwell to stay with the Moores, one of whose daughters he had been courting for more than a year. Jane liked being the mistress of Henry's house and going about in his carriage during her visits, but she faced the distinct possibility that he was going to marry again. She was reconciled to the idea and liked Miss Moore better than anybody else around. After he had been at Hanwell for a few days, his lawyer thought there was no need for him to keep out of London any longer. But Jane steeled herself. 'One knows the uncertainty of all this, but should it be so, we must think the best & hope the best & do the best.'[45] They waited.

Jane had kept steadily on her own course as soon as Henry began to recover from his illness. She had settled her business with Murray, agreeing to let the firm publish *Emma* on a profit-sharing plan and also bring out another edition of *Mansfield Park*. She liked attention, and Murray kindly provided it. He promptly answered her inquiries and lent her books while she was at Hans Place, important for both her and Henry during his convalescence. *Emma* went into press immediately, but the old problem of dilatory printers seemed to cause delays. Murray and the printer were quick to assure Jane that the fault lay with the stationer, who was slow to provide paper.

To try to hurry the production Jane played her trump – the book was to be dedicated by permission to the Prince Regent. At the height of Henry's illness one of the Prince Regent's personal physicians had been consulted. As Henry began to regain his strength, he could not forebear, in his usual way, telling the doctor who the sister caring for him really was. The physician in his turn, knowing the Prince admired Jane Austen's novels, told him he had met the author, and the Prince then instructed the librarian at Carlton House to invite her to see the library. On that visit, the librarian suggested she should dedicate her next novel to the Prince Regent, thereby using her as a means of flattering his own royal patron.

This episode was only an amusing diversion for Jane; but much more to her taste and far more interesting than the Prince Regent or his librarian was a young physician named Charles Haden, who had been consulted when Henry first fell ill. He was twenty-nine, unmarried, and said to be clever. Jane told Cassandra that she was impressed by his professional manner and skill: 'He is certainly very attentive & appears hitherto to have understood the complaint.' 46 (She also compliments Henry: he was a good patient, lying quietly in bed and taking his medicine without any moaning.) Six weeks later, with Henry on the mend, she wrote effusively about Haden to Cassandra. 'Tomorrow Mr Haden is to dine with us. There's Happiness! We really grow so fond of Mr Haden that I do not know what to expect.' 47

The 'we' included not only Jane and Henry but Fanny Knight, who had come to London to keep Jane company. Jane's expectation – a very Emma-like fantasy – centred on a romance between Haden and Fanny. Jane wrote to Cassandra about an evening in Hans Place:

Fanny played & [Haden] sat & listened & suggested improvements, till Richard came in to tell him that 'the Doctor was waiting for him at Captain Blake's' – and then he was off with a speed that you can imagine. He never does appear in the least above his Profession, or out of humour with it, or I should think poor Captain Blake, whoever he is, in a very bad way.[48]

Haden is fit to be the hero of one of Austen's novels – a man whose good character is reflected in his attention to his professional duties and his pleasure in his work.

He was also a reader. He admired *Pride and Prejudice* but had not read *Mansfield Park*. When he began reading it, he preferred it to the earlier novel. Jane must have waited with some amusement to hear what he would make of Fanny Price not being musical or of the use to which the Miss Bertrams put their duets and Mary Crawford her elegant harp, for about music, which was his avocation, she and Haden did not agree: 'I have been listening to dreadful Insanity', she wrote hyperbolically to Cassandra. 'It is Mr Haden's firm beleif that a person *not* musical is fit for every sort of Wickedness. I ventured to assert a little on the other side, but wished the cause in abler hands.' [49] Haden himself sang – but Jane never heard him because he would only perform with a piano accompaniment. Fanny had rented a harp, which she played for them.

Jane thought Charles Haden quite good enough for Miss Knight of Godmersham Park, his intelligence and professional values being of far greater merit in Jane's estimation than wealth or worldly rank. He was a gentleman, the son of a doctor, and had studied medicine at Edinburgh University. That was good enough to establish his social credentials with Jane. She hinted to Cassandra her hopes for Fanny and Haden.

So much for the morning; then came the dinner & Mr Haden who brought good Manners & clever conversation; from 7 to 8 the Harp; at 8 Mrs L. & Miss E. arrived, & for the rest of the evening the Drawing-room was thus arranged, on the Sopha-side the two Ladies Henry & myself making the best of it, on the opposite side Fanny & Mr Haden in two chairs (I *beleive* at least they had *two* chairs) talking together uninterruptedly. Fancy the scene! And what is to be fancied next? Why that Mr H. dines here again tomorrow.[50]

But her hope was to be disappointed. Nothing came of the match she had been making between her niece and the man she described to her sister as 'a Haden, nothing but a Haden, a sort of wonderful nondescript

Creature on two Legs, something between a Man & an Angel – but without the least spice of an Apothecary'.⁵¹ Jane might have been a bit carried away by the romance of the situation, but her judgement of Charles Haden was right.

He had a successful medical career, and introduced the stethoscope into use in England. He had a special sensitivity to the healthcare needs of women and children, and wrote sensibly on the subject.⁵² His son was Sir Seymour Haden, not only a successful physician and man of science but one of the leading etchers in England in the mid nineteenth century. Sir Seymour married Deborah Whistler, half-sister of the painter James McNeill Whistler, on whose work Haden is said to have exerted a considerable influence.

We seldom see Jane swept away by her own enthusiasm as she was in promoting the romance between Charles Haden and Fanny Knight. We can easily guess the kind of things Cassandra wrote to Jane in times of disappointment and crisis – gentle, affectionate exhortations to patience and forbearance and acceptance, and loving words of sympathy. Or comic letters to take her out of herself and make her forget her troubles. But what did Cassandra make of the romance of Haden and Fanny? Did she see that Jane was playing Emma? Did she know Fanny well enough to know that, though the girl was susceptible to the attentions of an attractive man, she belonged to the landed gentry and there she meant to stay? She would never have married a doctor, no matter what his personal charms and merits. No more than Mr Elton would have married Harriet Smith. And did she see that the Harriet Smith in this business was Charles Haden, who could have been (perhaps was) deeply hurt? Did Cassandra perceive any of this, and did she attempt to make Jane see the reality? If she saw, I think we can be sure that she gave Jane a warning. Jane had put more of herself into the character of Emma than perhaps even she realised.

Emma was published around Jane's fortieth birthday. It is a novel 'lively and at ease', as Austen at one point describes the mind of the heroine. Like *Pride and Prejudice*, it is of the present and reflects the state of her spirits at the time it was written. It also reflects some of the very things she was thinking about in her real life as she wrote. Her letters to Fanny Knight while the novel was being written carry us again and again back to the novel – to the ideas about love and perfection that she was expressing in the book. Of her impatience with Anna's secretiveness and criticism of her lack of openness, Austen takes an amused and indulgent, if not altogether approving view, in her treatment of Frank Churchill and Jane Fairfax.

Frank may have something of Tom Lefroy in his character. He is in love with and secretly engaged to a young woman called Jane, a girl who has no money. He is the adopted son of a rich, demanding aunt, whom he fears will disapprove of the engagement because Jane Fairfax is not rich or grand enough to suit the aunt's expectations. Frank is clever, lively and good-natured, but he is also a bit frivolous and careless of the feelings of others. He never quite realises how hard their situation is on Jane and how much she suffers. He just happily assumes that everything will work out. And it does, owing to the opportune death of his difficult aunt.

Austen followed what was now her custom. She gives one of Mrs Elton's grand friends the name of Mrs Partridge, the surname of Tom Jones's boon companion and putative father. But she makes an even more specific connection between *Emma* and Tom Lefroy by having Robert Martin and Harriet Smith go to Astley's, as Jane and Tom had in August 1796. Perhaps Austen was looking back on Tom Lefroy and trying to be just to him, as she had to Eliza in *Mansfield Park*.

While celebrating in *Emma* life in a country village and 'all those little matters on which the daily happiness of private life depends',[53] Austen looks closely at the potential dangers of the isolation of village life on an imaginative and intelligent young woman. Emma's imagination has no outlet in writing novels. And yet, though Jane Austen could write about Emma's unwarranted meddling in the affairs of others, she herself did exactly the same thing with Fanny Knight and Charles Haden.

Emma acknowledges Jane Austen's personal sense that Chawton with all its blessings had come to her almost haphazardly, imposed by some outside force. She could take no credit for getting what she had longed for for eight years, just as Emma Woodhouse and Frank Churchill do nothing to merit the happiness that comes to them at the end of the novel. Emma calls Frank 'the child of good fortune,'[54] a phrase equally applicable to herself. The outside world fortuitously flows into Highbury and into Emma's life. *Emma*, like *Northanger Abbey*, is a novel of reconciliation.

The publication of the novel marked the height of Jane Austen's fame in her own lifetime. It was published by John Murray, the most distinguished British publisher, and was dedicated to the Prince Regent, who was said to admire her work and to keep a set of her novels in each of his houses. *Emma* was reviewed, most notably in Sir Walter Scott's anonymous piece in the prestigious *Quarterly Review*. The increasing popularity of Austen's work seemed a guarantee of the success of her new novel.

She had a copy of *Emma* sent to the Countess of Morley, whom she had probably met in London through Henry. The countess wrote to thank her just after Christmas: 'I am already become intimate in the Woodhouse family, & feel that they will not amuse & interest me less than the Bennetts, Bertrams, Norriss & all their admirable predecessors. I *can* give them no higher praise.'[55] Jane replied to her on New Year's Eve: 'Accept my Thanks for the honour of your note & for your kind Disposition in favour of Emma. In my present State of Doubt as to her reception in the World, it is particularly gratifying to me to receive so early an assurance of your Ladyship's approbation.'[56]

Encouraging as such a sign of approval was to Jane Austen the artist, it was even more important as an indicator of the possible financial success of the novel. More than ever she was concerned with how much money the work would bring her. She had taken a risk in refusing Murray's offer to buy the copyright of *Emma*, along with that of *Sense and Sensibility* and *Mansfield Park*, for £450. But each novel had so far shown a substantial increase in earnings over the previous one. She had made £140 from *Sense and Sensibility*, and while she herself only got £110 from *Pride and Prejudice*, Egerton, as owner of the copyright, had made a considerable profit. *Mansfield Park* had earned her £350. Before the publication of *Emma*, then, Austen had made £600, which she invested to provide herself with a small income. She had sound reason for thinking *Emma* would also do well.

She certainly knew 'Susan' was worth a lot more than £10, and early in 1816, using Henry as intermediary, she bought back the manuscript. She was marshalling her assets. She had 'Susan' in hand again, and she persevered in writing her new novel, *Persuasion*. She had built up a store of strength and determination since coming to live at Chawton, and now she needed it all.

12

The Body

At the beginning of 1816, Jane Austen's becoming self-supporting was not just desirable but began to seem a necessity. If all that appeared to be going wrong did go wrong, she might find herself homeless and her brothers unable to continue their support. She could not let herself be overwhelmed by these dark possibilities, and she did not wait in wretched passivity to see what the outcome of her brothers' troubles would be. She kept writing *Persuasion*.

Henry was still trying to shore up his business to prevent the collapse of the Henrietta Street bank. A few days after Jane left London on her fortieth birthday, Henry had borrowed £10,000 from Edward, a loan Edward had to make to protect his own interests – he stood to lose a lot more if the London bank failed. Jane may not have known all the particulars of Henry's business affairs, but she was well aware that they remained in a precarious state.

Potentially even more devastating to Jane's own life were Edward's troubles that were wholly unrelated to Henry's. In the autumn of 1814 distant relatives of Edward's benefactor, Thomas Knight, threatened to bring a lawsuit claiming their legal right to the Chawton and Steventon estates. If it was successful, Edward would be deprived of a large part of his income and property. That such a catastrophe was pending rather than actual must have made it all the worse by creating a constant, wearing sense of uncertainty. Jane could not have failed to grasp the implications to herself of Edward's possible loss.

If the Chawton estate were lost, Chawton Cottage would go with it. Jane would lose her home again, lose the place that had restored her equanimity and made it possible for her to get on with her writing. She knew what the loss of Steventon had done to her ability to work; she now had to live with the prospect of a repetition of that if she had to give up Chawton. She might for a while have been able to keep such thoughts from getting a hold in her conscious mind, but one disaster seems to presage, however irrationally, the inevitability of another.

On 15 March 1816 the Henrietta Street bank failed and Henry was declared bankrupt. The financial stability of the whole family was undermined by the collapse of the bank. All four of his brothers had been involved in Henry's affairs. The inescapable impression is that Henry's appearance of being rich had been founded in part on capital provided by his brothers, and on pledges in the form of their names as guarantors and sureties. The agreeable Henry turned out to be the monumentally selfish Henry with a careless, callous and heedless disregard for the well-being of his brothers and their families. He had built his career not on what he was but on what he felt he had the right to be.

James and Frank and even Charles lost money calculated in hundreds of pounds, considerable sums to them. But the greatest losses were incurred by Edward and by their uncle Leigh-Perrot, both of whom had stood surety for Henry when he was made Receiver of General Taxes for Oxfordshire in 1813. Their losses ultimately amounted to thousands, even tens of thousands of pounds – the amount calculated at today's value is more than a million. Only Mrs Leigh-Perrot's opinion of the debacle has survived; she never forgave Henry: 'Nor would I have Henry's feelings (if he does feel)', she later wrote to James Austen, 'for [what] he has occasioned us to lose by his imprudence.'[1] For once it is hard not to share her indignation.

Jane lost about £25, not an insignificant sum to her, and she and her mother and sister felt the more lasting effects in the reduction of their income by £100 a year. Henry's bankruptcy meant the end of his contribution to them, and Frank had to stop his gift because of his own losses in the failure of the bank, coupled with a set-back in his professional life. He was on half-pay owing to the decrease in naval activity following the French defeat at Waterloo. He could find no command. Charles had never been able to afford to give anything to supplement the income of his mother and sisters, and when the ship he commanded ran aground and sank in February 1816, although he was absolved of personal responsibility for the loss of the ship, he too seemed further from financial security than ever. Nothing could be hoped for from him. The Austen women were now dependent on Edward and James alone. And while the lawsuit against Edward remained pending, the security of their house itself was threatened.

A decline in health of the Austen women coincided with the financial crises of the men. It is a strange coincidence. By January 1816 Anna had become pregnant again, hardly two months after the birth of her first child, and by midsummer Mary Gibson was pregnant with her seventh child. Mary Lloyd had a serious illness from which she was slow to recover. And sometime in the summer, as Jane Austen moved towards the finish of *Persuasion*, she too began to feel unwell but did not tell anyone, perhaps not even Cassandra. She was easily fatigued and suffered from what seemed to be rheumatism, especially in her back. Nothing really inconsistent with the strain of hard work and nagging worries. She kept silent and kept working.

She finished *Persuasion* on 18 July, pressing herself hard to reach the conclusion. On rereading it she was not satisfied with the final chapters and so rethought the denouement. She wrote the last chapters again, completing the novel on 6 August.

Persuasion was the last novel Austen lived to finish, and in that sense it is her valediction to Tom Lefroy. Yet it alone of her novels does not contain a character with a surname from *Tom Jones*. Jane's allusion is to the name Tom itself, not directly but by implication. She named the hero Frederick Wentworth, taking the surname of the husband of a distant relative by marriage. Her grandfather Leigh's brother had a sister-in-law called Elizabeth Lord, who fell in love with and secretly married a young army officer called Thomas Wentworth, whom her mother had forbidden her to marry. After her husband's death, she went to live with her sister and brother-in-law at Adlestrop, where she died. Jane Austen could not have helped seeing her memorial plaque in the church at Adlestrop because it is set in the wall directly over the pulpit; Elizabeth Lord is identified there as the wife of Lieutenant-General Thomas Wentworth. Jane would have read the Wentworths' story in Mary Leigh's family history when she was at Adlestrop in the summer of 1794.

The given name of Thomas had great resonance for several women in the Leigh family. Jane's grandmother had married Thomas Leigh, whose sister Cassandra had remained unwaveringly devoted to her cousin Thomas Wight. She had waited for him for ten years before they finally were able to marry. And in Jane's own generation, all three of Thomas Leigh's granddaughters fell in love with men named Tom: Jane herself was in love with Tom Lefroy, Cassandra was engaged to Tom Fowle, and Jane Cooper married Tom Williams. All of these relationships, each in its own particular way, were doomed: Jane spurned; Cassandra 'widowed' before she had even married; and Jane Cooper dead in a carriage accident after a five-year childless marriage. Their histories all converge in the story of Anne Elliot and Frederick Wentworth.

Persuasion does not carry any explicit internal evidence of the financial uncertainties dominating Austen's life during its composition, but in a general way these worries are deeply present in the instabilities of life itself as reflected in the novel. Running counter to these is an insistence on the need for patience, and also for self-reliance through personal exertion and activity.

The novel is often considered Austen's most romantic work, but although the quality of autumnal romanticism is present, it is a blind, making more bearable the harsher reality that emerges in the work. The love of Anne Elliot and Captain Wentworth is tender rather than romantically intense, consoling rather than fulfilling. What Anne feels more intensely than thwarted love is loneliness and alienation. She sometimes seems a hapless victim of her own virtues, virtues deriving as much from self-denying passivity as from genuine goodness.

Anne's family are egotistical fools, bordering on monsters. But Austen has something more subtle to tell us about families. In the cheerful Musgroves we get a double view. They are a happy family, open and trusting, right-feeling and considerate to each other, but they are an exclusive and excluding unit. They like Anne Elliot, and even admire her, but they use and exploit her to maintain their own family harmony.

There is something of Martha Lloyd and Cassandra Austen in Anne's eternally patient, capable, smoothing and soothing attempts to keep everyone satisfied and in good spirits. Jane Austen is at last looking at these women whom she so much admired and is understanding their limitations as well as their disappointments. They must sometimes have yearned for escape from their own virtues as Jane did from her own dissatisfactions.

Anne Elliot is not a self-portrait. Jane knew herself better than that. She could see that she herself was an exploiter, a recipient of much of the good done by excellent women like Martha and Cassandra and Anne Elliot. Like Mary Musgrove, Jane was the sister who complained of being left all alone, neglected, having more to cope with than she could bear. She had no housekeeping talents. She would have found it a trial to attend to the needs of little children, hour after hour, day after day: not at all the same thing as being the attentive aunt who sweeps in, exerts herself to train unruly children to be more orderly, and then sends them home and disappears to write novels.

We would like to think, of course, that Jane would have made a better job of it than Mary Musgrove, and maybe we are right. Jane had the intelligence and imagination that Mary does not possess. But perhaps Jane's meditation on herself through Mary led her to another place: at forty she might not have been asking herself what kind of wife and mother she would have been. She might now have been asking herself if she would have *wanted* to put her intelligence and imagination to the service of those roles. She had escaped becoming a Mary Musgrove.

In her niece Anna and her sister-in-law Mary Gibson, Jane Austen had been confronted with the fact that women were required to possess that supposedly very masculine virtue of physical courage: facing threats to their own lives. When we look back at the earlier novels we see that the prospect of physical danger does not belong to the men's lives but to those of their wives. By getting married Elinor and Marianne, Lizzy, Fanny and Emma all face in the natural course of things the prospect of putting their lives at risk every couple of years in childbirth. The men, however, only have to have moral courage. In *Persuasion* Austen makes her hero the equal of her heroine in a new particular: she gives Wentworth a profession in which he has to risk his life. When she wrote at the end of the novel, 'The prospect of another war was all that could cloud Anne's sunshine', she must have hoped women at least would add 'or the prospect of another pregnancy'.[2] Austen had done all she could for Anne Elliot; she had made her with any luck too old to have eleven children in less than twenty years.

Beneath its surface of autumnal calm and acceptance, *Persuasion* is the most unsettled of Austen's novels. When she wrote of Anne Elliot's having travelled from prudence to romance, 'the natural sequel of an unnatural beginning',[3] she was not speaking of romantic love but of a way of looking at the world, courageously and confidently, of approaching life boldly not timidly, imaginatively not conventionally. The world does not come to pay a visit to Anne Elliot; she is forced into the world.

After his bankruptcy Henry spent as little time as possible in London: 'London is become a hateful place to him, & he is always depressed by the idea of it', Jane wrote to Fanny Knight.[4] He took refuge with his family, spending time at Chawton, Steventon and Godmersham. Whatever matrimonial plans he had had were dropped. He could not afford to marry and had to find a way to support himself. He had one last possible chance to recoup his fortune. In the summer he went to France to try to claim for himself some of the Feuillide property that had been confiscated by the French government on the death of the Comte de Feuillide in 1794. But his attempt failed, and he returned to England empty-handed.

In September Cassandra went to Cheltenham with Mary Lloyd, who was still recuperating from her illness of the summer. Jane wrote to her sister that Anna's pregnancy had again undermined her health and that she was in a weakened state:

> We go on very well here; [James] Edward [James's son] is a great pleasure to me; he drove me to Alton yesterday; I went principally to carry news of you & Henry, & made a regular handsome visit, staying there while Edward went on to Wyards with an invitation to dinner; it was declined, & will be so again today probably, for I really beleive Anna is not equal to the fatigue.[5]

In her next letter she said: 'I have not seen Anna since the day you left us, her Father & Brother visited her most days.'[6] Four days later, Jane observed that Mary Gibson was not well either: 'Mrs F. A. seldom either looks or appears quite well. Little Embryo is troublesome I suppose.'[7] In spite of the cuteness of the phrase 'Little Embryo', Jane now knew what pregnancy meant physically to these women. She no longer had to imagine what it was like to have a body that was wearing out; she felt it in her own body. Anna had her baby, another daughter, on 27 September.

All that autumn Jane was weak, and on her forty-first birthday, 16 December 1816, she wrote to her nephew James Edward that she had not been able to accept an invitation to dine at Wyards: 'Ben was here on Saturday, to ask Uncle Charles & me to dine with them, as tomorrow, but I was forced to decline it, the walk is beyond my strength (though I am otherwise very well) & this is not a Season for Donkey Carriages.'[8] Although she could not give a completely favourable report of her own health, she was able to tell her nephew that his half-sister, Anna, had at last regained her strength: 'You will hear from Uncle Henry how well Anna is. She seems perfectly recovered.'[9]

Henry and Charles were at Chawton, so Jane had the pleasure of spending her birthday quietly with two of her adored brothers. She worried about Henry because of the collapse of his career, and about Charles, who not only had professional worries but had been slow to recover his spirits after the death of his wife two years before. She wrote to James Edward:

> We think Uncle Henry in excellent Looks, ... & we have the great comfort of seeing decided improvement in Uncle Charles, both as to Health, Spirits & Appearance. And they are each of them so agreable in their different way, & harmonize so well, that their visit is thorough Enjoyment.[10]

Henry had decided to be ordained and become a clergyman at last. This gave an odd twist to his life; he was finally ending up in the profession his family had always thought him best suited to. Jane was very much in favour of lively, agreeable, engaging parsons; she knew that religion is not made attractive by dour, humourless, unfeeling clergymen. At the time of Elizabeth's death, she had written to Cassandra that she hoped their cousin Edward Cooper, a parson, would 'not send one of his Letters of cruel comfort to my poor Brother'.[11] Henry, she trusted, would be a clergyman with a better sense of other people's feelings.

Before Henry's ordination she wrote to Cassandra that in his letters he did 'not write diffusely, but chearfully'.[12] It was not in his nature to be uncheerful – a temperament that Jane, who so often had to struggle against her own tendency to querulousness, particularly admired and envied. He was ordained on 19 December 1816 and took up the curacy of Bentley near Alton, which Edward had secured for him. Before Jane heard him preach herself, she was told he brought it off, as she informed her friend Alethea Bigg, 'with as much ease & collectedness, as if he had been used to it all his Life'.[13]

Jane jokingly suggested to her nephew James Edward that he and she might try to get hold of one of Henry's sermons to use in a novel. For James Edward, like his half-sister, Anna, and even his little sister, Caroline, was following his aunt by writing a novel. Her career was having quite an impact on James's children. She must have been pleased and at the same time amused. Jane enjoyed having such influence and seeing the talent the young people showed. 'Edward is writing a Novel', she wrote to Cassandra, 'we have all heard what he has written. It is extremely clever; written with great ease and spirit; if he can carry it on in the same way, it will be a firstrate work, & in a style, I think, to be popular.' 14 Writing to Cassandra, Jane could be honest in her opinion of their nephew's writing; she must have been telling the truth, and it is high praise indeed.

Later she heard from his mother that James Edward had lost two and a half chapters of the novel, and she wrote to him teasingly, her fancy warming to her subject as she developed it:

> It is well that *I* have not been at Steventon lately, & therefore cannot be suspected of purloining them; two strong twigs & a half towards a Nest of my own, would have been something. I do not think however that any theft of that sort would be really very useful to me. What should I do with your strong, manly, spirited Sketches, full of Variety & Glow? How could I possibly join them on to the little bit (two Inches wide) of Ivory on which I work with so fine a Brush, as produces little effect after much labour? 15

This is Jane at her most charming – but there is more to it than the manner and the meaning. The rhythm and cadences are those of Jane in good health, of Jane as a *writer*. James Edward would have felt it; we feel it. Jane is really getting better. Perhaps even she herself believed it.

Early in the new year Jane was giving optimistic but truthful accounts of her condition. To her twelve-year-old niece, Caroline, she wrote: '*I* feel myself getting stronger than I was half a year ago, & can so perfectly well walk to Alton, *or* back again, without the slightest fatigue that I hope to be able to do both when Summer comes.' 16 The next day to her old friend Alethea Bigg in Winchester she reported: 'We are all in good health [&] *I* have certainly gained strength through the Winter & am not far from being well; & I think I understand my own case now so much better than I did, as to be able by care to keep off any serious return of illness.' 17

She was encouraged too by Anna's continuing improvement, as she wrote to Alethea Bigg: 'Anna has not been so well or so strong or looking so much like herself since her Marriage, as she is now; she is quite equal to walking to Chawton, & comes over to us when she can, but the rain & dirt divide us a good deal.' 18 A month later she was even able to make a joke to Fanny about Anna – a sign of Jane's feeling a kind of relief; Anna was fine after all:

> Ben & Anna walked here last Sunday to hear Uncle Henry [preach], & she looked so pretty, it was quite a pleasure to see her, so young & so blooming & so innocent, as if she had never had a wicked Thought in her Life – which yet one has some reason to suppose she must have had, if we beleive the Doctrine of Original Sin, or if we remember the events of her girlish days.19

But Jane had not forgotten what Anna had been through during the past two years, nor grown indifferent to the decline of Mary Gibson, whose seventh child was due in April. This was not the fate Austen had envisioned for her heroines.

She had written six novels that celebrate courtship ending in the marriage of couples who are temperamentally, intellectually and morally well-suited to one another and have the joy of passionate fulfilment as well. The marriages represent social affirmation and deep personal good – the attainment of a state, she wrote near the end of *Mansfield Park*, 'as secure as earthly happiness can be'.20 So she had thought; now she saw something else.

She had perhaps drawn a curtain over the consequences of physical passion, although her brother James had observed, jokingly, in a *Loiterer* piece that pretended to argue against marriages of affection: 'My first and greatest objection to them arises from observing the large families with which those who marry for affection are commonly blessed.' 21 Now Jane perceived this was not a joke but a problem. A wearing parade of pregnancies was the likely result of a marriage for love. A marriage based on affection and respect meant harmonious companionship, but with sexual passion added it probably also meant almost continuous breeding. This is where Austen's amused, sensible, high-minded engagement with the theme of courtship had led her. She began to look at marriage from a different angle. Her reflections on the problems that she had become conscious of are first articulated in letters to Fanny Knight.

Fanny felt uneasily left behind because one of her close friends had been married for a year. She doesn't seem particularly to have wanted to be married; she just wanted to be sure she would not remain *unmarried*. Jane spoke kindly and sensibly to her about her situation:

> Well, I shall say, as I have often said before, Do not be in a hurry; depend upon it, the right Man will come at last; you will in the course of the next two or three years, meet with somebody more generally unexceptionable than anyone you have yet known, who will love you as warmly as ever *He* [John Plumptre] did, & who will so completely attach you, that you will feel you never really loved before.[22]

Jane had more to say, more she *had* to say. Beginning gently, she said to Fanny: 'Oh! what a loss it will be to me when you are married' – she erased *to me* – 'You are too agreable in your single state, too agreable as a Neice. I shall hate you when your delicious play of Mind is all settled down into conjugal & maternal affections.'[23] She was taking a light, teasing tone. But she had seen women made dull, narrowed and preoccupied by the demands of husband and children and housekeeping. And indeed she had noticed a similar effect of marriage on some men, including her brothers Charles and James. If Austen's novels had given the impression that marriage was a panacea, she now tried to amend that view to Fanny.

Her solace at the prospect of the changes marriage would effect in Fanny lay in thinking her niece at twenty-four had escaped early marriage and would very likely not marry for a few more years. In remarking on this, she approaches what she most wanted to say to Fanny: 'And then, by not beginning the business of Mothering quite so early in life, you will be young in Constitution, spirits, figure & countenance, while Mrs William Hammond [Fanny's friend who had already married] is growing old by confinements and nursing.'[24] A young married woman gave up her youth to a succession of pregnancies and to the sometimes very long process of being slowly used up, an expendable commodity.

When Jane felt stronger in January 1817 she had done what she wanted to do and what she *had* to do. She began a new novel. This act insists on her confidence in her ultimate recovery. Recovered, she would have to have money. She could not afford to stop writing.

The unfinished *Sanditon*, which Austen intended calling 'The Brothers', has much about it, even in twelve chapters, to show she was breaking new ground, both in form and themes. She creates mysteries, not expectations. The story unfolds leisurely with subtle tensions and potential conflicts. The only reason we know Charlotte Heywood is the heroine is that the narrator tells us so. Charlotte herself picks out another character as her idea of a heroine, creating an ambiguity as to who the heroine really is. Anna may have influenced Jane a little: she had thought of calling her novel 'Which Is the Heroine?' We never know quite where we are.

The narrator abjures more and more the role of moral arbiter. Austen was closing the gap between what it is to read a novel and what it is to know people in real life. The experience of her hated and resisted time in Bath now appears in her fiction. She accepts that we do not, even cannot, know other people perfectly. *Emma* hinted at this. *Persuasion*, in Anne Elliot's respect for the Harvilles, Captain Benwick and the Crofts, confirms that, willing or not, you must accept that limitation and trust your own judgement. One of the first lessons Charlotte Heywood learns in *Sanditon* is this: 'I must judge for myself.'[25]

Austen puts the reader in the position Charlotte is in – and the same one that had made her so uneasy in Bath. The characters in *Sanditon* are mixtures of the rational and the foolish, the selfish and the generous, the good and the bad, and we are not sure what to make of most of them. Even Charlotte's opinion, though you suspect it is sound, does not point to what might happen. No one can be pinned down.

Clara Brereton knows Sir Edward has marked her out for seduction but does not mean to be seduced; yet she meets him for secret trysts. We are a long way from Lydia Bennet and Maria Bertram. We know from beginning to end where we are with them. But Clara has a density, an unsettling mysteriousness not found in characters in

Austen's earlier work. We cannot see what Clara's faults are or what her fate will be.

More than in any of Austen's other novels, the characters speak not for effect but from what they *are*. This makes them in general much more transparent, but their very transparency makes them more complicated. It is impossible to guess what these characters are going to do or say. They are undefined and full of surprises, and this creates the effect of remarkable naturalness. We are in the same position as their interlocutors.

If you compare the twelve chapters of *Sanditon* to the first twelve chapters of Austen's completed novels, you see how radically different *Sanditon* was to have been. The story has hardly begun. It was apparently to have been a very long novel. The man assumed to be the hero only appears at the end of chapter 12, and though we have heard about him (from a pretty unreliable source) we know enough to see that he is not like Austen's other heroes – he lives too much in the world. But he is clever and frank and has a satirical eye.

Maybe he will fall in love with Charlotte, or maybe with Clara or even Esther Denham. Maybe Sir Edward won't carry off Clara but will slouch away, a bit ashamed, with one of the more willing Miss Beauforts. That leaves another Beaufort for Arthur – or perhaps Miss Lambe is for him, her sickliness being sure to create a bond between them. The point of these fanciful speculations is to show how much Austen keeps us in the dark while at the same time keeping us interested.

The sense of uncertainty, of the unpredictable, is echoed in the economic theme of the novel. *Sanditon* has a financial context quite different from that of Austen's earlier novels, in which characters are straightforwardly prudent or imprudent about money. The sensible ones live within their incomes and some, even more prudently, put aside money for the future or channel money back into their estates. The imprudent live beyond their means or fail to make provisions for the future. The picture in *Sanditon* is not so simple.

Austen is surprisingly vague about just how much money the characters actually have, but everyone, even the women, with the single exception of Clara Brereton, are independent. The rich Lady Denham, each of the Parkers – brothers and sisters – and the Heywood family (though their having thirteen children raises questions) all have at least enough to live quietly and comfortably. Sir Edward Denham is poor for someone of his rank (not at all the same thing as being poor) and his sister has only a small provision. But no one except Clara is a dependant.

Several of them, nevertheless, are involved in business speculations, all centred on turning the village of Sanditon into a fashionable seaside resort. But the speculators do not all have the same motive. Lady Denham is simply greedy. Mr Parker speculates out of enthusiasm and a love of being active, of *doing* something. Sir Edward speculates in a small way by building a 'Cottage Ornée' to rent out, bringing an increase in his income that will make him less poor for someone of his rank. Mr Parker's brothers and sisters are not speculators – at least not as far as we know. And Mr Heywood, who lives on dividends he goes to London twice a year to collect, is determinedly opposed to speculation.

Austen seems less interested in whether speculation is good or bad, right or wrong, than in the question of *why* people speculate. She understood why men like her brothers Frank and Charles risked their lives in a dangerous profession – they had to in order to support themselves and with luck make their fortunes. But why did men risk their security, though not their lives, when they were already independent? Henry had married independence in the form of Eliza's money, on which they could certainly have lived quite well. Moreover, he had no children, which might have provided a motive to get richer. Even more puzzling, what made rich men like Edward and uncle Leigh-Perrot risk so much money? Or James, who had far less margin to absorb a loss? Jane Austen seems to have intended exploring this mysterious and perhaps to her masculine phenomenon. The mystery is very much a part of the unknown and indefinite in *Sanditon*.

The novel itself begins with people who are literally not where they think they are. And it leads to trouble: a carriage accident. This is a startling departure from Austen's other novels, which all begin with a description of a character or a family. Austen is taking us to a new place in every sense.

In *Sanditon*, the physical scene itself is precisely described. The carriage has left the high road onto a 'very rough lane' and is 'overturned toiling up its' long ascent half rock half sand'.[26] But the topography is not there just to be described; it is there to *be*; and we are never long unaware of it, whether in the narrative flow or in the conversation of the characters: the weald, the down, long hills, heavy bits of road, a stream, a valley winding to the sea. The sea, the sea: dancing and sparkling in sunshine and freshness; here fine hard sand, no mud, no weeds, no slimy rocks; there a stagnant marsh, a bleak moor, a ridge of putrefying seaweed, brackish water, cold soil. The face of the earth exists but how it is perceived depends on who you are, what you want to see.

The land has houses on it, and each house has its own particular landscape – well fenced and planted, and rich in the garden, orchard and meadows which are the best embellishments of such a dwelling; the absence of a vegetable garden with the yearly nuisance of decaying vegetation is noted. A small lawn has a very young plantation around it, about a hundred yards from the brow of a steep, but not very lofty, cliff; the land around another house has a proper park paling in excellent condition 'with clusters of fine elms, or rows of old thorns following its line almost every where. *Almost* must be stipulated – for there were vacant spaces.' 27

A romantic-looking cottage is situated on a high eminence – but it turns out to be an ordinary labourer's cottage; a gentleman's house has a most intelligent portentous countenance; one house is snug-looking in a sheltered dip (or from a different point of view, in a hole, a contracted nook, without view or air); another is a light elegant building at the top of a hill; lodging houses are identified by To Let signs in the windows. Even houses may not be what they appear.

Details are there as casually as if they have always been there and always will be: canvas awnings, white curtains, low French windows, ample Venetian ones, blinds to be opened or closed, a flowerpot and a telescope on a balcony. Inside the houses there are phials of medicine on a mantelpiece; bedrooms to be dusted, furniture to be moved away from windows and huddled close to the fire, furniture that frolicking little Misses might damage.

The needs of the populace are provided for. The price of butcher's meat is discussed, a greengrocer is not flourishing, but a gardener will bring whatever fruits and vegetables are wanted. Asses' milk is to be flogged; cocoa is coddled and cooked; green tea, bitters 'of my own decocting', and wine are talked of and drunk (not always in moderation). 28 Bread is toasted and buttered. Shop windows have blue shoes, nankeen boots, straw hats, pendant laces.

Never before has Austen so insistently made us aware of the physical world: topography, houses and their trappings, food, clothes. The people who move through the landscape, live in the houses, take the medicine, eat the food, drink the drinks, wear the clothes are no less physically substantial than the world they inhabit: they themselves have bodies.

At the beginning of the novel the coachman shrugs his shoulders when directed to take the road where the accident occurs. Mr Parker sprains his foot extricating himself from the overturned carriage. Shoulders and foot: Diana Parker puts a shawl over *her* shoulders. She asks to feel her brother's sprained ankle, comments on his sinews, claims to have once rubbed a coachman's hurt ankle with her own hand for six hours straight. Mr Parker takes her hand to quiet her. Gums are diseased, teeth are pulled, internal organs are catalogued: lungs, stomach, liver. Curls are glossy, blood comes to cheeks, Arthur Parker sweats.

The characters are tall, elegantly tall, of middle height; they are upright and alert, have upright decided carriage, walk nimbly or are hardly able to crawl from bed to sofa; they are stout, slender, with a healthy frame, hale, broad, robust, lusty, sickly, have delicate or sodden complexions. We know their ages very exactly.

They inhabit the space where they stand, sit, move, and each sees from a particular physical perspective. The opening carriage accident is discerned from a hayfield and the workers – men, women and children – come to see what is happening. On the drive into Sanditon Mrs Parker looks at their old house through the back window of the carriage, and as she talks she keeps looking back. Esther Denham feels her poverty with discontent and is 'immediately gnawed by the want of an hand-somer equipage than the simple gig in which they travelled, & which their groom was leading about still in her sight'.[29] Everybody can see, but all find their own individual significance in what is seen.

Charlotte stands at her window and looks 'over the miscellaneous foreground of unfinished buildings, waving linens, & tops of houses, to the sea'.[30] Later at tea with the hypochondriacal Parkers she finds herself, on a very fine English summer day, by a brisk fire, but she 'drew back her chair to have all the advantage of [Arthur's] person as a screen, & was very thankful for every inch of back and shoulders'.[31] On a visit to

Sanditon House she spies Sir Edward and Clara, who think themselves well hidden: '[Charlotte] was glad to perceive that nothing had been discerned by Mrs Parker; If Charlotte had not been considerably the tallest of the two, Miss B.'s white ribbons might not have fallen within the ken of *her* more observant eyes.'[32] Charlotte's height, like Arthur's back and shoulders, the coachman's shrug of disbelief, and Diana's noticing the position of her brother's foot, keeps in our consciousness that everyone has a body, a body that identifies us to the world and gives us literally a very particular personal way of seeing the world. With our bodies we respond to the world. This is new in Austen's work.

She now moves into new territory, beyond the theme that she had inherited from her family and from the philosophical debates of her time: The theme of reason and feeling had dominated her first stories and bore extraordinary fruit in the six novels of her maturity. Now she has found a new theme: the body. Our feelings, our tempers, our dispositions and thoughts are all contained in and dependent on the vessel of the body.

Austen is as chary of taking a sentimental view of the human body as she had been of human emotions. In her earlier novels the characters can be physically affected by their faults: by emotional self-indulgence – Marianne Dashwood walking in wet shrubbery and getting pneumonia; by wilful stupidity – Mrs Bennet sending Jane on horseback to Netherfield when it is threatening rain, causing the girl to get sick; by some moral flaw – Dr Grant's gluttony which brings on apoplexy and death after three great institutional dinners in one week. But in *Sanditon* the body has a life of its own.

Hypochondria, which has generally been taken as the dominant theme of the *Sanditon* fragment, is only a pointer, an aspect of the wider and all-pervasive theme of the body. Sir Edward Denham is not a hypochondriac, but he is obsessed with his body. He is preoccupied with himself as a sexual entity to be gratified and with women as objects for his gratification. Austen makes his language so ridiculous that she can have him say what could not, in that time, perhaps otherwise have been said in a novel. In defending Robert Burns's poetry, Sir Edward says to Charlotte:

The coruscations of talent, elicited by impassioned feeling in the breast of man, are perhaps incompatible with some of the prosaic decencies of life, nor can any woman be a fair Judge of what a man may be propelled to say, write or do, by the sovereign impulses of illimitable ardour.[33]

In plain English (as the young James Austen says in the *Loiterer*), sexual desire will drive a man to anything. Denham's insistence that women cannot understand means he thinks women do not experience sexual desire – at least not as intensely as men.

Charlotte knows perfectly well what he is saying, as would, Austen implies, any woman clever enough to penetrate his obtuse manner of expressing himself. Her female characters are not ignorant of sexual desire, and the clever ones know that, whatever cant a man like Denham might use to hide the fact, in him the great driving force of the body is not 'in the breast of man', but in another part.[34] Sir Edward does not have a clue what a woman may feel for a man.

Sublimely stupid, he tells Charlotte that the characters he most admires in novels are seducers like Richardson's Lovelace. He fancies himself to be a seducer. Austen presents this as satire on the way a weak head can be influenced by literature. But this strategy for approaching the theme of sex contains within it a deeper purpose. Sir Edward is not driven by vanity, as Henry Crawford is in *Mansfield Park*; he is driven by sexual desire.

Here Austen is at her most subversive. Sir Edward does not just represent the sexual appetite of a fool; he represents the sexuality of all men, whether stupid or intelligent, seducers or husbands, whether their erotic impulses are illicit or morally sanctioned by marriage. As her working title, 'The Brothers', may indicate, Austen was approaching a confrontation with her respect for her own brothers – two of whose wives had already died in childbirth, while a third was being exhausted by one pregnancy after another before Jane's very eyes. The problem Jane had to grapple with was, quite bluntly, why her own brothers did not respect their wives enough to restrain their sexual desires.

She does not put all the blame on men. Charlotte Heywood is at first attracted to Sir Edward because he is handsome ('very well to look at', Lady Denham says),[35] and has a 'very good address & wish of paying attention & giving pleasure'.[36] Charlotte is aware from the first that his conversation is 'rather commonplace perhaps, but doing very well from the lips of a handsome Sir Edward'.[37] The important words are 'lips' and 'handsome', not 'Sir'. This is sexual attraction, but it is soon dampened by Charlotte's discovering Sir Edward is a fool.

Cruder than Charlotte, the Beaufort sisters with their 'shewey figures' know very well they are sexual objects.[38] Colluding with men, they rejoice in being so: they exhibit themselves on the balcony of their house; the telescope is their prop. Arthur Parker, already known for his love of the sensual pleasures of food and drink, makes a little detour in his walk every day, in spite of his indolence, to see the Beauforts parading their bodies. In retrospect we understand his motive for being so attentive to Charlotte when she has tea with him and his sisters. Austen knew what was on men's minds – and women's too. We get only a glimpse of Miss Whitby, whose mother owns the Sanditon lending library, when she tears herself away from her toilette and hurries down to show off all her glossy curls and smart trinkets. Austen knew what was on her mind too.

Sex itself is not new to Austen's work. It is a moving force in all of her novels. *Sense and Sensibility* has its emotional aspects but the erotic comes into its own in *Pride and Prejudice*, especially in the relationship of Elizabeth and Darcy. When Lizzy and Jane Bennet speak of their determination to marry only for love, sex is a distinct, if unspecified, part of their meaning. Jane Austen was not a Victorian, and it is wrong of us to allow the shadow of Victorian values and assumptions to be cast back over her. Sex is a strong though inexplicit element in all of her novels.

She looked all around the subject but obliquely. She knew that sexual attraction can be stronger than rational judgement, even – or perhaps especially – in choosing a marriage partner. Why else did Mr Bennet marry his wife? Or Sir Thomas marry Lady Bertram or Mr and Mrs Price each other in *Mansfield Park*? *Persuasion* introduces a variation: Lady Elliot married Sir Walter, showing that sexual attraction can overcome a woman's good judgement too. Lady Elliot is presented as having been much too good and upright to have married Sir Walter for his wealth and social position. Being carried away by sexual desire is treated sometimes comically, sometimes with light irony. But it is there, distinct if implicit. In *Pride and Prejudice* sex lends an almost sinister element to Charlotte Lucas's marriage to Mr Collins, a repulsive man in every way.

Not until *Sanditon* does the body take its own place as a theme in Austen's work. Being energetic or fatigued, getting warm or cooling off, eating and drinking, complaining of maladies real or imagined, parading sex in words or actions: the characters in *Sanditon* bring us back inexorably to the body, its needs and desires. Where the theme might have led her remains unknown. She did not have the time or energy to complete the novel. In mid March 1817 she stopped writing, and her business became dying. The body had its way.

In February Jane was trying to pass off her illness as rheumatism, something no one ever *died* of. 'I am almost entirely cured of my rheumatism', she wrote to Fanny Knight, 'just a little pain in my knee now & then, to make me remember what it was, & keep on flannel.' [39] To her niece Caroline she persisted in this myth until the end of March: 'A great deal of Wind does not suit me, as I have still a tendency to Rheumatism. [In] short I am a poor Honey at present.' [40] 'Poor Honey' is a phrase Jane had coined much earlier as a name for all women who enjoyed being sick and enjoyed their 'spasms & nervousness & the consequences' they gave them. [41] Calling herself one is like saying she is only pretending to be sick.

By mid March she had given up the pretence of the rheumatism story when writing to Fanny, but she tried to be optimistic:

> I am got tolerably well again, quite equal to walking about & enjoying the Air; & by sitting down & resting a good while between my Walks, I get exercise enough. I have a scheme however for accomplishing more, as the weather grows springlike. I mean to take to riding the Donkey. It will be more independant & less troublesome than the use of the Carriage, & I shall be able to go about with Aunt Cassandra in her walks to Alton & Wyards.[42]

Two weeks later she wrote Fanny something closer to the truth but tried to keep up her spirits:

> Many thanks for your kind care for my health; I certainly have not been well for many weeks, & about a week ago I was very poorly, I have had a good deal of fever at times & indifferent nights, but I am considerably better now, & recovering my Looks a little, which have been bad enough, black & white & every wrong colour. I must not depend upon being ever very blooming again. Sickness is a dangerous Indulgence at my time of Life ... We are going

to have Rain, & after that, very pleasant genial weather, which will exactly do for me, as my Saddle will then be completed, and air & exercise is what I want.[43]

She ended the letter by announcing she had taken her first ride on the donkey. This was a kind of proof. She could go places. She was getting better.

The same could not, however, be said for Anna. The sunny picture of Anna's health that Jane had sent to Fanny in January did not hold. By March Anna had 'a bad cold, looks pale, & we fear something else. She has just weaned Julia'.[44] Anna was pregnant again, only seven months after her second child was born. Ten days later, Jane wrote Fanny that 'Anna has not a chance of escape; her husband called here the other day, & said she was *pretty well* but not *equal* to so long a walk; she must come in her Donkey Carriage. Poor Animal, she will be worn out before she is thirty. I am very sorry for her'.[45] Poor Animal. Strong words, a bitter phrase. This is far from Jane's being gentle with Fanny about the loss of a girl's play of mind once she has settled into conjugal and maternal affections. Marriage could turn a woman into a poor animal.

Jane Austen might have begun by feeling deeply for the plight of Anna alone and then to fear that Fanny's destiny would be the same. But her sympathy led her further. In *Sanditon* she says: 'Woman feels for woman very promptly and compassionately.' [46] Well, in truth, not promptly in Jane Austen's own case. If she had felt before, she had not expressed it. Now, though, she *did* feel. She wrote to Fanny in the same letter in which she speaks of Anna's situation: 'Mrs Clement too is in that way again. I am quite tired of so many children.' [47] She was not tired of the children; she was tired of what pregnancy and childbearing did to women, tired of the apparent indifference of their husbands to their share in causing their wives' state. Tired of the death that sooner or later very likely awaited the poor animals.

In the last week of March, Mrs Austen's brother Leigh-Perrot lay dying at Scarlets, his house in Berkshire. This impending event brought up again all Mrs Austen's past feelings about her brother's failure to provide her with financial assistance. 'Indeed I shall be very glad when the Event at Scarlets is over', Jane wrote to Fanny Knight, 'the expectation of it keeps us in a worry, your Grandmama especially; She sits brooding over

Evils which cannot be remedied & Conduct impossible to be understood.' [48] What kept them in a worry, moreover, was not just the past
or even Leigh-Perrot's approaching death itself, but the contents of his
will. With the recent financial reverses of the brothers, the Austen
women needed more than ever before a legacy from Leigh-Perrot. A
couple of thousand pounds would have given them some sense of
security and would have relieved the Austen men of the burden of
having to support them.

But when Leigh-Perrot died on 28 March, his will revealed he had
left nothing at all to his sister. To his wife he left the houses at Scarlets
and Bath, as well as the land he owned in the parish of Wargrave (where
Scarlets was located) and £10,000 in cash. The rest of the estate was left
in trust, the income from it to go to his wife for her lifetime. When
she died, the property held in trust would go to James Austen, except
for £1000 apiece to each of James's brothers and sisters. (The disabled
George was not included in the bequest.) This was a heavy blow,
especially to the women, who had immediate needs.

Jane wrote to Charles that their mother bore 'the forgetfulness of *her*
extremely well; her expectations for herself were never beyond the
extreme of moderation, & she thinks with you that my Uncle always
looked forward to surviving her. She ... heartily wishes that her younger
Children had more, & all her Children something immediately'.[49] The
crux of the matter is stated in the last clause: Mrs Austen felt the pressing
urgency of her children's needs.

The person who actually showed herself most strongly affected by the
will was Jane. Perhaps she had not brooded like her mother, but she
too had apparently been unable to give up some last hope that her
uncle's will would bring immediate relief to the whole family. 'A few
days ago my complaint appeared removed, but I am ashamed to say',
she wrote to Charles, 'that the shock of my Uncle's Will brought on a
relapse ... I am the only one of the Legatees who has been so silly, but
a weak Body must excuse weak Nerves.' [50] Many years before, when
Eliza's son was suffering from epileptic fits, she had written to Philadelphia Walter that she believed 'mental and bodily sufferings are ever
closely related'.[51] She may have written something similar to Jane; in any
case, Jane had come to the very same perception. Shock is a strong word
and suggests that in spite of all that had gone before – Leigh-Perrot's

consistently ignoring Mrs Austen's financial plight over the past twelve years – Jane had clung to the hope that he would finally do something for them.

When she wrote to Charles on 6 April, she said that two days before she had been so ill

> & thought myself so likely to be worse that I could not but press for Cassandra's returning [from Scarlets] with Frank after the Funeral last night, which she of course did, & either her return, or my having seen Mr Curtis, or my Disorder's chusing to go away, have made me better this morning. I live upstairs [in bed] however for the present & am coddled.[52]

The next three weeks, though, confirmed to her the seriousness of her decline. On 27 April she made her will. She left everything to Cassandra except for a £50 legacy to Henry and another £50 to his former servant Madame Bigeon, who had lost her life's savings in the collapse of Henry's bank – Jane could not forget a penniless woman.

On 22 May she wrote her last surviving letter from Chawton. Writing to Anne Sharp, a former governess at Godmersham, she claimed she had been recovering her strength since the beginning of the month:

> Your kind Letter my dearest Anne found me in bed, for inspite of my hopes & promises when I wrote to you I have since been very ill indeed ... *Now*, I am getting well again, & indeed have been gradually though slowly recovering my strength for the last three weeks. I can sit up in my bed & employ myself, as I am proving to you at this present moment, & *really* am equal to being out of bed, but that the posture is thought good for me. How to do justice to the kindness of all my family during this illness, is quite beyond me! Every dear Brother so affectionate & so anxious! And as for my Sister! Words must fail me in any attempt to describe what a Nurse she has been to me.[53]

Jane strove to see her situation from the viewpoint of others, to give them their due. She perceived the effects of her decline on both her mother and Martha Lloyd:

> I have not mentioned my dear Mother; she suffered much for me when I was at the worst, but is tolerably well. Miss Lloyd too has been all kindness. In short, if I live to be an old Woman I must expect to wish I had died now, blessed in the tenderness of such a Family, & before I had survived either them or their affection.[54]

For us, this was Jane's leave-taking of her mother and her friend Martha.

During the April attack the Alton apothecary had been at a loss as to treatment and had called in a physician from Winchester. Giles Lyford was the nephew of Mrs Austen's old favourite medical adviser, John Lyford the Basingstoke surgeon. Jane had kept insisting that she was suffering from nothing but a temporary indisposition which would soon pass. But now her illness was acknowledged to be serious – it is believed today she had Addison's disease, tuberculosis of the adrenal glands. She was advised to seek treatment in Winchester or London and decided to put herself directly in Lyford's hands by going to Winchester. On 24 May Jane and Cassandra left Chawton, and Martha Lloyd remained with Mrs Austen.

They made the journey in James Austen's carriage; his wife, Mary Lloyd, had arranged it all, as Jane wrote to Anne Sharp:

> Now, that's a sort of thing which Mrs J. Austen does in the kindest manner! But still she is in the main *not* a liberal-minded Woman, & as to this reversionary Property's amending that part of her Character, expect it not my dear Anne; too late, too late in the day; & besides, the Property may not be theirs these ten years. My Aunt [Leigh-Perrot] is very stout [healthy].[55]

The reference is to James Austen's being heir to the Leigh-Perrot fortune after their aunt's death, but Jane rightly perceived that Jane Leigh-Perrot was in good health and would live long – she lived for nearly twenty more years, until 1836.

It rained most of the way to Winchester, drenching Henry and their nephew William Knight, who accompanied the carriage on horseback. William, who was nineteen, and his brother Henry, twenty, had spent a good deal of time at Chawton since the beginning of the year. Jane had grown very fond of them and had written her praise of both to their sister Fanny. 'William & I are the best of friends. I love him very much. Everything is so *natural* about him, his affections, his Manners & his Drollery. He entertains & interests us extremely.'[56] To the end Jane believed nothing could make any sister happier than to hear good of her brother.

Winchester had something of home about it. Since 1814 Jane's old friend Eliza Bigg Heathcote had lived in the Close at Winchester with her spinster sister, Alethea. Mrs Heathcote arranged lodgings for

Jane and Cassandra in College Street, not far from her own house; her sister Alethea had, as Jane put it, 'frisked off like half England, into Switzerland'.[57]

On 27 May in writing to James Edward, Jane described what she insisted was her convalescence:

> I know no better way my dearest Edward, of thanking you for your most affectionate concern for me during my illness, than by telling you myself as soon as possible that I continue to get better. I will not boast of my hand-writing; neither that, nor my face have yet recovered their proper beauty, but in other respects I am gaining strength very fast. I am now out of bed from 9 in the morning to 10 at night – Upon the Sopha t'is true – but I eat my meals with Aunt Cassandra in a rational way, & can employ myself, & walk from one room to another.[58]

The next day she wrote to an unidentified correspondent:

> My attendant is encouraging, and talks of making me quite well. I live chiefly on the sofa, but am allowed to walk from one room to the other. I have been out once in a sedan-chair, and am to repeat it, and be promoted to a wheel-chair as the weather serves. On this subject I will only say further that my dearest sister, my tender, watchful, indefatigable nurse, has not been made ill by her exertions. As to what I owe to her, and to the anxious affection of all my beloved family on this occasion, I can only cry over it, and pray to God to bless them more and more.[59]

Jane was stable for the first few days but then her symptoms returned. Her pulse sometimes rose to a hundred and twenty. Mr Lyford told the family the case was desperate. James, in bad health himself, came to Winchester for a while and then his wife, Mary Lloyd, took his place. Jane's state remained dangerous but unchanging through June and the first two weeks of July. Cassandra and Mary cared for her, the brothers came as often as they could. Fanny Knight wrote cheerful and amusing letters that Jane enjoyed until she became too weak to take an interest even in Fanny's news. Of Jane's spiritual life, Henry later wrote: 'She made a point of receiving the sacrament before excessive bodily weakness might have rendered her perception unequal to her wishes.'[60]

Now we hear at last Cassandra's voice, not that of the woman who wrote platitudinous letters to Philadelphia Walter, but of the beloved sister who had been Jane's bulwark in the difficult years and her companion in the times of contentment. She wrote to Fanny Knight after Jane's death, rehearsing the details of her sister's last days and hours:

> Since Tuesday evening, when her complaint returned, there was a visible change, she slept more & much more comfortably, indeed during the last eight & forty hours she was more asleep than awake. Her looks altered & she fell away, but I perceived no material diminution of strength & though I was then hopeless of a recovery I had no suspicion how rapidly my loss was approaching.[61]

On Thursday, Jane recovered sufficiently to realise that death was at hand. She created a reason to get Cassandra out of the house, as Cassandra reported to Fanny without, perhaps, understanding her dying sister's motive: 'Immediately after dinner on Thursday I went into the Town to do an errand which your dear Aunt was anxious about.'[62]

While Cassandra was out, Jane tried to die. She had another seizure but survived it. She was able to tell Cassandra about it when she returned from the errand:

> I returned about a quarter before six & found her recovering from faintness & oppression, she got so well as to be able to give me a minute account of her seisure & when the clock struck 6 she was talking quietly to me.[63]

Soon after this she had another fainting spell 'which was followed by the sufferings she could not describe'.[64] Mr Lyford was sent for and gave her something for the pain; 'she was in a state of quiet insensibility by seven oclock at the latest'.[65]

But Jane did not slip away so quietly as this seems to imply. In the half hour between six-thirty and seven came the crisis:

> She felt herself to be dying about half an hour before she became tranquil & apparently unconscious. During that half hour was her struggle, poor Soul! she said she could not tell us what she suffered, though she complained of little fixed pain. When I asked her if there was any thing she wanted, her answer was she wanted nothing but death & some of her words were 'God grant me patience, Pray for me Oh Pray for me.'[66]

Cassandra sat for six hours with a pillow in her lap to assist in supporting Jane's head, which in her restless movement lolled off the bed. At one o'clock in the morning of 18 July, Cassandra was relieved by Mary Lloyd. She rested for about two hours and a half and then resumed her place. Jane died an hour later, her head in her sister's lap.

In the midst of the facts, Cassandra told Fanny what Jane had been to her: 'She was the sun of my life, the gilder of every pleasure, the soother of every sorrow, I had not a thought concealed from her, & it is as if I had lost a part of myself.' [67] But she was still Cassandra and would not be overcome by grief:

> You know me too well to be at all afraid that I should suffer materially from my feelings, I am perfectly conscious of the extent of my irreparable loss, but I am not at all overpowered & very little indisposed, nothing but what a short time, with rest & change of air will remove. [68]

Four days later Jane was buried in Winchester Cathedral. Cassandra again wrote to Fanny and described her own view of the scene as the coffin was taken from the house in College Street and carried to the cathedral:

> I watched the little mournful procession the length of the Street & when it turned from my sight & I had lost her for ever – even then I was not overpowered, nor so much agitated as I am now in writing of it. [69]

APPENDIX

The 'Nameless, Dateless Romance'

Caroline Austen, the daughter of James Austen and Mary Lloyd, related that her aunt Cassandra told her about an incident that had occurred at a seaside resort involving Jane Austen and a young clergyman. Since Jane is known to have gone to Devon and Dorset several times between 1801 and 1804, it is assumed the meeting took place on one of these visits.

What Cassandra said, according to Caroline, was that the family met a man who Cassandra thought fell in love with Jane and could have won her heart. At the end of the holiday, the man asked where the Austens planned to be the following summer and said he would join them. But, soon after he departed, the Austens heard that he had died.

The most important thing in this account seems to me to be that Cassandra didn't say Jane was in love – only that Cassandra thought the parson was a man Jane would have fallen in love with. It seems unlikely that either Cassandra or Caroline fabricated this tale; perhaps the fault lies with some biographers who have taken for granted that Jane herself was in love.

If she was, she had recovered sufficiently to accept (however briefly) Harris Bigg-Wither's proposal in December 1802. And the following year she indicated that Tom Lefroy still had an important place in her imagination by naming the family of the title of her new novel, *The Watsons*, after a family in *Tom Jones*, Lefroy's favourite novel. The parson who loved Jane Austen didn't supplant Tom Lefroy in her imagination.

Notes

References to Jane Austen's work are from the *Oxford Illustrated Jane Austen*, 6 vols, ed. R. W. Chapman; the usual abbreviations for the titles of the novels are used and MW (Minor Works) for the volume containing Austen's other work. The following short titles are used for frequently cited works:

Letters: Deirdre Le Faye, ed. *Jane Austen's Letters* (Oxford, 1995).

Austen Papers: R. A. Austen-Leigh, ed. *Austen Papers, 1704–1856* (London, 1942).

Notes to Chapter 1: 'Legacies'

1. *Austen Papers*, p. 9, Elizabeth Weller's 'Memorandum'.
2. *Austen Papers*, p. 8, 'Memorandum'.
3. *Austen Papers*, p. 8, 'Memorandum'.
4. Within Jane Austen's family, the situation of her father's uncle Cope Freeman has the closest parallel to the situation of John Austen. Freeman died when his children were very young, but his will carefully provides for each of them, and indeed even for any child born subsequent to his making the will or to any child with whom his wife might be pregnant at the time of his death. His eldest son inherited the bulk of the fortune, his younger son inherited both land and capital (£1000), and the daughters £1500 a piece. He further provides separate money for the maintenance and education of all the children. The wills of Jane Austen's Leigh and Perrot connections follow, in general, this pattern, leaving the bulk of an estate to the eldest son but amply providing for daughters and younger sons. For these wills, *A Century of Wills from Jane Austen's Family* (Sydney, 2001). The will of John Austen, PROB 11/483, sig. 163, is transcribed here.
5. *Austen Papers*, p. 3, 'Memorandum'.
6. *Austen Papers*, p. 4, 'Memorandum'.
7. *Austen Papers*, p. 9, 'Memorandum'.
8. *Austen Papers*, p. 8, 'Memorandum'.

9. *Letters*, p. 122, Jane Austen to Cassandra Austen, Southampton, 20 February 1807.

10. *Austen Papers*, pp. 13–14, 'Memorandum'.

11. *Austen Papers*, p. 8, 'Memorandum'.

12. *Austen Papers*, p. 8, 'Memorandum'.

13. Margaret Wilson, *Jane Austen's Family and Tonbridge* (Chawton, Hampshire, 2001), p. 16, maintains that it is 'almost certain' that Betty's husband was George Hooper, a lawyer in Tonbridge.

14. Will of William Austen, PROB 11/686, sig. 264; transcription in *Century of Wills*.

15. Will of William Austen.

16. Will of William Austen.

17. Will of William Austen.

18. Will of Cope Freeman, PROB 11/668, sig. 262; transcription in *Century of Wills*

19. Will of Cope Freeman.

20. George Tucker, *A History of Jane Austen's Family*, revised edition (Stroud, 1998), p. 22. (Originally titled *A Goodly Heritage*, Manchester, 1983.)

21. Will of Stephen Austen, PROB 11/785, sig 1; transcription in *Century of Wills*.

22. Maggie Lane, *Jane Austen's Family Through Five Generations* (London, 1984), pp. 43–44; Deirdre Le Faye, 'Leonora Austen', *Jane Austen Society Annual Report, 1998*, pp. 55–57.

23. James Edward Austen-Leigh, *A Memoir of Jane Austen*, ed. R. W. Chapman (2nd edn, London, 1951), p. 4.

24. Wilson, *Tonbridge*, p. 57, says the Hoopers had three children, though no other information is given. It may be that they died in infancy and that George was placed with them because they were childless.

25. Robin Vick, 'The Hancocks', *Jane Austen Society Annual Report, 1999*, p. 22.

26. Robin Vick, 'The Hancocks', p. 22.

27. *Austen Papers*, p. 61, Tysoe Hancock to Mary Freeman, Calcutta, 29 March 1772. This letter is mistakenly indexed as being to Stella Freeman.

28. Will of Stephen Austen.

29. *Austen Papers*, p. 35.

30. Robin Vick, 'The Hancocks', p. 20.

31. See *Austen Papers*, p. 32, Cassandra Leigh Austen to Susannah Walter, Steventon, 20 August 1775. Mrs Austen's letter suggests Freeman was known to be sympathetic to the plight of orphans.

32. Deirdre Le Faye, *Jane Austen: Her Life and Letters. A Family Record* (London, 1989), p. 4.

33. Austen-Leigh, *Memoir*, pp. 7–8.

34. *Austen Papers*, p. 177, Henry Austen to Warren Hastings, 5 June 1802.

35. See Lane, *Jane Austen's Family*, pp. 39–40.
36. Tucker, *History*, p. 39.
37. *Austen Papers*, p. 65, Tysoe Hancock to Philadelphia Hancock, Calcutta, 23 September 1772.
38. Mark Bence-Jones, *Clive of India* (London, 1974), p. 220.

Notes to Chapter 2: Home

1. Will of Thomas Leigh, PROB 11/896, sig. 56; transcription in *A Century of Wills from Jane Austen's Family* (Sydney, 2001).
2. *Austen Papers*, pp. 23–24, George Austen to Susannah Walter, Steventon, 8 July 1770.
3. *Austen Papers*, pp. 25–26, Cassandra Leigh Austen to Susannah Walter, Steventon, 26 August 1770.
4. *Austen Papers*, pp. 26–27, Cassandra Leigh Austen to Susannah Walter, Steventon, 9 December 1770.
5. *Austen Papers*, p. 23, George Austen to Susannah Walter, Steventon, 8 July 1770.
6. *Austen Papers*, p. 27, Cassandra Leigh Austen to Susannah Walter, Steventon, 9 December 1770.
7. *Austen Papers*, p. 66, Tysoe Hancock to Philadelphia Hancock, Calcutta, 23 September 1772.
8. *Austen Papers*, pp. 65–66, Tysoe Hancock to Philadelphia Hancock, Calcutta, 23 September 1772.
9. *Austen Papers*, p. 72, Tysoe Hancock to Philadelphia Hancock, Calcutta, 9 August 1773.
10. *Austen Papers*, p. 32, George Austen to Susannah Walter, Steventon, 17 December 1775.
11. *Austen Papers*, p. 82, John Woodman to Warren Hastings, London, 11 June 1776.
12. *Austen Papers*, p. 83.
13. *Austen Papers*, p. 50, Tysoe Hancock to Philadelphia Hancock, Calcutta, 7 September 1770.
14. *Austen Papers*, p. 38.
15. *Austen Papers*, p. 73, Tysoe Hancock to Philadelphia Hancock, Calcutta, 3 September 1773.
16. *Austen Papers*, p. 56, Tysoe Hancock to Philadelphia Hancock, Calcutta, 28 August 1771.
17. *Austen Papers*, p. 82, John Woodman to Warren Hastings, London, 11 June 1776.

18. Philadelphia Hancock's account for 1777 at Hoare's Bank; details given by Claire Tomalin, *Jane Austen* (New York, 1997), note 18 to chapter 1, p. 296.

19. Deirdre Le Faye, *Jane Austen: Her Life and Letters. A Family Record* (London, 1989), p. 38.

20. *Letters*, p. 526, 'Biographical Index'.

21. Will of John Cope Freeman, PROB 11/1161, sig. 16; transcription in *Century of Wills*.

22. Le Faye, *Family Record*, p. 38.

23. Le Faye, *Family Record*, p. 40.

24. Le Faye, *Family Record*, pp. 40–41; quoted from MS notes for family history by Anna Lefroy.

25. James Edward Austen-Leigh, *Memoir of Jane Austen*, ed. R. W. Chapman (2nd edn, London, 1951), p. 40.

26. Le Faye, *Family Record*, p. 40, quotes MS by Anna Lefroy.

27. *Austen Papers*, p. 31, Cassandra Leigh Austen to Susannah Walter, Steventon, 20 August 1775.

28. Le Faye, *Family Record*, p. 40, quotes MS by Anna Lefroy.

29. Will of Thomas Knight, PROB 11/1252.

30. Maggie Lane, *Jane Austen's Family Through Five Generations* (London, 1984), p. 78, quotes the MS memoirs of Admiral Sir Francis Austen.

31. George Tucker, *A History of Jane Austen's Family* (Stroud, Gloucestershire, 1998), p. 66.

32. David Selwyn, ed., *Collected Poems and Verse of the Austen Family* (Manchester, 1996) 'Epistle to G. East Esq.', p 25, lines 1–6.

33. Selwyn, ed., *Collected Poems*, 'Epistle to G. East Esq.', p. 26, lines 43–48.

34. Selwyn, ed., *Collected Poems*, 'The Humble Petition of R. Buller & W. Goodenough', p. 28.

35. Selwyn, ed., *Collected Poems*, 'To F. S. who Accused the Author of Partiality in Writing Verses for F C Fowle, & Not for Him', pp. 27–28.

36. Will of Ann Cooper, PROB 11/967, sig. 2000.

37. *Letters*, p. 240, Jane Austen to Cassandra Austen, Godmersham, 14 October 1813.

38. *Letters*, p. 248, Jane Austen to Cassandra Austen, Godmersham, 3 November 1813.

39. Austen-Leigh, *Memoir*, p. 16.

40. Tucker, *History*, p. 151.

41. Will of Ann Cawley, PROB 11/1158.

42. 'To the Memory of Mrs Lefroy', verses 5 and 6, MW p. 441.

43. To the Memory of Mrs Lefroy,' verse 9, line 2, MW p. 441.

44. Samuel Egerton Brydges, *The Autobiography, Times, Opinions and Contemporaries of Sir Egerton Brydges* (London, 1834), p. 41.

45. Brydges, *Autobiography*, p. 5.

46. *Poetical Register and Repository of Fugitive Poetry* (3rd edn, London, 1815), p. v.

47. Miss [Anne] Brydges, 'On Seeing Some School-Boys', *Poetical Register*, p. 30.

48. Miss [Anne] Brydges, 'Poetical Epistle', *Poetical Register*, pp. 90–91.

49. *Gentleman's Magazine* (1797), p. 983; F. J. Darton, *The Life and Times of Mrs Sherwood* (London, 1910), p. 128.

50. Le Faye, *Family Record*, p. 48; Tucker, *History*, p. 153; J. J. Cooper, *Some Worthies of Reading* (Reading, 1923), p. 72.

51. Darton, *Mrs Sherwood*, p. 128.

52. *Letters*, p. 5, Jane Austen to Cassandra Austen, Rowling, 1 September 1796.

53. Deirdre Le Faye, 'Three Austen Family Letters', *Notes & Queries* (September 1985), p. 333, Cassandra Leigh Austen to Philadelphia Walter, Steventon, 31 December 1786.

54. Edward Austen, MS volume, Journal through Switzerland, August 1786. Hampshire Record Office, 39M89, fol. 87.

55. Edward Austen, Journal, 6 August 1786.

56. Edward Austen, Journal, 13 August 1786.

57. Edward Austen, Journal, 13 August 1786.

58. Edward Austen, Journal, 10 August 1786.

Notes to Chapter 3: Scenes

1. *Austen Papers*, p. 115, Eliza de Feuillide to Philadelphia Walter, Château de Jourdan (Guienne), 17 January 1786.

2. Deirdre Le Faye, ed., 'Three Austen Family Letters', *Notes & Queries* (September 1985), p. 334, Cassandra Leigh Austen to Philadelphia Walter, Steventon, 31 December 1786.

3. [James Austen], *Loiterer*, no. 52, 23 January 1790.

4. [James Austen], *Loiterer*, no. 52.

5. *Letters*, p. 120, Jane Austen to Cassandra Austen, Southampton, 8 February 1807.

6. Le Faye, ed., 'Three Austen Family Letters,' p. 333, Cassandra Leigh Austen to Philadelphia Walter, Steventon, 31 December 1786.

7. *Austen Papers*, p. 125, Philadelphia Walter to James Walter, Seale, 19 September 1787.

8. Le Faye, ed., 'Three Austen Family Letters,' p. 333, Cassandra Leigh Austen to Philadelphia Walter, Steventon, 31 December 1786.

9. *Austen Papers*, p. 119, Eliza de Feuillide to Philadelphia Walter, Guienne, 23 May 1786.

10. *Letters*, p. 237, Jane Austen to Cassandra Austen, Godmersham, 14 October 1813.

11. *Austen Papers*, p. 170, Eliza de Feuillide to Philadelphia Walter, Ipswich, 16 February 1798.

12. *Austen Papers*, p. 122, Eliza de Feuillide to Philadelphia Walter, London, 9 April 1787.

13. *Austen Papers*, p. 129, Philadelphia Walter to James Walter, London, 21 April 1788.

14. It is not possible to date some of the early juvenile pieces very specifically. 'Jack & Alice' does, though, show Jane at her most playful on the subject of her cousin Eliza.

15. *Austen Papers*, p. 133, Eliza de Feuillide to Philadelphia Walter, London, 22 August 1788.

16. *Austen Papers*, p. 138, Eliza de Feuillide to Philadelphia Walter, Paris, 11 February 1789.

17. *Austen Papers*, p. 148, Eliza de Feuillide to Philadelphia Walter, Steventon, 26 October 1792.

18. 'Jack & Alice', MW, p. 13.

19. 'Jack & Alice', MW, p. 15

20. 'Jack & Alice', MW, p. 15.

21. *Austen Papers*, p. 115, Eliza de Feuillide to Philadelphia Walter, Château de Jourdan (Guienne), 17 January 1786.

22. *Austen Papers*, p. 124, Philadelphia Walter to James Walter, Seale, 19 September 1787.

23. *Austen Papers*, p. 149, Eliza de Feuillide to Philadelphia Walter, Steventon, 26 October 1792.

24. *Austen Papers*, p. 125, Philadelphia Walter to James Walter, Seale, 19 September 1787.

25. David Garrick, *Bon Ton: or High Life above Stairs* (London, 1775), act 1, scene 1.

26. Garrick, *Bon Ton*, act 1, scene 1.

27. Hannah Cowley, *Which is the Man?* (5th edn, London, 1785), act 2, scene 1.

28. Cowley, *Which is the Man?*, act 5, scene 1.

29. *Austen Papers*, p. 127, Eliza de Feuillide to Philadelphia Walter, London, 16 November 1787.

30. See *Austen Papers*, p. 126, Philadelphia Walter to James Walter, Seale, 19 September 1787.

31. *Austen Papers*, p. 128, Eliza de Feuillide to Philadelphia Walter, London, 23 November 1787.

32. *The Poetical Register and Repository of Fugitive Poetry*, ii, *1802* (London, 1803), pp. 58–59. See George Holbert Tucker, *Jane Austen the Woman* (London, 1994), p. 91.

33. Samuel Egerton Brydges, *The Autobiography, Times, Opinions and Contemporaries of Sir Egerton Brydges* (London, 1834).

34. Chawton MSS, poem 53.

35. Susannah Centlivre, *The Wonder! A Woman Keeps a Secret* (London, 1781), and David Garrick and John Fletcher, *The Chances* (London, 1773).

36. James Edward Austen-Leigh, *A Memoir of Jane Austen*, ed. R. W. Chapman (2nd edn, London, 1951), p. 27.

37. *Letters*, p. 583, 'Biographical Index'; *Austen Papers*, p. 30, Cassandra Leigh Austen to Susannah Walter, Steventon, 12 December 1773.

38. *Austen Papers*, p. 131, Philadelphia Walter to James Walter, Seale, 23 July 1788.

39. *Austen Papers*, p. 131, Philadelphia Walter to James Walter, Seale, 23 July 1788.

40. *Austen Papers*, p. 148, Eliza de Feuillide to Philadelphia Walter, Seventon, 26 October 1792.

41. *Letters*, p. 68, Jane Austen to Cassandra Austen, Steventon, 3 January 1801.

42. 'The Beautifull Cassandra', MW, p. 45.

43. *Austen Papers*, p. 24, Cassandra Leigh Austen to Susannah Walter, Steventon, 26 August 1770.

44. 'The Beautifull Cassandra', MW, p. 47.

45. 'The Beautifull Cassandra', MW, p. 46.

46. *Letters*, p. 287, Jane Austen to Fanny Knight, London, 30 November 1814.

Notes to Chapter 4: The Good Apprentice

1. *Austen Papers*, p. 130, Philadelphia Walter to James Walter, Seale, 23 July 1788.

2. *Austen Papers*, p. 133, Eliza de Feuillide to Philadelphia Walter, London, 22 August 1788.

3. *Letters*, p. 264, Jane Austen to Cassandra Austen, Chawton, 23 June 1814.

4. [James Austen], *Loiterer*, no. 1, 31 January 1789.

5. [Henry Austen], *Loiterer*, no. 8, 21 March 1789.

6. [James Austen or Jane Austen], *Loiterer*, no. 9, 28 March 1789.

7. *Austen Papers*, pp. 134–35, Philadelphia Hancock to John Woodman, Paris, 5 Febrary 1789; Deirdre Le Faye, *Jane Austen's 'Outlandish Cousin'* (London, 2002), p. 96.

8. [Henry Austen], *Loiterer*, no. 32, 5 September 1789.

9. [Henry Austen], *Loiterer*, no. 32.

10. [Henry Austen], *Loiterer*, no. 48, 26 December 1789.

11. [Henry Austen] *Loiterer*, no. 47, 19 December 1789.

12. [James Austen], *Loiterer*, nos 52 and 53, 23 and 30 January 1790.

13. [James Austen], Loiterer, no. 52.

14. [James Austen], Loiterer, no. 52.

15. *Austen Papers*, p. 130, Philadelphia Walter to James Walter, Seale, 23 July 1788.

16. 'Love and Freindship', MW, p. 105.

17. MW, p. 76.

18. David Garrick, *Bon Ton: or High Life Above Stairs* (London, 1775), act 1, scene 1.

19. 'Love and Freindship', MW, p. 76.

20. Le Faye, 'Outlandish Cousin', p. 100, Eliza de Feuillide to Philadelphia Walter, London, 23 June 1791.

21. *Austen Papers*, p. 140, Eliza de Feuillide to Philadelphia Walter, Margate, 7 January 1791.

22. 'Lesley Castle', MW, p. 110.

23. 'Lesley Castle', MW, p. 119.

24. 'Lesley Castle' MW, p. 119.

25. 'Lesley Castle', MW, p. 113.

26. 'History of England', MW, p. 146.

27. Henry Austen, 'Biographical Notice', NA, pp. 7–8.

28. 'Catharine', MW, p. 194.

29. *Austen Papers*, pp. 66–67, Tysoe Hancock to Philadelphia Hancock, Calcutta, 23 September 1772.

30. *Austen Papers*, p. 325, appendix 2, extract from Philip Dormer Stanhope, *Genuine Memoirs of Asiaticus* (1784).

31. *Austen Papers*, p. 326, appendix 2, extract from Stanhope.

32. 'Catharine', MW, p. 205.

33. 'Catharine', MW, p. 203.

34. *Emma*, p. 300.

35. *Letters*, p. 186, Jane Austen to Cassandra Austen, London, 30 April 1811.

36. Deirdre Le Faye, *Jane Austen: Her Life and Letters. A Family Record* (London, 1989), p. 9, quotes MS by Anna Lefroy.

37. *Austen Papers*, p. 147, Eliza de Feuillide to Philadelphia Walter, London, 16 July 1792.

38. *Austen Papers*, p. 148, Eliza de Feuillide to Philadelphia Walter, Steventon, 26 October 1792.
39. *Austen Papers*, p. 150, Eliza de Feuillide to Philadelphia Walter, Steventon, 26 October 1792.
40. *Austen Papers*, p. 148, Eliza de Feuillide to Philadelphia Walter, Steventon, 26 October 1792.
41. Quoted by B. C. Southam, *Jane Austen's Literary Manuscripts* (Oxford, 1964), p. 36.

Notes to Chapter 5: History

1. *Austen Papers*, p. 323; p. 36.
2. *Austen Papers*, pp. 97–98, John Woodman to Warren Hastings, London, 7 August 1781.
3. 'Lesley Castle', MW, p. 120.
4. *Lady Susan*, MW, p. 303.
5. *Austen Papers*, p. 125, Philadelphia Walter to James Walter, Seale, 19 September 1787.
6. *Lady Susan*, MW, p. 251.
7. *Lady Susan*, MW, p. 313.
8. *Lady Susan*, MW, p. 258.
9. *Victoria County History of Gloucestershire*, vi, pp. 9–10.
10. Quoted in C. H. C. Baker, *The Life and Circumstances of James Brydges* (London, 1949), p. 262.
11. Cf. Baker, *James Brydges*, p. 263, and note for the various versions of this story; also G. E. Cokayne, *The Complete Peerage* (rep. Gloucester, 1982), iii, p. 131.
12. Mary Leigh, MS of Family History of the Leighs of Adlestrop, dated 1788, Stoneleigh Papers, Shakespeare Birthplace Trust, Stratford-upon-Avon, DR/18/.
13. *Letters*, p. 549, 'Biographical Index'.
14. Leigh MS.
15. Leigh MS.
16. Leigh MS.
17. MP, p. 99.
18. Leigh MS.
19. Leigh MS.
20. *Victoria County History of Middlesex*, v, p. 115.
21. Deidre Le Faye, *Jane Austen: Her Life and Letters. A Family Record* (London, 1989), p. 7.

22. Leigh MS.
23. Boyd's Marriage Register for Middlesex 1712.
24. Leigh MS.
25. Leigh MS.
26. Leigh MS.
27. Will of Theophilus Leigh, PROB 11/604, sig. 157; transcription in *A Century of Wills from Jane Austen's Family* (Sydney, 2001).
28. Leigh MS.
29. Boyd's Marriage Register for Middlesex 1728; and Leigh MS.
30. Leigh MS.
31. MP, p. 7.
32. *Letters*, p. 10, Jane Austen to Cassandra Austen, Rowling, 15 September 1796; and p. 57, Jane Austen to Cassandra Austen, Steventon, 8 November 1800.
33. Le Faye, *Family Record*, p. 84, quotes Fanny Caroline Lefroy MS Family History.
34. MW, facing p. 242.
35. *Austen Papers*, p. 330.

Notes to Chapter 6: Love and Art

1. J. A. P. Lefroy, 'Jane Austen's Irish Friend', in *Proceedings of the Huguenot Society of London*, 23 (1979), p. 149.
2. *Letters*, p. 1, Jane Austen to Cassandra Austen, Steventon, 9 January 1796.
3. *Letters*, p. 1, Jane Austen to Cassandra Austen, Steventon, 9 January 1796.
4. *Letters*, p. 1, Jane Austen to Cassandra Austen, Steventon, 9 January 1796.
5. *Letters*, p. 4, Jane Austen to Cassandra Austen, Steventon, 14 January 1796.
6. *Letters*, p. 1, Jane Austen to Cassandra Austen, Steventon, 9 January 1796.
7. *Letters*, p. 2, Jane Austen to Cassandra Austen, Steventon, 9 January 1796.
8. Henry Fielding, *Tom Jones*, book 17, chapter 9.
9. *Letters*, p. 3, Jane Austen to Cassandra Austen, Steventon, 14 January 1796.
10. *Letters*, p. 4, Jane Austen to Cassandra Austen, Steventon, 14 January 1796.
11. *Letters*, p. 4, Jane Austen to Cassandra Austen, Steventon, 14 January 1796.
12. *Letters*, p. 1, Jane Austen to Cassandra Austen, Steventon, 9 January 1796.
13. *Letters*, p. 2, Jane Austen to Cassandra Austen, Steventon, 9 January 1796.
14. *Letters*, p. 355, letter 3, note 2. Le Faye speculates the Austens probably stayed with Langlois.
15. *Letters*, p. 5, Jane Austen to Cassandra Austen, London, 23 August 1796.
16. Samuel Egerton Brydges, *The Autobiography, Times, Opinions and Contemporaries of Sir Egerton Brydges* (London, 1834), p. 40.

17. Lefroy, 'Irish Friend', p. 149

18. Lefroy, 'Irish Friend', p. 149.

19. Lefroy, 'Irish Friend', p. 150.

20. *Letters*, p. 6, Jane Austen to Cassandra Austen, Rowling, 1 Sepember 1796.

21. *Letters*, p. 2, Jane Austen to Cassandra Austen, Steventon, 9 January 1796.

22. *Letters*, p. 12, Jane Austen to Cassandra Austen, Rowling, 18 September 1796.

23. *Austen Papers*, p. 155, Eliza de Feuillide to Philadelphia Walter, London, 7 November 1796.

24. The editor of Eliza's letters seems to misinterpret her use of the word 'late'. He takes her to mean that by early November Mary was no longer Henry's fiancée, but in the eighteenth century the word 'late' was also used simply to mean 'recent'. Jane Austen sometimes uses it in that sense, as when she wrote to Cassandra: 'You will have had such late accounts from this place as (I hope) to prevent your expecting a Letter from me immediately.'

25. A character called Tom Bennet is mentioned in book 4, chapter 8 of Fielding's novel – another Tom in addition to Jones and Lefroy.

26. Howe, M. A. DeWolfe, 'A Jane Austen Letter, with Other "Janeana" from an Old Book of Autographs', *Yale Review* (January 1926), pp. 321–22.

27. PP, p. 189.

28. NA, p. 239.

29. *Letters*, p. 201, Jane Austen to Cassandra Austen, Chawton, 29 January 1813.

30. *Letters*, p. 1, Jane Austen to Cassandra Austen, Steventon, 9 January 1796.

31. *Letters*, p. 3, Jane Austen to Cassandra Austen,, Steventon, 14 January 1796.

32. *Austen Papers*, p. 228, Cassandra Leigh Austen to Mary Lloyd, Steventon, 30 November 1796.

33. *Austen Papers*, p. 157, Eliza de Feuillide to Philadelphia Walter, London, 30 December 1796.

34. *Austen Papers*, pp. 156–57, Eliza de Feuillide to Philadelphia Walter, London, 13 December 1796.

35. *Austen Papers*, p. 168, Eliza de Feuillide to Warren Hastings, London, 28 December 1797.

36. *Austen Papers*, p. 159, Eliza de Feuillide to Philadelphia Walter, London(?), 3 May 1797.

37. *Austen Papers*, p. 159, Eliza de Feuillide to Philadelphia Walter, London(?), 3 May 1797.

38. *Austen Papers*, p. 166, Eliza de Feuillide to Philadelphia Walter, Lowestoft, 22 September 1797.

39. *Austen Papers*, p. 166, Eliza de Feuillide to Philadelphia Walter, Lowestoft, 22 September 1797.

40. It appears in book 8, chapter 11 of *Tom Jones*.

41. *Austen Papers*, pp. 229–30, Edward Austen to Catherine Knight, Rowling, 23 November 1797.

42. *Austen Papers*, p. 231, Catherine Knight to Edward Austen, Godmersham, 24 November 1797.

43. *Austen Papers*, p. 231, Catherine Knight to Edward Austen, Godmersham, 24 November 1797.

44. *Letters*, p. 19, Jane Austen to Cassandra Austen, Steventon, 17 November 1798.

45. Deirdre Le Faye, 'Tom Lefroy and Jane Austen', *Jane Austen Society Collected Reports, 1976–1985*, pp. 336–38, quotes text of letter written by Anna Austen Lefroy to Emma Austen-Leigh, Reading, 24 May 1869.

46. Deirdre Le Faye, *Jane Austen: Her Life and Letters. A Family Record* (London, 1989), p. 87, quotes letter from Tom Lefroy's nephew to James Edward Austen-Leigh.

47. *Letters*, p. 286, Jane Austen to Fanny Knight, London, 30 November 1814.

48. *Letters*, p. 19, Jane Austen to Cassandra Austen, Steventon, 17 November 1798.

49. *Letters*, p. 19, Jane Austen to Cassandra Austen, Steventon, 17 November 1798.

50. *Letters*, p. 281, Jane Austen to Fanny Knight, Chawton, 18 November 1814.

51. James Edward Austen-Leigh, *A Memoir of Jane Austen*, ed. R. W. Chapman (2nd edn, Oxford, 1951), p. 17.

52. *Letters*, p. 5, Jane Austen to Cassandra Austen, Rowling, 1 September 1796.

53. *Letters*, p. 33, Jane Austen to Cassandra Austen, Steventon, 8 January 1799.

54. *Letters*, p. 38, Jane Austen to Cassandra Austen, Steventon, 21 January 1799.

55. *Letters*, p. 17, Jane Austen to Cassandra Austen, Steventon, 27 October 1798.

56. *Letters*, pp. 16–17, Jane Austen to Cassandra Austen, Steventon, 27 October 1798.

57. *Letters*, p. 20, Jane Austen to Cassandra Austen, Steventon, 17 November 1798.

58. *Letters*, p. 29, Jane Austen to Cassandra Austen, Steventon, 24 December 1798.

59. *Letters*, p. 38, Jane Austen to Cassandra Austen, Steventon, 21 January 1799.

60. See Geoffrey Gorer, 'Poor Honey: Some Notes on Jane Austen and her Mother', *London Magazine*, 4 (August 1957), pp. 35–48. Gorer was the first

to look closely at Jane Austen's relationship with her mother, and also at the economic realities of Jane Austen's life at Steventon.

61. *Letters*, p. 26, Jane Austen to Cassandra Austen, Steventon, 18 December 1798.
62. *Letters*, p. 29, Jane Austen to Cassandra Austen, Steventon, 26 December 1798.
63. *Letters*, p. 32, Jane Austen to Cassandra Austen, Steventon, 28 December 1798.
64. *Letters*, p. 34, Jane Austen to Cassandra Austen, Steventon, 8 January 1799.
65. *Letters*, pp. 37–38, Jane Austen to Cassandra Austen, Steventon, 21 January 1799. This is the same letter in which Jane mentions that Charles appeared to more advantage at Steventon among people he knew and felt at ease with than he had at Godmersham.
66. *Letters*, p. 191, Jane Austen to Cassandra Austen, Chawton, 31 May 1811.
67. *Letters*, p. 37, Jane Austen to Cassandra Austen, Steventon, 21 January 1799.
68. *Letters*, p. 37, Jane Austen to Cassandra Austen, Steventon, 21 January 1799.
69. *Letters*, pp. 29–30, Jane Austen to Cassandra Austen, Steventon, 24 December 1798.
70. *Letters*, p. 35, Jane Austen to Cassandra Austen, Steventon, 8 January 1799.
71. MW, facing p. 242.
72. Deirdre Le Faye, *Jane Austen's 'Outlandish Cousin'* (London, 2002), p. 127, Eliza de Feuillide to Philadelphia Walter, London, 7 November 1796.
73. Fielding mentions the name Allen in book 13, chapter 1 of *Tom Jones*.
74. *Letters*, p. 39, Jane Austen to Cassandra Austen, Steventon, 21 January 1799.

Notes to Chapter 7: Place

1. E, p. 117.
2. *Letters*, p. 47, Jane Austen to Cassandra Austen, Bath, 19 June 1799.
3. *Letters*, p. 45, Jane Austen to Cassandra Austen, Bath, 11 June 1799.
4. *Letters*, p. 47, Jane Austen to Cassandra Austen, Bath, 19 June 1799.
5. *Letters*, p. 41, Jane Austen to Cassandra Austen, Bath, 17 May 1799.
6. *Austen Papers*, p. 124, Philadelphia Walter to James Walter, London, 19 September 1787.
7. *Letters*, p. 44, Jane Austen to Cassandra Austen, Bath, 11 June 1799.
8. *Letters*, p. 82, Jane Austen to Cassandra Austen, Bath, 5 May 1801.
9. *Letters*, p. 103, Jane Austen to Cassandra Austen, Bath, 21 April 1805.
10. *Letters*, p. 42, Jane Austen to Cassandra Austen, Bath, 2 June 1799.
11. *Letters*, p. 44, Jane Austen to Cassandra Austen, Bath, 11 June 1799.

12. *Letters*, pp. 47–48, Jane Austen to Cassandra Austen, Bath, 19 June 1799.

13. *Letters*, p. 120, Jane Austen to Cassandra Austen, Southampton, 8 February 1807.

14. *Letters*, p. 45, Jane Austen to Cassandra Austen, Bath, 11 June 1799.

15. *Letters*, pp. 46–47, Jane Austen to Cassandra Austen, Bath, 19 June 1799.

16. *Letters*, p. 47, Jane Austen to Cassandra Austen, Bath, 19 June 1799.

17. *Austen Papers*, p. 194, Jane Leigh-Perrot to Mountague Cholmeley, Ilchester, 10 November 1799.

18. *Letters*, p. 154, Jane Austen to Cassandra Austen, Southampton, 20 November 1808.

19. *Austen Papers*, p. 210, Jane Leigh-Perrot's speech to the judge and jury, related in her letter to Mountague Cholmeley, Bath, 1 April 1800.

20. *Austen Papers*, p. 210, Jane Leigh-Perrot's speech to the judge and jury, related in her letter to Mountague Cholmeley, Bath, 1 April 1800.

21. *Austen Papers*, p. 207, Jane Leigh-Perrot to Mountague Cholmeley, Ilchester, 6 March 1800.

22. *Austen Papers*, p. 209, Jane Leigh-Perrot to Mountague Cholmeley, Bath, 1 April 1800.

23. *Letters*, p. 67, Jane Austen to Cassandra Austen, Steventon, 3 January 1801.

24. *Letters*, p. 49, Jane Austen to Cassandra Austen, Steventon, 28 October 1800.

25. *Letters*, p. 50, Jane Austen to Cassandra Austen, Steventon, 25 October 1800.

26. *Letters*, p. 55, Jane Austen to Cassandra Austen, Steventon, 8 November 1800.

27. *Letters*, p. 55, Jane Austen to Cassandra Austen, Steventon, 8 November 1800.

28. *Letters*, p. 49, Jane Austen to Cassandra Austen, Steventon, 25 October 1800.

29. *Letters*, p. 64, Jane Austen to Cassandra Austen, Ibthorpe, 30 November 1800.

30. *Letters*, p. 64, Jane Austen to Cassandra Austen, Ibthorpe, 30 November 1800.

31. *Letters*, p. 65, Jane Austen to Cassandra Austen, Ibthorpe, 30 November 1800.

32. *Sanditon*, MW, p. 402.

33. R. W. Chapman, *Facts and Problems* (Oxford, 1948), p. 46; Deirdre Le Faye, *Jane Austen: Her Life and Letters. A Family Record* (London, 1989), p. 113.

34. *Letters*, p. 73, Jane Austen to Cassandra Austen, Steventon, 14 January 1801.

35. *Letters*, p. 245, Jane Austen to Cassandra Austen, Godmersham, 26 October 1813.
36. *Letters*, p. 69, Jane Austen to Cassandra Austen, Steventon, 8 January 1801.
37. *Letters*, p. 68, Jane Austen to Cassandra Austen, Steventon, 3 January 1801.
38. *Letters*, pp. 68–69, Jane Austen to Cassandra Austen, Steventon, 3 January 1801.
39. *Letters*, p. 73, Jane Austen to Cassandra Austen, Steventon, 14 January 1801.
40. *Letters*, p. 73, Jane Austen to Cassandra Austen, Steventon, 14 January 1801.
41. *Letters*, pp. 71–72, Jane Austen to Cassandra Austen, Steventon, 8 January 1801.
42. *Letters*, p. 79, Jane Austen to Cassandra Austen, Steventon, 25 January 1801.
43. *Letters*, p. 71, Jane Austen to Cassandra Austen, Steventon, 8 January 1801.
44. *Letters*, p. 78, Jane Austen to Cassandra Austen, Steventon, 25 January 1801.
45. *Letters*, p. 80, Jane Austen to Cassandra Austen, Manydown, 11 February 1801.
46. *Letters*, p. 67, Jane Austen to Cassandra Austen, Steventon, 3 January 1801.
47. *Letters*, p. 86, Jane Austen to Cassandra Austen, Bath, 12 May 1801.
48. *Letters*, p. 87, Jane Austen to Cassandra Austen, Bath, 21 May 1801.
49. *Letters*, p. 88, Jane Austen to Cassandra Austen, Bath, 21 May 1801.

Notes to Chapter 8: Ways of Escape

1. Deirdre Le Faye, *Jane Austen: Her Life and Letters. A Family Record* (London, 1989), p. 122.
2. *Letters*, p. 3, Jane Austen to Cassandra Austen, Steventon, 14 January 1796.
3. *Letters*, p. 22, Jane Austen to Cassandra Austen, Steventon, 25 November 1798.
4. Samuel Egerton Brydges, *The Autobiography, Times, Opinions and Contemporaries of Sir Egerton Brydges* (London, 1834), p. 40.
5. Brydges, *Autobiography*, p. 40.
6. Brydges, *Autobiography*, p. 41.
7. In book 8, chapter 12, of *Tom Jones*.
8. *The Watsons*, MW, pp. 361–62.
9. *Letters*, p. 97, Jane Austen to Frank Austen, Bath, 22 January 1805.
10. *Letters*, p. 96, Jane Austen to Frank Austen, Bath, 21 January 1805.
11. *Austen Papers*, p. 233, Henry Austen to Frank Austen, Bath, 27 January 1805.

12. *Austen Papers*, p. 235, Henry Austen to Frank Austen, Bath, 28 January 1805.
13. *Letters*, p. 100, Jane Austen to Cassandra Austen, Bath, 8 April 1805.
14. *Letters*, p. 99, Jane Austen to Cassandra Austen, Bath, 8 April 1805.
15. *Letters*, p. 82, Jane Austen to Cassandra Austen, Bath, 5 May 1801.
16. See Robin Vick, 'Cousins in Bath', in *Jane Austen Society Collected Reports, 1986–1995*, pp. 394–99.
17. *Letters*, p. 100, Jane Austen to Cassandra Austen, Bath, 8 April 1805.
18. *Letters*, p. 104, Jane Austen to Cassandra Austen, Bath, 21 April 1805.
19. *Letters*, p. 104, Jane Austen to Cassandra Austen, Bath, 21 April 1805.
20. *Letters*, p. 137–38, Jane Austen to Cassandra Austen, Godmersham, 30 June 1808.
21. *Letters*, p. 107, Jane Austen to Cassandra Austen, Godmersham, 24 August 1805.
22. *Letters*, p. 110, Jane Austen to Cassandra Austen, Goodnestone, 27 August 1805.
23. *Letters*, p. 145, Jane Austen to Cassandra Austen, Southampton, 7 October 1808.
24. MP, p. 315.
25. MP, p. 353.
26. *Austen Papers*, p. 237, Cassandra Leigh Austen to Mary Lloyd, Bath, 10 April 1806.

Notes to Chapter 9: Money

1. *Letters*, p. 138, Jane Austen to Cassandra Austen, Godmersham, 30 June 1808.
2. *Austen Papers*, p. 240, James Leigh-Perrot to Jane Leigh-Perrot, London, 4 July 1806.
3. *Austen Papers*, p. 241, James Leigh-Perrot to Jane Leigh-Perrot, London, 4 July 1806.
4. *Austen Papers*, p. 241, James Leigh-Perrot to Jane Leigh-Perrot, London, 5 July 1806.
5. *Austen Papers*, p. 243, James Leigh-Perrot to Jane Leigh-Perrot, London, 5 July 1806.
6. *Austen Papers*, pp. 243–44, James Leigh-Perrot to Jane Leigh-Perrot, London, 5 July 1806.
7. *Austen Papers*, p. 245, Cassandra Austen to Mary Lloyd, Stoneleigh, 13 August 1806.
8. *Letters*, p. 114, Jane Austen to Cassandra Austen, Southampton, 7 January 1807.

9. *Letters*, p. 121, Jane Austen to Cassandra Austen, Southampton, 8 February 1807.

10. *Letters*, p. 119, Jane Austen to Cassandra Austen, Southampton, 8 February 1807.

11. *Letters*, p. 117, Jane Austen to Cassandra Austen, Southampton, 7 January 1807.

12. *Letters*, p. 115, Jane Austen to Cassandra Austen, Southampton, 7 January 1807.

13. *Letters*, p. 119, Jane Austen to Cassandra Austen, Southampton, 8 February 1807.

14. *Letters*, p. 119, Jane Austen to Cassandra Austen, Southampton, 8 February 1807.

15. *Letters*, p. 120, Jane Austen to Cassandra Austen, Southampton, 8 February 1807.

16. *Letters*, p. 117, Jane Austen to Cassandra Austen, Southampton, 7 January 1807.

17. *Letters*, p. 117, Jane Austen to Cassandra Austen, Southampton, 7 January 1807.

18. *Letters*, p. 116, Jane Austen to Cassandra Austen, Southampton, 7 January 1807.

19. *Letters*, p. 116, Jane Austen to Cassandra Austen, Southampton, 7 January 1807.

20. *Letters*, p. 116, Jane Austen to Cassandra Austen, Southampton, 7 January 1807.

21. *Letters*, p. 122, Jane Austen to Cassandra Austen, Southampton, 20 February 1807.

22. *Letters*, p. 126, Jane Austen to Cassandra Austen, Godmersham, 15 June 1808.

23. *Letters*, p. 133, Jane Austen to Cassandra Austen, Godmersham, 26 June 1808.

24. *Letters*, p. 138, Jane Austen to Cassandra Austen, Godmersham, 30 June 1808.

25. *Letters*, p. 134, Jane Austen to Cassandra Austen, Godmersham, 26 June 1808.

26. *Letters*, p. 138, Jane Austen to Cassandra Austen, Godmersham, 30 June 1808.

27. *Letters*, p. 163, Jane Austen to Cassandra Austen, Southampton, 10 January 1809.

28. *Letters*, p. 126, Jane Austen to Cassandra Austen, Godmersham, 15 June 1808.

29. *Letters*, p. 133, Jane Austen to Cassandra Austen, Godmersham, 26 June 1808.

30. *Letters*, p. 142, Jane Austen to Cassandra Austen, Southampton, 1 October 1808.

31. *Letters*, p. 151, Jane Austen to Cassandra Austen, Southampton, 24 October 1808.

32. *Letters*, p. 149, Jane Austen to Cassandra Austen, Southampton, 15 October 1808.

33. *Letters*, p. 144, Jane Austen to Cassandra Austen, Southampton, 7 October 1808.

34. *Letters*, p. 148, Jane Austen to Cassandra Austen, Southampton, 15 October 1808.

35. *Letters*, p. 40, Jane Austen to Cassandra Austen, Bath, 17 May 1799.

36. *Letters*, p. 54, Jane Austen to Cassandra Austen, Steventon, 1 November 1800.

37. *Letters*, p. 61, Jane Austen to Cassandra Austen, Steventon, 20 November 1800.

38. *Letters*, p. 150, Jane Austen to Cassandra Austen, Southampton, 24 October 1808.

39. *Letters*, p. 150, Jane Austen to Cassandra Austen, Southampton, 24 October 1808.

40. *Letters*, p. 150, Jane Austen to Cassandra Austen, Southampton, 24 October 1808.

41. *Letters*, p. 17, Jane Austen to Cassandra Austen, Steventon, 27 October 1798.

42. *Letters*, p. 151, Jane Austen to Cassandra Austen, Southampton, 24 October 1808.

43. *Letters*, p. 152, Jane Austen to Cassandra Austen, Southampton, 24 October 1808.

44. *Letters*, p. 151, Jane Austen to Cassandra Austen, Southampton, 24 October 1808.

45. *Letters*, p. 173, Jane Austen to Cassandra Austen, Southampton, 30 January 1809.

46. *Letters*, p. 154, Jane Austen to Cassandra Austen, Southampton, 20 November 1808.

47. *Letters*, p. 154, Jane Austen to Cassandra Austen, Southampton, 20 November 1808.

48. *Letters*, p. 154, Jane Austen to Cassandra Austen, Southampton, 20 November 1808.

49. Thomas Leigh was the mentally deficient brother of Mrs Austen and James

Leigh-Perrot. In the Hon. Mary Leigh's will she provided an annuity of £200 for the support of her cousin Thomas Leigh. See *A Century of Wills from Jane Austen's Family* (Sydney, 2001). James Austen, it appears, was in 1818 in charge of this money and was entitled to keep for himself whatever was not needed by his uncle. Thomas Leigh died in 1821.

50. *Austen Papers*, p. 258, James Austen to James Edward Austen, Steventon, 28 April 1818.

51. *Austen Papers*, p. 259, James Edward Austen to James Austen, Oxford, 1 May 1818.

52. *Letters*, p. 158, Jane Austen to Cassandra Austen, Southampton, 9 December 1808.

53. *Letters*, p. 164, Jane Austen to Cassandra Austen, Southampton, 10 January 1809.

54. *Letters*, p. 216, Jane Austen to Frank Austen, Chawton, 3 July 1813.

55. *Letters*, p. 157, Jane Austen to Cassandra Austen, Southampton, 9 December 1808.

56. *Letters*, pp. 174–75, Jane Austen to Crosby and Co. Southampton, 5 April 1809.

57. Henry Austen, 'Biographical Notice', NA, p. 6.

Notes to Chapter 10: Work

1. 'Author's Note', NA, p. 12.

2. Henry Austen, 'Biographical Notice', NA, p. 6.

3. Henry Austen, 'Biographical Notice', NA, p. 6.

4. Henry Fielding, *Tom Jones*, book 13, chapter 8.

5. James Edward Austen-Leigh, *A Memoir of Jane Austen*, ed. R. W. Chapman (2nd edn, London, 1951), p. 188.

6. *Letters*, p. 132, Jane Austen to Cassandra Austen, Godmersham, 20 June 1808.

7. *Letters*, p. 180, Jane Austen to Cassandra Austen, London, 18 April 1811.

8. *Letters*, p. 179, Jane Austen to Cassandra Austen, London, 18 April 1811.

9. *Letters*, pp. 180–81, Jane Austen to Cassandra Austen, London, 18 April 1811.

10. *Letters*, pp. 182–83, Jane Austen to Cassandra Austen, London, 25 April 1811.

11. *Letters*, p. 182, Jane Austen to Cassandra Austen, London, 25 April 1811.

12. *Letters*, p. 186, Jane Austen to Cassandra Austen, London, 30 April 1811.

13. *Austen Papers*, p. 248, Cassandra Austen to Philadelphia Walter, Chawton, 18 August 1811.

14. *Letters*, p. 202, Jane Austen to Cassandra Austen, Chawton, 29 January 1813.

15. *Letters*, p. 161, Jane Austen to Cassandra Austen, Southampton, 27 December, 1808.

16. *Letters*, p. 235, Jane Austen to Cassandra Austen, Godmersham, 11 October 1813.

17. *Letters*, p. 274, Jane Austen to Martha Lloyd, London, 2 September 1814.

18. *Letters*, p. 268, Jane Austen to Anna Austen, Chawton, 10 August 1814.

19. *Letters*, p. 319, Jane Austen to Cassandra Austen, Chawton, 4 September 1816.

20. *Letters*, p. 320, Jane Austen to Cassandra Austen, Chawton, 8 September 1816.

21. *Letters*, p. 278, Jane Austen to Anna Austen, Chawton, 28 September 1814.

22. *Letters*, p. 291, Jane Austen to Cassandra Austen, London, 17 October 1815.

23. Deirdre Le Faye, *Jane Austen: Her Life and Letters. A Family Record* (London, 1989), p. 168.

24. *Letters*, p. 197, Jane Austen to Martha Lloyd, Chawton, 29 November 1812.

25. *Letters*, p. 201, Jane Austen to Cassandra Austen, Chawton, 29 January 1813.

26. *Letters*, p. 201, Jane Austen to Cassandra Austen, Chawton, 29 January 1813.

27. *Letters*, p. 203, Jane Austen to Cassandra Austen, Chawton, 4 February 1813.

28. *Letters*, p. 217, Jane Austen to Frank Austen, Chawton, 3 July 1813.

29. *Letters*, pp. 212–13, Jane Austen to Cassandra Austen, London, 24 May 1813.

30. *Letters*, p. 218, Jane Austen to Cassandra Austen, London, 15 September 1813.

31. *Letters*, p. 231, Jane Austen to Frank Austen, Godmersham, 25 September 1813.

32. *Letters*, p. 203, Jane Austen to Cassandra Austen, Chawton, 4 February 1813.

33. *Letters*, p. 231, Jane Austen to Frank Austen, Godmersham, 25 September 1813.

34. *Letters*, p. 231, Jane Austen to Frank Austen, Godmersham, 25 September 1813.

35. *Letters*, p. 250, Jane Austen to Cassandra Austen, Godmersham, 3 November 1813. D'Arblay was the son of the novelist Fanny Burney.

36. Deirdre Le Faye, *Jane Austen's 'Outlandish Cousin'* (London, 2002), pp. 132–33, Eliza de Feuillide to Philadelphia Walter, London, 13 December 1796.

37. *Letters*, p. 277, Jane Austen to Anna Austen, Chawton, 28 September 1814.

38. *Letters*, pp. 215–16, Jane Austen to Frank Austen, Chawton, 3 July 1813.
39. *Letters*, pp. 213–14, Jane Austen to Cassandra Austen, London, 24 May 1813.
40. MP, p. 297.
41. *Letters*, p. 258, Jane Austen to Cassandra Austen, London, 5 March 1814.
42. *Letters*, p. 261, Jane Austen to Cassandra Austen, London, 9 March 1814.
43. *Letters*, p. 276, Jane Austen to Anna Austen, Chawton, 28 September 1814.
44. *Letters*, p. 137, Jane Austen to Cassandra Austen, Godmersham, 30 June 1808.
45. *Letters*, p. 134, Jane Austen to Cassandra Austen, Godmersham, 26 June 1808.
46. *Letters*, p. 184, Jane Austen to Cassandra Austen, London, 25 April 1811.
47. *Letters*, p. 184, Jane Austen to Cassandra Austen, London, 25 April 1811.
48. *Letters*, p. 193, Jane Austen to Cassandra Austen, Chawton, 6 June 1811.
49. *Letters*, p. 193, Jane Austen to Cassandra Austen, London, 6 June 1811.
50. *Letters*, p. 232, Jane Austen to Frank Austen, Godmersham, 25 September 1813.
51. *Letters*, p. 232, Jane Austen to Frank Austen, Godmersham, 25 September 1813.
52. *Letters*, pp. 231–32, Jane Austen to Frank Austen, Godmersham, 25 September 1813.
53. *Letters*, p. 225, Jane Austen to Cassandra Austen, Godmersham, 23 September 1813.
54. *Letters*, p. 246, Jane Austen to Cassandra Austen, Godmersham, 26 October 1813.
55. *Letters*, p. 246, Jane Austen to Cassandra Austen, Godmersham, 26 October 1813.
56. *Letters*, p. 246, Jane Austen to Cassandra Austen, Godmersham, 26 October 1813.
57. *Letters*, p. 196, Jane Austen to Martha Lloyd, Chawton, 29 November 1812.
58. *Letters*, p. 230, Jane Austen to Frank Austen, Godmersham, 25 September 1813.
59. *Letters*, p. 234, Jane Austen to Cassandra Austen, Godmersham, 11 October. 1813.
60. *Letters*, p. 230, Jane Austen to Frank Austen, Godmersham, 25 September 1813.
61. *Letters*, p. 227, Jane Austen to Cassandra Austen, Godmersham, 23 September 1813.
62. *Letters*, p. 227, Jane Austen to Cassandra Austen, Godmersham, 23 September 1813.

63. *Letters*, p. 238, Jane Austen to Cassandra Austen, Godmersham, 14 October 1813.
64. *Letters*, p. 216, Jane Austen to Frank Austen, Chawton, 3 July 1813.
65. *Letters*, p. 216, Jane Austen to Frank Austen, Chawton, 3 July 1813.
66. *Letters*, p. 216, Jane Austen to Frank Austen, Chawton, 3 July 1813.
67. *Letters*, p. 238, Jane Austen to Cassandra Austen, Godmersham, 14 October 1813.
68. *Letters*, p. 234, Jane Austen to Cassandra Austen, Godmersham, 11 October 1813.
69. *Letters*, p. 251, Jane Austen to Cassandra Austen, Godmersham, 6 November 1813.
70. *Letters*, p. 245, Jane Austen to Cassandra Austen, Godmersham, 26 October 1813.
71. *Letters*, p. 249, Jane Austen to Cassandra Austen, Godmersham, 3 November 1813.
72. *Letters*, p. 251, Jane Austen to Cassandra Austen, Godmersham, 6 November 1813.
73. *Letters*, p. 239, Jane Austen to Cassandra Austen, Godmersham, 14 October 1813.

Notes to Chapter 11: The World

1. *Letters*, p. 271, Jane Austen to Cassandra Austen, London, 23 August 1814.
2. *Letters*, p. 277, Jane Austen to Anna Austen, Chawton, 28 September 1814.
3. *Letters*, p. 277, Jane Austen to Anna Austen, Chawton, 28 September 1814.
4. *Letters*, p. 277, Jane Austen to Anna Austen, Chawton, 28 September 1814.
5. *Letters*, p. 267, Jane Austen to Anna Austen, ?Chawton, ?mid July 1814.
6. *Letters*, p. 269, Jane Austen to Anna Austen, Chawton, 10 August 1814.
7. *Letters*, p. 268, Jane Austen to Anna Austen, Chawton, 10 August 1814. Le Faye reads the last word 'indeed', whereas in his edition Chapman suggests 'instead'.
8. *Letters*, p. 268, Jane Austen to Anna Austen, Chawton, 10 August 1814.
9. *Letters*, p. 332, Jane Austen to Fanny Knight, Chawton, 13 March 1817.
10. See P, p. 169.
11. *Letters*, p. 231, Jane Austen to Frank Austen, Godmersham, 25 September 1813.
12. *Letters*, p. 277, Jane Austen to Anna Austen, Chawton, 28 September 1814.
13. *Letters*, pp. 328–29, Jane Austen to Fanny Knight, Chawton, 20 February 1817.

14. *Letters*, p. 226, Jane Austen to Cassandra Austen, Godmersham, 23 September 1813.
15. *Letters*, p. 280, Jane Austen to Fanny Knight, Chawton, 20 November 1814.
16. *Letters*, p. 279, Jane Austen to Fanny Knight, Chawton, 20 November 1814.
17. *Letters*, p. 279, Jane Austen to Fanny Knight, Chawton, 20 November 1814.
18. *Letters*, p. 233, Jane Austen to Cassandra Austen, Godmersham, 11 October 1813.
19. *Letters*, p. 280, Jane Austen to Fanny Knight, Chawton, 18 November 1814.
20. *Letters*, p. 280, Jane Austen to Fanny Knight, Chawton, 18 November 1814.
21. *Letters*, p. 280, Jane Austen to Fanny Knight, Chawton, 18 November 1814.
22. *Letters*, p. 286, Jane Austen to Fanny Knight, London, 30 November 1814.
23. *Letters*, p. 282, Jane Austen to Fanny Knight, Chawton, 18 November 1814.
24. *Letters*, p. 285, Jane Austen to Fanny Knight, London, 30 November 1814.
25. *Letters*, p. 286, Jane Austen to Fanny Knight, London, 30 November 1814.
26. *Letters*, p. 286, Jane Austen to Fanny Knight, London, 30 November 1814.
27. *Letters*, p. 281, Jane Austen to Fanny Knight, Chawton, 18 November 1814.
28. *Letters*, p. 281, Jane Austen to Fanny Knight, Chawton, 18 November 1814.
29. See *Letters*, p. 56, Jane Austen to Cassandra Austen, Steventon, 8 November 1800.
30. *Letters*, p. 283, Jane Austen to Anna Austen, ?London, 29 November 1814.
31. *Letters*, p. 285, Jane Austen to Fanny Knight, London, 30 November 1814.
32. *Letters*, p. 285, Jane Austen to Fanny Knight, London, 30 November 1814.
33. *Letters*, p. 284, Jane Austen to Anna Lefroy, London, 30 November 1814.
34. *Letters*, p. 284, Jane Austen to Anna Lefroy, London, 30 November 1814.
35. *Letters*, p. 289, Jane Austen to Anna Lefroy, ?between February–July 1815.
36. *Letters*, p. 325, Jane Austen to Caroline Austen, Chawton, 23 January 1817.
37. *Letters*, p. 336, Jane Austen to Fanny Knight, Chawton, 23 March 1817.
38. See John Wiltshire, *Jane Austen and the Body* (Cambridge, 1992).
39. *Letters*, p. 291, Jane Austen to Anna Lefroy, Chawton, 29 September 1815.
40. *Letters*, p. 332, Jane Austen to Fanny Knight, Chawton, 13 March 1817.
41. *Letters*, p. 291, Jane Austen to Cassandra Austen, London, 17 October 1815.
42. *Letters*, p. 292, Jane Austen to Cassandra Austen, London, 17 October 1815.
43. T. A. B. Corley, 'Jane Austen and her Brother Henry's Bank Failure, 1815–16', *Jane Austen Society Annual Report*, 1998, pp. 12, 23.
44. *Letters*, p. 299, Jane Austen to Cassandra Austen, London, 24 November 1815.
45. *Letters*, p. 301, Jane Austen to Cassandra Austen, London, 26 November 1815.
46. *Letters*, p. 292, Jane Austen to Cassandra Austen, London, 17 October 1815.

47. *Letters*, p. 298, Jane Austen to Cassandra Austen, London, 24 November 1815.
48. *Letters*, p. 298, Jane Austen to Cassandra Austen, London, 24 November 1815.
49. *Letters*, p. 300, Jane Austen to Cassandra Austen, London, 24 November 1815.
50. *Letters*, p. 301, Jane Austen to Cassandra Austen, London, 26 November 1815.
51. *Letters*, p. 303, Jane Austen to Cassandra Austen, London, 2 December 1815.
52. Winifred Watson, 'The Austens' London Doctor', in *Jane Austen Society Collected Reports, 1949–1965*, pp. 194–97.
53. E, p. 117.
54. E, p. 448.
55. *Letters*, p. 308, Countess of Morley to Jane Austen, Saltram, 27 December 1815.
56. *Letters*, p. 309, Jane Austen to the Countess of Morley, 31 December 1815.

Notes to Chapter 12: The Body

1. Jane Leigh-Perrot to James Austen, 31 January 1819, Hampshire Record Office, 23M93/60/1/7.
2. P, p. 252.
3. P, p. 30.
4. *Letters*, p. 337, Jane Austen to Fanny Knight, Chawton, 23 March 1817.
5. *Letters*, p. 318, Jane Austen to Cassandra Austen, Chawton, 4 September 1816.
6. *Letters*, p. 321, Jane Austen to Cassandra Austen, Chawton, 8 September 1816.
7. *Letters*, p. 320, Jane Austen to Cassandra Austen, Chawton, 8 September. 1816.
8. *Letters*, p. 323, Jane Austen to James Edward Austen, Chawton, 16 December 1816.
9. *Letters*, p. 323, Jane Austen to James Edward Austen, Chawton, 16 December 1816.
10. *Letters*, pp. 322–23, Jane Austen to James Edward Austen, Chawton, 16 December 1816.
11. *Letters*, p. 148, Jane Austen to Cassandra Austen, Southampton, 15 October 1808.
12. *Letters*, p. 318, Jane Austen to Cassandra Austen, ?Chawton, 4 September 1816.

13. *Letters*, p. 327, Jane Austen to Alethea Bigg, Chawton, 24 January 1817.

14. *Letters*, p. 319, Jane Austen to Cassandra Austen, Chawton, 4 September 1816.

15. *Letters*, p. 323, Jane Austen to James Edward Austen, Chawton, 16 December 1816.

16. *Letters*, p. 326, Jane Austen to Caroline Austen, Chawton, 23 January 1817.

17. *Letters*, p. 326, Jane Austen to Alethea Bigg, Chawton, 24 January 1817.

18. *Letters*, p. 327, Jane Austen to Alethea Bigg, Chawton, 24 January 1817.

19. *Letters*, p. 330, Jane Austen to Fanny Knight, Chawton, 20 February 1817.

20. MP, p. 473.

21. [James Austen], *Loiterer*, no. 29, 15 August 1789.

22. *Letters*, p. 332, Jane Austen to Fanny Knight, Chawton, 13 March 1817.

23. *Letters*, p. 329, Jane Austen to Fanny Knight, Chawton, 21 February 1817.

24. *Letters*, p. 332, Jane Austen to Fanny Knight, Chawton, 13 March 1817.

25. *Sanditon*, MW, p. 402.

26. *Sanditon*, MW, pp. 363–64.

27. *Sanditon*, MW, p. 426.

28. *Sanditon*, MW, p. 411.

29. *Sanditon*, MW, p. 394.

30. *Sanditon*, MW, p. 384.

31. *Sanditon*, MW, p. 415.

32. *Sanditon*, MW, p. 426.

33. *Sanditon*, MW, p. 398.

34. *Sanditon*, MW, p. 398.

35. *Sanditon*, MW, p. 400.

36. *Sanditon*, MW, p. 394.

37. *Sanditon*, MW, p. 396.

38. *Sanditon*, MW, p. 421.

39. *Letters*, p. 329, Jane Austen to Fanny Knight, Chawton, 20 February 1817.

40. *Letters*, p. 338, Jane Austen to Caroline Austen, Chawton, 26 March 1817.

41. *Letters*, p. 231, Jane Austen to Frank Austen, Godmersham, 25 September 1813.

42. *Letters*, p. 333, Jane Austen to Fanny Knight, Chawton, 13 March 1817.

43. *Letters*, pp. 335–36, Jane Austen to Fanny Knight, Chawton, 23 March 1817.

44. *Letters*, p. 332, Jane Austen to Fanny Knight, Chawton, 13 March 1817.

45. *Letters*, p. 336, Jane Austen to Fanny Knight, Chawton, 23 March 1817.

46. *Sanditon*, MW, p. 378.

47. *Letters*, p. 336, Jane Austen to Fanny Knight, Chawton, 23 March 1817.

48. *Letters*, p. 336, Jane Austen to Fanny Knight, Chawton, 3 March 1817.

49. *Letters*, p. 338–39, Jane Austen to Charles Austen, Chawton, 6 April 1817.

50. *Letters*, p. 338, Jane Austen to Charles Austen, Chawton, 6 April 1817.

51. Deirdre Le Faye, *Jane Austen's 'Outlandish Cousin'* (London, 2002), p. 156, Eliza de Feuillide to Philadelphia Walter, Dorking, 29 October 1799.

52. *Letters*, p. 338, Jane Austen to Charles Austen, Chawton, 6 April 1817.

53. *Letters*, p. 340, Jane Austen to Anne Sharp, Chawton, 22 May 1817.

54. *Letters*, p. 341, Jane Austen to Anne Sharp, Chawton, 22 May 1817.

55. *Letters*, pp. 340–41, Jane Austen to Anne Sharp, Chawton, 22 May 1817.

56. *Letters*, p. 333, Jane Austen to Fanny Knight, Chawton, 13 May 1817.

57. *Letters*, p. 341, Jane Austen to Anne Sharp, Chawton, 22 May 1817.

58. *Letters*, p. 342, Jane Austen to James Edward Austen, Winchester, 27 May 1817.

59. *Letters*, p. 343, Jane Austen to ?Frances Tilson, Winchester, ?28 May 1817.

60. Henry Austen, 'Biographical Notice', NA, p. 4.

61. *Letters*, p. 344, Cassandra Austen to Fanny Knight, Winchester, 20 July 1817.

62. *Letters*, p. 344, Cassandra Austen to Fanny Knight, Winchester, 20 July 1817.

63. *Letters*, pp. 344–45, Cassandra Austen to Fanny Knight, Winchester, 20 July 1817.

64. *Letters*, p. 345, Cassandra Austen to Fanny Knight, Winchester, 20 July 1817.

65. *Letters*, p. 345, Cassandra Austen to Fanny Knight, Winchester, 20 July 1817.

66. *Letters*, p. 344, Cassandra Austen to Fanny Knight, Winchester, 20 July 1817.

67. *Letters*, p. 344, Cassandra Austen to Fanny Knight, Winchester, 20 July 1817.

68. *Letters*, p. 344, Cassandra Austen to Fanny Knight, Winchester, 20 July 1817.

69. *Letters*, p. 347, Cassandra Austen to Fanny Knight, Winchester, 29 July 1817.

Bibliography

Unpublished

Austen, Cassandra Leigh, memorandum on the history of the Perrot family, Hampshire Record Office, Winchester.

Austen, Charles, diaries and journals, 1815–17, National Maritime Museum, Greenwich.

Austen (later Knight), Edward, Journal through Switzerland, August 1786, Hampshire Record Office, Winchester.

Austen, Francis, letterbooks, 1801–14, National Maritime Museum, Greenwich.

Austen, James, verses, Jane Austen Memorial Trust, Chawton.

Boyd's marriage register, Society of Genealogists, London.

Brydges, Cassandra (Duchess of Chandos), letterbook, North London Collegiate School.

Brydges, James (1st Duke of Chandos), letterbooks. Huntington Library.

Feuillide, Eliza de, letters, Hampshire Record Office, Winchester.

Leigh, Mary, History of the Leigh family of Adlestrop, Shakespeare Birthplace Trust, Stratford.

Westminster rate books, 1795–98.

Wills, Public Record Office and Family Records Centre, London.

Published

Andrews, S. M., *Jane Austen ... her Tonbridge Connections* (Tonbridge, 1949).

Austen, Caroline, *My Aunt Jane Austen* (Chawton, 1952).

—, *Reminiscences*, ed. Deidre Le Faye (Chawton, 1986).

Austen, James et al., *The Loiterer* (London, 1789–90).

Austen-Leigh, Emma, *Jane Austen and Steventon* (London, 1937).

—, *Jane Austen and Bath* (London, 1939).

Austen-Leigh, James Edward, *A Memoir of Jane Austen,* ed. R. W. Chapman (2nd edn, Oxford, 1951).

Austen-Leigh, Mary Augusta, *Personal Aspects of Jane Austen* (London, 1920).

Austen-Leigh, Richard, *Austen Papers, 1704–1856* (London, 1942).

—, *Jane Austen and Lyme Regis* (London, 1946).

—, *Jane Austen and Southampton* (London, 1949).

—, and William Austen Leigh, *Jane Austen: Her Life and Letters. A Family Record* (London, 1913); revised and enlarged by Deirdre Le Faye (London, 1989).

Austen-Leigh, William, and Montague George Knight, *Chawton Manor and its Owners* (London, 1911).

—, and Richard Arthur Austen-Leigh, *Jane Austen: Her Life and Letters* (London, 1913).

Baker, C. H. C., *The Life and Circumstances of James Brydges* (London, 1949).

Bence-Jones, Mark, *Clive of India* (London, 1974).

Bernstein, Jeremy, *The Dawning of the Raj* (Chicago, 1998).

Bigg-Wither, R. F., *Materials for a History of the Wither Family* (Winchester, 1907).

Blanc, Oliver, *Last Letters: Prisons and Prisoners of the French Revolution 1793–94* (London, 1987).

Boyle, Eliza, *Boyle's Court and Country Guide* (London, 1815).

Brabourne, Edward, *Letters of Jane Austen* (London, 1884).

Brydges, [Anne] Miss, 'On Seeing Some School-Boys', in *Poetical Register and Repository of Fugitive Poetry* (3rd edn, London, 1815), p. 30.

Brydges, [Anne] Miss, 'Poetical Epistle', in *Poetical Register and Repository of Fugitive Poetry* (3rd edn, London, 1815), p. 90–91.

Brydges, Samuel Egerton, *The Autobiography, Times, Opinions and Contemporaries of Sir Egerton Brydges* (London, 1834).

Burke, John *et al., Commoners* (London, 1838).

—, *Extinct Baronetcies* (London, 1838).

—, *Landed Gentry* (London, 1846).

Centlivre, Susannah, *The Wonder! A Woman Keeps a Secret* (London, 1781).

Chapman, R. W., *Jane Austen: Facts and Problems* (Oxford, 1948).

—, ed., *Jane Austen's Letters to her Sister Cassandra and Others* (2nd edn, Oxford, 1952).

Cokayne, G. E., *The Compete Peerage* (London 1887–98).

Collins, Irene, *Jane Austen and the Clergy* (London, 1994).

—, *Jane Austen: The Parson's Daughter* (London, 1998).

Cooper, J. J., *Some Worthies of Reading* (Reading, 1923).

Corley, T. A. B., 'Jane Austen and her Brother Henry's Bank Failure, 1815–16', *Jane Austen Society Annual Report* (1998), pp. 12–23.

Cowley, Hannah, *Which is the Man?* (London, 1783).

Darton, F. J., *The Life and Times of Mr Sherwood, 1775–1851* (London, 1910).

Dictionary of National Biography.

Doody, Margaret Anne, and Douglas Murray, eds, *Jane Austen: Catharine and Other Writings* (Oxford, 1993).

Feiling, Keith, *Warren Hastings* (London, 1954).

Fielding, Henry, *Tom Jones* (London, 1749).

Foster, Joseph, *Alumni Oxonienses, 1715–1886* (London, 1887).

Freeman, Jean, *Jane Austen in Bath*, Jane Austen Society (1969).

Garrick, David, *The Chances* (London, 1773).

—, *Bon Ton* (London, 1775).

Gentleman's Magazine.

Gilson, David, *A Bibliography of Jane Austen* (Oxford, 1982).

Gore, John, 'Sophia Sentiment: Jane Austen?', in *Collected Reports of the Jane Austen Society, 1966–1975*, pp. 9–12.

Gorer, Geoffrey, 'Poor Honey: Some Notes on Jane Austen and her Mother', *London Magazine*, 4 (August, 1957), pp. 35–48.

Grier, Sydney C., 'A God-Daughter of Warren Hastings', *Temple Bar*, 131, pp. 562–71.

Halperin, John, *Jane Austen* (Brighton, 1985).

Hasted, Edward, *History of Kent* (Canterbury, 1778–99).

Hill, Constance, *Jane Austen, her Homes and her Friends* (London, 1904).

Hodge, Joan Aiken, *The Double Life of Jane Austen* (London, 1972).

Hubback, J. H. and Edith C., *Jane Austen's Sailor Brothers* (London, 1906).

Jacob, Alexander, *A Complete English Peerage* (London, 1766).

Jane Austen Society, *Collected Reports*, i, *1949–65*; ii, *1966–75*; iii, *1976–85*; iv, *1986–95*; *Annual Reports*, 1996 and continuing.

Jane Austen Society of North America, *Persuasions*, 1979 and continuing.

Jane Austen Society of Australia, *A Century of Wills from Jane Austen's Family* (Sydney, 2001).

Jane Austen Society of Austrialia, *Sensibilities*, 1989 and continuing.

Jenkins, Elizabeth, *Jane Austen: A Biography* (London 1938).

Johnson, Joan, *Excellent Cassandra* (Gloucester, 1981).

—, *Princely Chandos* (Gloucester, 1984).

Lane, Maggie, *Jane Austen's Family Through Five Generations* (London, 1984).

Lascelles, Mary, *Jane Austen and her Art* (Oxford, 1963).

Le Faye, Deirdre, 'Fanny Knight's Diaries', *Persuasions*, Occasional Papers 2 (1986).

—, ed., *Jane Austen's Letters* (Oxford, 1995).

—, *Jane Austen's 'Outlandish Cousin'* (London, 2002).

—, 'Leonora Austen', *Jane Austen Society Annual Report, 1998*, pp. 55–57.

—, 'Three Austen Family Letters', *Notes and Queries*, 32 (September 1985), pp. 335–56.

—, 'Tom Lefroy and Jane Austen', *Jane Austen Society Collected Reports, 1976–85*, pp. 336–38.

Lefroy, Helen, *Jane Austen* (Winchester, 1997).

Lefroy, J. A. P., 'Jane Austen's Irish Friend', *Proceedings of the Hugenot Society of London*, 23 (1979), pp. 148–65.

Litz, A. Walton, '*The Loiterer*: A Reflection of Jane Austen's Early Environment', *Review of English Studies*, new series 12 (1961), pp. 251–61.

MacKinnon, Sir Frank Douglas, *Grand Larceny* (Oxford, 1937).

Mitford, Nancy, *The Stanleys of Alderley* (London, 1939).

Nabokov, Vladimir, *Lectures on Literature* (New York, 1981).

Poetical Register and Repository of Fugitive Poetry, ii, 1802 (London, 1803).

Pope, E. B., *History of Wargrave* (Hitchin, 1929).

Smithers, David, *Jane Austen in Kent* (Westerham, 1981).

Southam, Brian, *Jane Austen and the Navy* (London, 2000).

—, *Jane Austen's Literary Manuscripts* (Oxford, 1964).

—, ed., *Jane Austen's 'Sir Charles Grandison'* (Oxford, 1980).

—, ed., *Jane Austen: The Critical Heritage*, i , 1811–70 (London, 1968).

—, ed., *Jane Austen: The Critical Heritage*, ii, 1879–1940 (London, 1987).

Tomalin, Claire, *Jane Austen* (London, 1997).

Tucker, George Holbert, *A History of Jane Austen's Family* (Stroud, 1998; revised edition of *A Goodly Heritage* (Manchester, 1983)).

—, *Jane Austen the Woman* (London, 1994).

Vick, Robin, 'Cousins in Bath', *Jane Austen Society Collected Reports, 1986–95*, pp. 394–99.

—, 'The Hancocks', *Jane Austen Society Annual Report, 1999*, pp. 19–23.

Victoria County History of Berkshire.

Victoria County History of Durham.

Victoria County History of Essex.

Victoria County History of Gloucestershire.

Victoria County History of Hampshire.

Victoria County History of Herefordshire.

Victoria County History of Hertfordshire.

Victoria County History of Huntingtonshire.

Victoria County History of Kent.

Victoria County History of Oxfordshire.

Victoria County History of Warwickshire.

Victoria County History of Worcestershire.

Watson, Winifred, 'The Austens' London Doctor', *Jane Austen Society Collected Reports, 1949–65*, pp. 194–97.

Wilson, Margaret, *Almost Another Sister* (Maidstone, Kent, 1997).

—, *Jane Austen and Tonbridge* (Chawton, 2001).

Index